Teach Yourself VISUALLY

Power BI®

by Alexander Loth

Visual
A Wiley Brand

About the Author

Alexander Loth is a distinguished digital strategist and data scientist with over 14 years of experience advising numerous large companies on their digital transformations. He has a background in computational nuclear research, having worked at the European Organization for Nuclear Research (CERN) before transitioning to the tech industry.

Alexander holds an Executive MBA from the Frankfurt School of Finance & Management and is also a lecturer on the subject of digital society at the same institution. He has worked for several industry leaders, including Tableau (now part of Salesforce), Capgemini, and SAP. Since 2019, he has been a valuable member of the Microsoft team.

In addition to his industry experience, Alexander has an impressive academic background. He studied at the China Europe International Business School (CEIBS) in Shanghai and conducted postgraduate research at the University of the West of England's Department of Computer Science, focusing on machine-learning algorithms for geo-distributed petabyte-scale big data processing, data science, and cybersecurity.

Alexander's passion for sharing his knowledge and experience with others is evident in his role as co-founder of Futura Analytics, a fintech advisory. He has also written extensively on topics such as digital transformation, artificial intelligence, blockchain, and business analytics, and is the author of the best-selling books *Visual Analytics with Tableau* and *Decisively Digital*.

To stay up to date on the latest industry developments and insights, be sure to follow Alexander Loth on his blog at alexloth.com, on Twitter @xlth, and on LinkedIn at www.linkedin.com/in/aloth.

Author's Acknowledgments

I am deeply grateful to the numerous individuals who have helped bring this book to fruition. Their support, insights, and encouragement have been invaluable to me throughout this journey. They include the people at Wiley and my colleagues at Microsoft.

I would especially like to thank Sarah Hellert, who has edited several titles in the Teach Yourself VISUALLY series and provided valuable advice and practical guidance beyond expectation on this book; Jonathan Bartleson, for his sharp eye for technical detail in the book; and Christine O'Connor, who pulled the threads together for this book. I also express my deepest gratitude to Jim Minatel, who published this and my previous books with Wiley, for his many years of excellent cooperation.

Finally, I want to thank my family for their unwavering patience, encouragement, and support throughout this process. Their love and support have sustained me through many long hours and challenging moments.

Thank you to everyone who has contributed to this project. Your efforts have made this book a reality, and I am deeply grateful for your support.

How to Use This Book

Who This Book Is For

This book is for the reader who has never used this particular technology or software application. It is also for readers who want to expand their knowledge.

The Conventions in This Book

1 Steps

This book uses a step-by-step format to guide you easily through each task. Numbered steps are actions you must do; bulleted steps clarify a point, step, or optional feature; and indented steps give you the result.

2 Notes

Notes give additional information — special conditions that may occur during an operation, a situation that you want to avoid, or a cross reference to a related area of the book.

3 Icons and Buttons

Icons and buttons show you exactly what you need to click to perform a step.

4 Tips

Tips offer additional information, including warnings and shortcuts.

5 Bold

Bold type shows command names, options, and text or numbers you must type.

6 Italics

Italic type introduces and defines a new term.

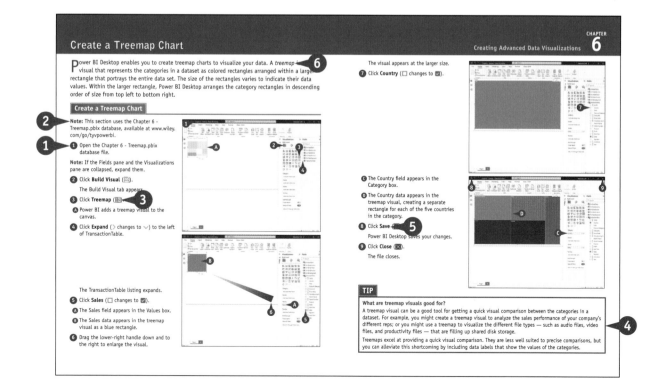

Table of Contents

Chapter 3 Cleaning and Shaping Data

Chapter 4 Modeling Data in Model View

Table of Contents

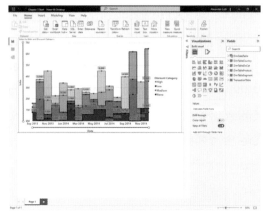

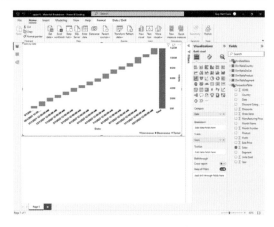

Chapter 7   Showing Geographic Data on Maps

Table of Contents

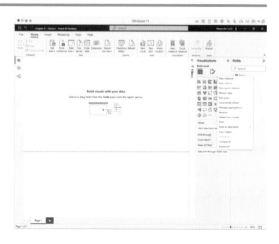

Chapter 11 — Publishing Reports and Dashboards

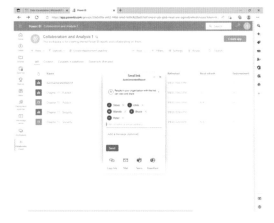

CHAPTER 1

Getting Started with Power BI

Power BI enables you to create visual analytics from data, allowing you to understand even complex data structures and effectively communicate insights gained. You need neither special mathematical skills nor programming experience to understand and acquire Power BI skills.

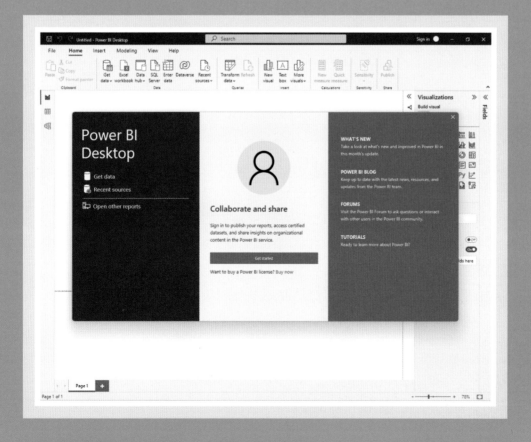

What Is Power BI?

Power BI is a data-visualization app that enables you to analyze data without technical expertise or programming knowledge. BI is a standard abbreviation for *business intelligence*. Instead of needing to type in complex data queries, you can create your queries by clicking and dragging items in Power BI's graphical interface. This ease of use allows you to quickly find insights in your data and to share them with others.

You do not have to know from the start what you are looking for or how you want to present the results. Rather, Power BI takes you on a journey through your data and helps you discover relationships you did not expect to exist through visual analysis. This approach is fundamentally different from other tools, whose use requires that you already know at the beginning of your analysis which data you want to present in which form.

Power Query, an Essential Part of Power BI

Power BI also offers complex techniques of data cleansing, data modeling, and data preparation with Power Query. *Power Query* is a data transformation and data preparation engine. Power Query has a graphical user interface for retrieving data from sources and a Power Query editor for applying transformations. You can use Power Query to perform ETL processing on data. *Extract, Transform, Load*, or *ETL*, is a process that unifies data from multiple, possibly differently structured, data sources.

Power BI's Vast Variety of Data Sources

Power BI Desktop enables you to connect to a wide variety of data sources. You can use data stored in Excel workbooks or in text files in the comma-separated values format, CSV. You can use data from databases such as Access or SQL Server. You can access data in *data cubes*, which are multidimensional arrays containing values. You can also connect to data warehouses, clusters of computers running the Apache Hadoop computing framework, or various cloud services such as Google Analytics.

After connecting to the appropriate data source, you interact with the Power BI user interface to query the data with a few mouse clicks and display the results in various charts and maps. You can then arrange these visualizations into dashboards to put them into meaningful context.

When communicating key insights, you have a variety of options depending on the product you use, from sharing interactive dashboards to embedding them in web pages. Power BI facilitates both the presentation of insights from data and the communication process, that is, data storytelling and interactive dashboards, without requiring any programming skills.

Data Analysis and Excel

Data analysis and visualization have always been an important topic in the professional environment and a fundamental tool for business decision-making. In this environment, Microsoft Excel quickly became popular and established itself as one of the most important tools for data analysis. However, with the exponential growth of data in the world, often referred to as *big data*, and the growth of the culture of analytics and data science, Excel is reaching its limits and is being replaced by more efficient tools for data analysis such as Power BI.

Power BI, the Big Leap from Excel

Year after year, companies are focusing more on data and how to get value from it in order to sell more products, attract more customers, and increase the efficiency of the process. In this scenario, a tool that handles a large amount of data and is able to analyze data quickly and easily to present information clearly to businesses becomes essential. To address this need, Microsoft has developed Power BI, a visualization tool that is capable of handling large and complex amounts of data while changing the way you deal with charts or visualizing data.

Excel has excellent features and allows the user to work easily and effectively to analyze data. Excel is the most widespread spreadsheet tool, where it can indisputably show its full power. With the introduction of Pivot Tables in Excel in 1994 and Power Query functions in Excel 2010, Excel gained functions for editing and analyzing data in tables up to 1 million rows. Nevertheless, Excel's strength remains the calculation of complex formulas more than the processing of large amounts of data. Excel also brings good functionalities for analysis and good graphical visualizations. Ultimately, even with smaller data sets, Power BI offers better performance, more comprehensive analytics and visualizations, and the ability to share dashboards or apps across the enterprise for a "one-stop solution." In these cases, Power BI proves to be extremely useful with advantages over Excel, making data analysis more agile and efficient.

With a wide range of graphics and widgets, a good ability to handle big data, integration with different platforms and ease of use, and centralization of different data sources, Power BI is proving to be increasingly popular, both among experienced Excel users and beginners new to the world of data.

How This Book Guides You into Power BI

This book is designed to provide you with a step-by-step introduction to creating visual analytics, enabling you to understand even complex data structures and effectively communicate insights gained. Therefore, this book is of interest to a variety of audiences, such as people who have access to and want to understand data, executives who make decisions based on data, analysts and developers who create visualizations and dashboards, and aspiring data scientists.

You need neither special mathematical skills nor programming experience to understand this book and develop skill in using Power BI effectively. The book is suitable for beginners and for users who want to approach the topic of data visualization and analysis in a practical way, without extensive theoretical treatises.

Understanding the Different Components of Power BI

Microsoft groups various software products and services for data analysis under the umbrella name Power BI. For this book's purposes, the three key Power BI components are Power BI Desktop, the Power BI cloud service, and the Power BI Report Server.

Power BI Desktop is a desktop application that you use to create analyses and reports from data sources. You can then make these analyses and reports available to consumers via either the Power BI cloud service or the Power BI Report Server — or indeed both. This section explains how the different Power BI components and licensing models interact with reports.

Power BI Desktop

Power BI Desktop is a free application for Windows that is popular among analysts and business users. On the one hand, Power BI Desktop allows you to connect to local files, such as Excel and CSV, and save report files locally. On the other hand, Power BI Desktop allows you to connect to many external data sources and store them on your own report server or the Power BI cloud service. The focus of this book is Power BI Desktop, which allows you to quickly create advanced analytics and reports and gain data-driven insights.

Power BI Pro

Power BI Pro is a user-based license for the Power BI service that lets you share reports and analytics with other users. You can use collaborative functions and integrate a role and rights concept. You can also embed published reports in other applications such as Microsoft SharePoint, Microsoft Teams, or other Microsoft Power Platform applications. At the time of this writing, the Pro license cost $9.99 per user per month; see powerbi. microsoft.com/en-us/pricing for current pricing. Power BI Pro is already included in the Microsoft 365 Enterprise E5 subscription plan.

Power BI Premium

Power BI is a platform for data analysis and is used by small companies as well as large, publicly traded corporations. Power BI Premium is used to provide company-wide visualizations and dashboards, which can also be operated in the web browser and can also be embedded in the company intranet. As of this writing, Microsoft offers a free 30-day trial for Power BI Premium; go to powerbi.microsoft.com/en-us/ power-bi-premium and click **Try Power BI for free**.

Power BI Embedded

With Power BI Embedded, you can integrate reports and analyses on your website and make them available to your customers without them having to log in to the Power BI service. Power BI Embedded uses a different licensing model: Your company pays for Power BI capacity that you make available for your customers to use, rather than customers needing to have their own Power BI accounts.

Power BI Report Server

The Power BI Report Server is a server platform on which you can publish and view reports in the same way as Power BI Premium. However, this is not a cloud platform but a so-called "on-premise" solution that you can integrate into your own network.

Power BI Mobile

Power BI Mobile is an application for iOS and Android smartphones and tablets and Windows devices that lets you access your data and the Power BI service on the go.

Understanding Power BI as Part of the Power Platform

Power BI is part of Microsoft's Power Platform, a set of tools for creating data-driven solutions to business needs. In addition to Power BI, Power Platform includes the Power Apps development environment, the Power Automate framework, the Power Virtual Agents tool for creating chatbots, and the Power Pages tool for building business-oriented websites quickly.

Power Apps

Power Apps is a development environment with little or no code, where you can develop your own applications to solve various business challenges. For example, you could develop a Power App that accesses a SharePoint list for data display and data entry. You could then deploy that app to your organization's iPhones, iPads, and Android devices.

Power Automate

Power Automate is a framework that allows end users to create "flows" that automate organizational processes. For example, you might develop a flow that automatically sends an email notification to supervisors when an employee submits a particular electronic form.

Power Virtual Agents

Power Virtual Agents is a no-code tool that lets you create chatbots to communicate with customers and employees.

Using the Power Platform

Each of these components — Power Apps, Power Automate, and Power Virtual Agents — can be used by Power BI to provide insights that drive your work forward. What follows are some examples of how each component might work with Power BI.

For example, in Power Apps, you could set up an application that allows an inspector to take notes in the field and upload that data to a SQL Server database. A Power BI report could also connect to that SQL Server database, retrieve the information uploaded by the Power App, and update the report based on the new data added by the multiple inspectors in the field using the Power App.

As another example, consider *virtual agents*, which are software programs that provide customer service to humans and mimic a customer service representative. With virtual agents, large amounts of data are collected as end users interact with your chatbots. All of this data is collected and stored, which means Power BI can generate reports on it. This creates an end-to-end reporting solution that allows your business to get textual insights into what your customers really want from your business.

Install Power BI Desktop

You can install Power BI Desktop in only a few minutes and begin creating visual data analytics. Before you start installing Power BI Desktop, make sure that your computer meets the necessary system requirements; see the tip for details.

The requirements of Power BI Desktop on your system are comparable to other Microsoft Office applications. However, how much data you connect and how many visualizations you display at the same time also play a major role. For complex analyses and large amounts of data, you will get a more comfortable experience with a powerful processor and more memory.

Install Power BI Desktop

Ⓐ If Microsoft Store (🛍) appears on the taskbar, click **Microsoft Store** (🛍) and go to step **4**.

① In Windows, click **Start** (⊞).

The Start menu opens.

② Type **store**.

The search results appear.

③ Click **Microsoft Store** (🛍).

The Microsoft Store app opens.

④ Click **Search** (🔍).

The Search field becomes active.

⑤ Type **power bi desktop**.

The search results appear.

⑥ Click **Power BI Desktop** (📊).

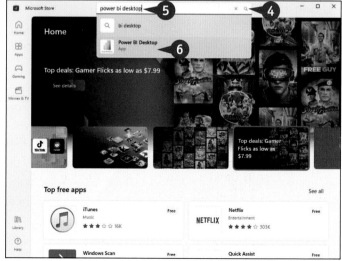

The product page for Power BI Desktop appears.

Note: To determine whether Power BI Desktop will run on your computer, scroll down to the System Requirements section on the product page and look for the message *This product should work on your device*. See the tip for more information on system requirements.

7 Click **Get**.

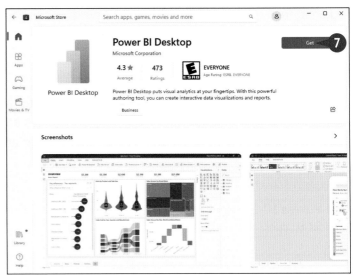

B Power BI Desktop begins downloading and installing on your computer.

When the download and installation is complete, the Open button appears.

C You can click **Open** to open Power BI Desktop directly from the Microsoft Store app.

8 Click **Close** (■).

The Microsoft Store app closes.

TIP

What are the system requirements for Power BI Desktop?
To run Power BI Desktop, you need a PC running Windows 10 version 14393.0 or later, such as Windows 11, with at least 2 GB of disk space free. Microsoft recommends a Windows 10 PC with a minimum of 2 GB of RAM, but for reasonable performance, 4 GB is a realistic minimum, and 8 GB or more will give better performance. Windows 11 requires at least 4 GB of RAM; for good performance, treat 8 GB as a realistic minimum, and get 16 GB or more if possible.

Start and Pin Power BI Desktop

After you have successfully installed Power BI Desktop, as described in the previous section, you can launch the app from the Windows Start menu. If you want to launch Power BI Desktop more quickly in the future, you can pin Power BI Desktop to your Start menu, making it always appear there. For even faster launching without opening the Start menu, you can pin Power BI Desktop to the taskbar.

This section shows Windows 11. If your computer has Windows 10, the Start menu is located in the lower-left corner of the screen by default.

Start and Pin Power BI Desktop

Start Power BI Desktop

1 Click **Start** (■).

The Start menu opens.

A If Power BI Desktop (📊) appears in the Recommended section, click **Power BI Desktop** (📊) and go to step **4**.

2 Start typing **power bi desktop**.

The Start menu displays search results as you type.

3 Click **Power BI Desktop** (📊).

Power BI Desktop opens.

Ⓑ The Power BI Desktop splash screen appears.

Ⓒ The right pane contains links you can click to display various types of information about Power BI.

④ Click **Get Started**.

The splash screen closes.

You can now start using Power BI Desktop.

Pin Power BI Desktop

① Click **Start** (▦).

The Start menu opens.

② Right-click **Power BI Desktop** (▮).

③ To pin Power BI Desktop to the Start menu, click **Pin to Start** (✧).

④ To pin Power BI Desktop to the taskbar, click **Pin to taskbar** (✧).

After pinning the Power BI Desktop icon to the Start menu or the taskbar, you can start Power BI Desktop quickly by clicking the icon on the Start menu or the taskbar.

TIP

Is Power BI available for the Mac or Linux?
As of this writing, Power BI Desktop is available only for Windows, so Mac users and Linux users cannot install and use Power BI Desktop natively. On either macOS or Linux, you can install virtual-machine software, such as Parallels Desktop for macOS, from www.parallels.com, or the free VirtualBox for either macOS or Linux, from www.virtualbox.org. Install Windows on the virtual machine, and then install Power BI Desktop. Another approach is to use a cloud PC, such as Microsoft's Windows 365 Cloud PC service, which you can access from macOS, Linux, Windows, iOS and iPadOS, Android, and most other current operating systems.

Explore the Power BI Workspace

Like many of Microsoft's professional apps, Power BI Desktop has a ribbon-driven interface rather than menus. If you are familiar with Microsoft apps such as Word or Excel, the Power BI Desktop ribbon will look familiar; if not, you can quickly master how to use it.

Below the ribbon is the Canvas, the area on which you create visualizations. To the left of the Canvas is the View bar; to the right of the Canvas are the Filters pane, the Visualizations pane, and the Fields pane, which you can collapse and expand as needed. At the bottom of the Power BI Desktop window is the status bar.

A **Quick Access Toolbar**

The Quick Access toolbar provides easy access to the Save, Undo, and Redo commands.

B **Ribbon**

The ribbon is the primary interface element for giving commands. The ribbon contains six fixed tabs: File, Home, Insert, Modeling, View, and Help. Other tabs, such as the Format tab and the Data/Drill tab, are context sensitive and appear only when you have selected an object with which such a tab is associated.

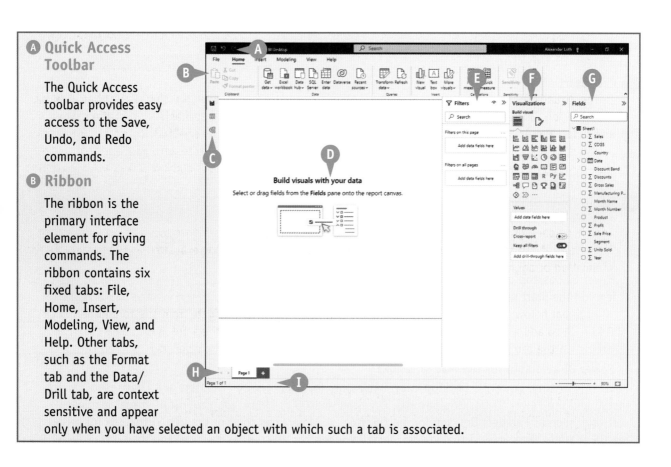

ⓒ View Bar

The View bar, on the left side of the Power BI Desktop window, enables you to switch between three views: Report, Data, and Model. By default, Report view is selected.

ⓓ Canvas

The Canvas is the area on which you create and manipulate your visualizations.

ⓔ Filters Pane

In the Filters pane, you can filter data fields to limit the analysis to the relevant data range. You can control whether the filtering applies to a single visualization, a single page, or all pages of your file. You can expand the Filters pane, the Visualizations pane, and the Fields pane by clicking **Expand** (《), and you can collapse them by clicking **Collapse** (》).

ⓕ Visualizations Pane

In the Visualizations pane, you can create a new data visualization, change the chart type of an existing visualization, and adjust the formatting. A series of icons shows you the available visualization types and helps to quickly select the desired chart. Here, also depending on the selected visualization, you can assign data fields or calculation results to the visualizations and add visual features such as tool tips, drill-through references, and additional analyses. You can also load various other powerful visualizations from the Microsoft Store.

ⓖ Fields Pane

The Fields pane gives you an overview of which data fields and calculations are available in your source. A sum sign, Σ, in front of a field name indicates a field that Power BI has evaluated as being suitable for summation or aggregation.

ⓗ Tab Bar

The tab bar below the Canvas enables you to create new pages and navigate from one to another. Click **Add** (➕) to add a page. Click a page's tab to display that page. When there are more pages than can appear on the tab bar, click **Go to Start** (◀) or **Go to End** (▶) to scroll the displayed tabs left or right.

ⓘ Status Bar

The status bar, at the bottom of the Power BI Desktop window, displays current information, such as the page number and the number of pages, and contains the zoom slider, the Zoom Menu button (such as 90%), and the Fit to Page button (⌗).

continued ▶

Explore the Power BI Workspace (continued)

The Power BI Desktop ribbon contains six fixed tabs: File, Home, Insert, Modeling, View, and Help, looking from left to right. This section gives you an overview of these six tabs.

Power BI Desktop also has context-sensitive tabs, which appear when you have selected an object for which the tabs are relevant. For example, when you select a visual, the Format tab appears, giving you access to controls for configuring interactions with the visual and arranging it on the canvas.

The Files Tab and Backstage View

Clicking the File tab at the left end of the ribbon opens Backstage view, which gives you access to commands for creating, saving, and managing documents. For example, you can click **New** (A) to open a new Power BI Desktop window, click **Save** (B) to save the active report, click **Get Data** (C) to display the Get Data commands, or click **Options and settings** (D) to configure Power BI Desktop.

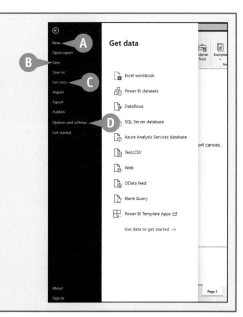

The Home Tab

The Home tab contains seven groups of controls. The Clipboard group

enables you to use the Cut, Copy, Paste, and Format Painter commands. The Data group allows you to create connections to data sources. The Queries group lets you transform data and refresh your existing queries. From the Insert group, you can insert visuals and text boxes. The Calculations group enables you to create new *measures*, or calculations. The Sensitivity group allows you to apply sensitivity labels to reports. The Share group lets you upload the report to the Power BI service.

The Insert Tab

The Insert tab contains six groups. The Pages group enables you to add new

pages to the report. The Visuals group provides controls for adding visuals to the report. The AI Visuals group lets you add elements such as a Q&A section and a decomposition tree. The Power Platform group helps you add Power Apps to the report; see the section "Understanding Power BI as Part of the Power Platform," earlier in this chapter, for more about Power Apps. The Elements group lets you insert text boxes, buttons, shapes, and images. The Sparklines group allows you to add *sparklines*, miniature charts that illustrate a single data series.

The Modeling Tab

The Modeling tab contains six groups. The Relationship group contains the Manage

Relationships button, which you click to open the Manage Relationships dialog box, where you configure the relationships between different tables you are using. The Calculations group enables you to create new measures, columns, and tables. The Page Refresh group allows you to configure the frequency at which Power BI Desktop checks your data sources for changes. The What If group lets you add new parameters to your report. The Security group provides controls for managing security roles for other users and for viewing your report from another user's point of view. The Q&A group enables you to configure a Q&A section, set its language, and import and export linguistic schemas.

The View Tab

The View tab contains five groups. From the Themes group, you can

apply a preset visual theme to the report. The Scale to Fit group lets you choose whether to view the report at its actual size, fit it to a page, or fit it to the window width. The Page Options group enables you to add gridlines, control whether objects snap to the grid, and lock objects to prevent movement. The Show Panes group allows you to control which panes appear in the report window.

The Help Tab

The Help tab contains four groups. The Info group contains only the About button, which you

can click to display information about Power BI Desktop and your current session. The Help group gives you access to specific help resources. The Community group provides links to community support and external tools. The Resources group lets you access examples and Power BI consulting services.

CHAPTER 2

Connecting Power BI to Your Data

Power BI enables you to analyze data from many different sources. The data can be either local — stored on your computer — or remote, stored on a network or the Internet. In this chapter, you learn to connect Power BI to local files, such as Excel workbooks; to Power BI datasets; to SharePoint lists; and to Microsoft SQL Server.

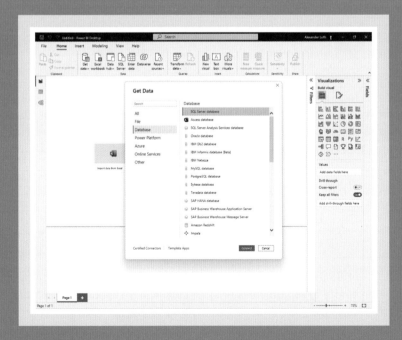

Grasp How Power Query Editor Works with Power BI Desktop

If all your data were stored in a single database and perfectly organized, you would be able to access and query it easily. But usually this is not the case. Instead, your data is typically scattered across multiple databases, files such as text files and Excel workbooks, and cloud services. To work with this data, you must locate it, connect to it, and often cleanse and shape it.

Power BI Desktop connects to a wide range of data sources — more than 120 types as of this writing. Power BI Desktop uses Microsoft's Power Query Editor to explore, cleanse, and shape data.

Understanding How Power Query Editor and Power BI Desktop Work Together

Power BI Desktop and Power Query Editor work together almost seamlessly. The process typically goes as follows.

First, you create a report in Power BI Desktop and use a Get Data command to connect it to the data source that contains the data you want to use. Power BI Desktop offers various Get Data commands for connecting to different data sources — text files, Excel workbooks, SharePoint lists, SQL Server databases, and so on.

Second, after establishing the connection to the data source, you select the data you want to load into the Power BI report. Normally, this will be a subset of the available data, but in some cases, you may want to load all the data.

Third, once the data you want is loaded into the Power BI report, you can issue the Transform Data command, which launches Power Query Editor and loads the data into it. Power Query Editor opens as a separate window in front of Power BI Desktop, and you use its capabilities to examine, cleanse, and transform the data, as needed. For example, you might remove errors, strip out duplicate values, correct any incorrect data types, and split a single column into multiple columns.

Fourth, when you have gotten the data in your preferred shape, you give the Close & Apply command, which closes Power Query Editor and applies your changes to the data, returning you to Power BI Desktop.

Fifth, you can use Power BI Desktop's features and tools to analyze the data and create visualizations. When your report or dashboard is finished, you can publish it on the Power BI service.

Understanding the Benefits of Power Query Editor

High-quality analysis relies on well-organized, error-free data that comes from a single reliable source. Power Query Editor enables you to process, combine, and transform data with simple, repeatable procedures instead of needing to spend hours sorting out the data manually.

Power Query Editor is one of the most transformative tools available to any analyst working with data in Excel or the Microsoft Power Platform. Not only can Power Query Editor save you valuable time, but it also leads to fewer manual errors and delivers a greater capability to pull data from a single source.

Understanding Data Types in Power Query

Power Query uses 13 data types to classify values in data sets. A field must have a data type assigned so that Power Query can work effectively with the data. Assigning a suitable data type increases the quality of your data and helps you identify errors when they creep in.

Normally, each field should contain the same type of data in each record. However, you can apply the Any data type to a field that contains different data types in different records. You might apply the Any data type as a temporary measure until you can separate the different data types into different files.

Table 2-1 explains the data types, including the icons Power Query uses for quick identification.

		Table 2-1: Data Types in Power Query	
Data Type	**Icon**	**Explanation**	**Examples**
Any	ABC 123	The default data type when no specific data type has been assigned	11 text
Decimal number	1.2	A number that includes a decimal point and one or more decimal places	2.3 144.65
Fixed decimal number	$	A number that includes a decimal point and four decimal places; also known as the Currency type	3.2126 98.4938
Whole number	1²3	An integer — no decimal point or decimal places	1 916,826
Percentage	%	A decimal number formatted as a percentage	29%
Date/Time	🗓	A date and a time	2023-12-25 16:00
Date	📅	A date with no time	2023-06-03
Time	🕐	A time with no date	17:25
Date/Time/ Timezone	🌐	A Date/Time value with a Timezone offset; converts to a Date/Time value in the data model	2023-05-01 12:03:15 AM -05:00
Duration	⏱	A period of time	9:00:00:01
Text	A$C	A string of up to 268,535,546 Unicode characters	Operations
True/False	×ᵥ	A Boolean value, one that can be either only True or False	True False
Binary	▤	Any data with a binary format, such as a JPEG image	—

Connect Power BI Desktop to a Local File

Before you can analyze data in Power BI Desktop, you must connect it to a data source. To connect, you use the Power Query tool, which enables you to access data sources that range from local files, such as Excel workbooks, to databases stored on remote servers.

In this section, you connect Power BI to a sample Excel workbook called Financial Sample.xlsx, which contains a dataset of sales data from a fictional company. Before starting the steps, download this file from docs.microsoft.com/bs-latn-ba/power-bi/create-reports/sample-financial-download. You can also access this workbook through Power BI Desktop, as explained in the first tip.

Connect Power BI Desktop to a Local File

1 Open Power BI Desktop.

For example, if you pinned Power BI Desktop to the Start menu, click **Start** (⊞), and then click **Power BI Desktop** (▮).

Note: If the splash screen appears, click **Show this screen on startup** (☑ changes to ☐), and then click **Close** (✖).

2 Click **Home**.

The Home tab of the ribbon appears.

3 Click **Get Data** (∨).

The Get Data drop-down menu opens.

4 Click **Excel workbook** (🗎).

The Open dialog box appears.

5 Navigate to the folder that contains the file you want to open.

6 Click the file.

7 Click **Open**.

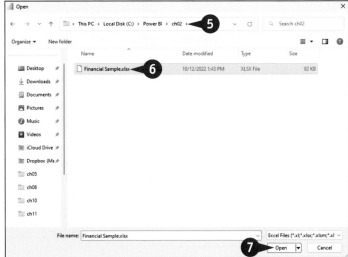

The Open dialog box closes.

Power Query connects to the data source.

The Navigator dialog box opens.

Ⓐ The Financial Sample.xlsx workbook appears on the left, showing the worksheets it contains.

8 Click **Sheet1** (☐ changes to ☑).

Ⓑ The data in the Sheet1 worksheet appears.

9 Click **Load**.

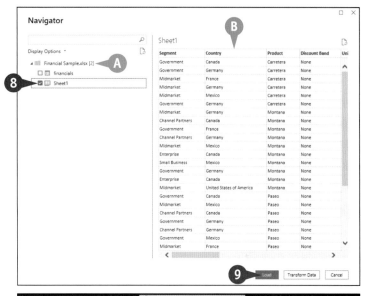

The Navigator dialog box closes.

Ⓒ The Fields pane expands automatically.

Note: If the Sheet1 list of fields is collapsed, click **Expand** (⟩) to expand it.

Ⓓ The list of fields in the Sheet1 worksheet appears.

Note: You can now save the report file. See the next section, "Save, Close, and Open Power BI Reports," for instructions.

How do I access the sample Excel workbook through Power BI Desktop?

Open Power BI Desktop and click **Try a Sample Dataset** (🗂) on the Add Data to Your Report screen. The Two Ways to Use Sample Data dialog box opens. Click **Load Sample Data** (✎). The Navigator dialog box opens. In the left pane, click **financials** (☐ changes to ☑), and then click **Load**.

How do I connect Power BI Desktop to a PDF?

Click **Home**, click **Get Data** (⌄), and then click **More** to open the Get Data dialog box. In the left pane, click **File**; in the right pane, click **PDF** (📄); and then click **Connect**. In the Open dialog box that appears, click the file, and then click **Open**.

Save, Close, and Open Power BI Reports

After creating a new report in Power BI Desktop, you can save the report to preserve its contents. As normal, when you save a report for the first time, you select the folder in which to store it and specify the filename. You can then quickly save subsequent changes to the report in the same file; and you can close the report and reopen it later, as needed.

This section assumes you have created a new report, as explained in the previous section, "Connect Power BI Desktop to a Local File," but not yet saved it.

Save, Close, and Open Power BI Reports

Save and Close a Report

1 With an unsaved report open, click **Save** (⊟).

The Save As dialog box opens.

2 Navigate to the folder in which you want to save the report.

3 Type the report name. This example uses **Sample Dataset**.

4 Click **Save**.

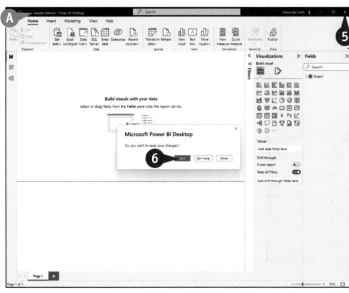

The Save As dialog box closes.

Ⓐ The filename appears in the Power BI Desktop title bar.

Note: You can now save subsequent changes by clicking **Save** (⊟) or by pressing **Ctrl** + **S**.

5 Click **Close**.

If the report contains any unsaved changes, a Microsoft Power BI Desktop dialog box opens. If not, skip step **6**.

6 Click **Save**.

Power BI Desktop saves the changes.

The report window closes.

Open a Report

1 Open Power BI Desktop if it is not already open.

For example, if you have pinned Power BI Desktop to the taskbar, click **Power BI Desktop** ( ) on the taskbar.

2 Click **File**.

The Backstage view opens, with the Open Report category selected in the left pane.

B The Recent Reports list shows reports you have opened recently in Power BI Desktop.

C You can click **Pin** (—☐ changes to ✧) to pin a report to the Recent Reports list.

D If the report you want to open appears on the list, click it to open it. Skip the rest of this list.

3 Click **Browse Reports** (☐).

The Open dialog box appears.

4 Navigate to the folder that contains the report you want to open.

5 Click the report.

6 Click **Open**.

Power BI opens the report.

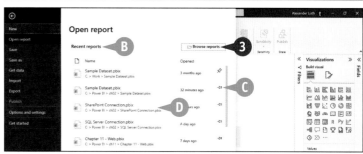

TIPS

How do I save a report under a new name?
Click **File** to open Backstage view, and then click **Save As** in the left column. The Save As dialog box opens. You can then specify a different filename, select a different folder, or both. After making your choices, click **Save**.

What other way can I open a Power BI report file?
You can open a Power BI report file by double-clicking it in a File Explorer window. You may find it more convenient to use a File Explorer window to browse to the file you want to open rather than use the Open dialog box for browsing.

Start Working with the Sample Dataset

Once you have loaded the sample dataset and saved it to a file, as explained in the previous two sections, you can start working with the data. In this section, you learn to explore the structure of a dataset and examine the types of data columns it contains.

When you import data, Power Query analyzes the data and automatically assigns a data type to each column. Power Query often assigns the most suitable data type, but you should always review each column and assign different data types manually where needed. For this review, you use the Power Query Editor.

Start Working with the Sample Dataset

Open the Sample Dataset in Power Query Editor

1 In Power BI Desktop, open the Sample Dataset.pbix report.

Note: See the previous section, "Save, Close, and Open Power BI Reports," for instructions on opening a report.

2 Click **Home**.

3 Click **Transform data** (⊞).

Note: Click the icon part (⊞) of the Transform Data button, not the drop-down menu (∨).

A The Power Query Editor window opens.

Power Query Editor loads the data from the Sample Dataset report.

B Power Query Editor has a ribbon as its main control interface.

C The Home tab of the ribbon appears at first.

D The Queries pane shows the Sheet1 query.

E The main part of the window shows the dataset laid out in columns and rows.

F The Query Settings pane shows the query that produced the dataset.

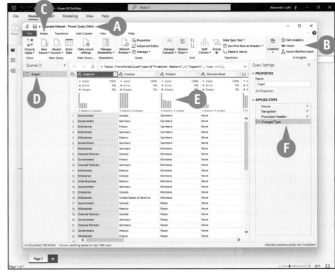

Check the Data Type of Each Column

1 Click **Transform**.

2 Verify that Power Query Editor has assigned the correct data type for each column.

Note: Scroll right to see other columns.

G The column heading icon shows the current data type.

Note: Refer to Table 2-1, earlier in this chapter, for a breakdown of the icons.

H The Data Type drop-down list shows the name of the current data type.

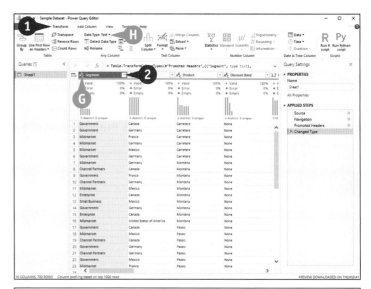

Change the Data Type of a Column

1 Click the column heading.

I Power Query Editor selects the column.

2 Click **Data Type**.

The Data Type drop-down menu opens.

3 Click the data type you want to assign.

Power Query Editor changes the column to the new data type.

Note: If the Change Column Type dialog box opens, see the first tip for advice.

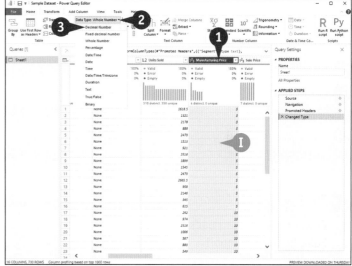

What button should I click in the Change Column Type dialog box?
The Change Column Type dialog box opens when you change the data type of a column whose values already have a conversion applied to them. Click **Replace current** if you want to replace the current conversion with a conversion to the new data type. Click **Add new step** if you want Power Query Editor to maintain the current conversion and add a separate step containing the new conversion.

Can different rows in a column have different data types?
Yes, but only if you or Power Query Editor assign the Any data type to the column. Otherwise, each row must have the data type applied to the column.

continued ▶

As well as the data type, Power Query Editor lets you view the distribution of each column. The *distribution* enables you to determine how many distinct values the column contains, see how many of those values are unique, and see the approximate share of each nonunique value.

Power Query Editor also allows you to assess a column's quality — how many of a column's values are valid, how many values contain errors, and how many values are empty. You can use the Replace Errors dialog box to replace values that contain errors with valid data.

Start Working with the Sample Dataset (continued)

View the Column Distribution and Column Quality

1 Click **View**.

2 Click **Column Quality** (☐ changes to ☑).

A A quality table showing the percentages of Valid values, Error values, and Empty values appears below the column header.

3 Click **Column Distribution** (☐ changes to ☑).

B A histogram showing the column distribution appears below the quality table.

Note: Scroll the table left to see the quality table and distribution histograms for other columns.

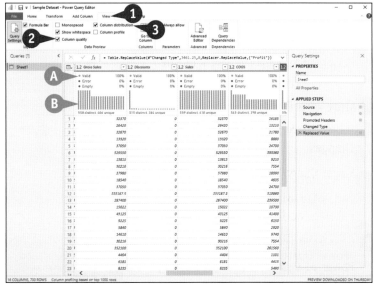

Correct Errors

1 Scroll horizontally to locate a column that contains errors.

C The red bar and green-and-white shading indicates that a column contains errors.

2 Scroll up or down to locate the errors.

D The word *Error* indicates an error value.

3 Right-click the column heading.

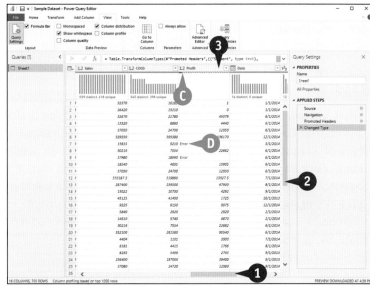

The contextual menu opens.

④ Click **Replace Errors**.

The Replace Errors dialog box opens.

⑤ In the Value text box, type **0**.

Note: Power BI identifies an error when a data value does not match the data type for the field. For example, a decimal value in an integer field causes an error.

⑥ Click **OK**.

The Replace Errors dialog box closes.

Ⓔ Power Query Editor replaces all the errors with the value you specified.

⑦ Click **Close & Apply** (⌐×↑).

Power Query Editor saves your changes.

Power Query Editor closes.

The Power BI Desktop window becomes active again.

⑧ Click **Save** (💾).

Power BI Desktop saves your changes.

⑨ Click **Close** (✕).

The file closes.

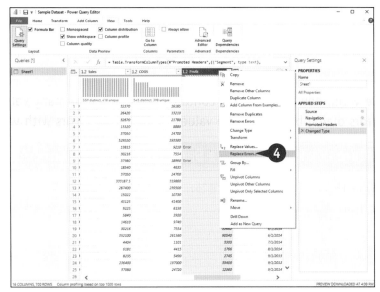

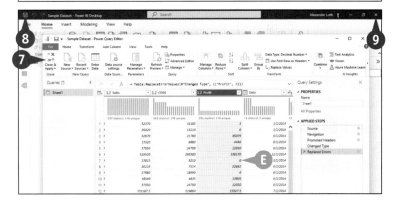

TIP

What causes errors in imported data?

Errors can result from a variety of causes. Many common errors result from Power BI not correctly recognizing special characters in the source data and substituting incorrect characters. However, errors may also be present in the source data. For example, if you import Excel worksheet data that contains, say, divide-by-zero errors, those errors show up as errors in Power Query Editor too. Even not-available values from Excel, #N/A, appear as errors in Power Query Editor.

Connect to a Power BI Dataset

Instead of connecting to a data source that you need to clean and transform, you can connect to an existing Power BI dataset, a dataset that has already been cleaned up and organized for data analytics. Such a dataset contains information on data models, calculated columns and measures, and other information helpful for analysis.

Ideally a Power BI dataset should be plug-and-play, so all you have to do is connect to it. No additional data cleanup should be required. But this is not always the case.

Connect to a Power BI Dataset

1 In Power BI Desktop, click **Home**.

The Home tab of the ribbon appears.

2 Click **Get data**.

Note: Click the icon part of the Get Data button, not the button's text.

The Get Data dialog box opens.

3 In the left pane, click **Power Platform**.

The Power Platform list appears in the right pane.

4 Click **Power BI datasets** (⊞).

5 Click **Connect**.

The Get Data dialog box closes.

The Data Hub dialog box opens.

6 Click the dataset you want to load. In this example, you would click **Financial Sample Dataset**.

7 Click **Connect**.

The Data Hub dialog box closes.

Ⓐ Power BI loads the dataset's data in the Fields pane.

8 Click **Save** (💾).

The Save As dialog box opens.

9 Navigate to the folder in which you want to save the file.

10 Type the filename.

11 Click **Save**.

The Save As dialog box closes.

Power BI Desktop saves the file.

12 Click **Close** (❌).

The file closes.

TIP

Can I also use a Power BI dataset in Excel?

Yes. First, enable the connection. In Excel, click **File**, click **Options** to open the Excel Options dialog box, click **Trust Center** in the left pane, and then click **Trust Center Settings**. In the Trust Center dialog box, click **Privacy Options** in the left pane, click **Privacy Settings**, and then click **Enable optional connected experiences** (☐ changes to ☑). Click **OK**, click **OK**, and then click **OK** again.

After this rigmarole, you can connect to a Power BI dataset in two ways. First, click **Insert** on the ribbon, click **PivotTable**, and then click **From Power BI (Microsoft)**. Second, click **Data** on the ribbon, click **Get Data**, and then click **From Power BI (Microsoft)**.

Connect to a SharePoint List

If your company or organization uses SharePoint, Microsoft's collaborative software platform, you can connect Power BI Desktop to access the data stored in SharePoint lists. Power BI Desktop enables you to analyze your SharePoint list data visually, rendering the data much easier to understand than in the list format.

To work through this section, you need access to a SharePoint server. If your company or organization has a SharePoint server, ask the SharePoint administrator what URL and credentials to use. If not but you have a Microsoft 365 subscription, you may be able to set up your own SharePoint server.

Connect to a SharePoint List

1 In Power BI Desktop, click **Home**.

The Home tab of the ribbon appears.

2 Click **Get data**.

Note: Click the icon part of the Get Data button, not the button's text.

The Get Data dialog box opens.

3 In the left pane, click **Other**.

The Other list appears.

4 Click **SharePoint list** (⬛).

5 Click **Connect**.

The Get Data dialog box closes.

The SharePoint Lists dialog box opens.

6 Type or paste the SharePoint URL into the Site URL box.

7 Click **OK**.

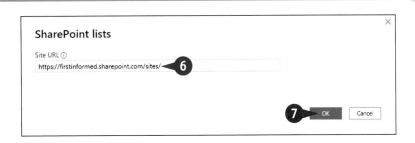

The SharePoint Lists dialog box closes.

The SharePoint dialog box opens.

A At first, the Anonymous tab of the SharePoint dialog box appears.

Note: To connect to the SharePoint server using anonymous access, skip step **8** and continue with step **9**.

8 Click **Windows** to use Windows authentication to connect to the SharePoint server, or click **Microsoft account** to authenticate via your Microsoft account. This example uses **Windows**.

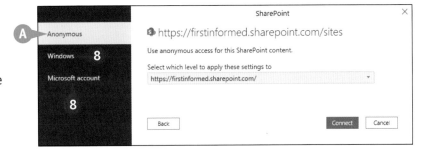

TIP

What are my authentication choices for connecting to SharePoint?
The SharePoint dialog box offers you three choices for authentication. First, you can connect using anonymous access; this can be handy if the SharePoint server allows anonymous access, but many servers do not. Second, you can use Windows credentials — either the credentials under which you are currently signed in to Windows or alternate credentials you specify. Third, you can use your Microsoft account credentials, such as your Microsoft 365 account.

continued ▶

Connect to a SharePoint List (continued)

Each SharePoint list can store up to 30 million rows of data, making lists ideal for small and medium-size enterprises that need a dynamic, simple, and fast data source. SharePoint lists have additional features that allow for seamless connectivity to Power BI Desktop, PowerApps, Power Automate, and Power BI Services.

After connecting Power BI Desktop to a SharePoint list, you may need to clean up the list's data in Power Query before using it. See Chapter 3 to learn the techniques you may need.

Connect to a SharePoint List (continued)

The Windows tab of the dialog box appears.

9 Click **Use my current credentials** (○ changes to ◉) if you want to use the credentials with which you are signed in to Windows.

Ⓐ You can click **Use alternate credentials** (○ changes to ◉) and type your username and password.

10 Click **Connect**.

The SharePoint dialog box closes.

Power BI Desktop establishes the connection to the SharePoint list.

The Navigator dialog box opens.

11 In the left pane, click the list you want to import (☐ changes to ☑). This example uses **Financial Sample Data**.

Ⓑ The list's data appears in the right pane.

12 Click **Load**.

The Navigator dialog box closes.

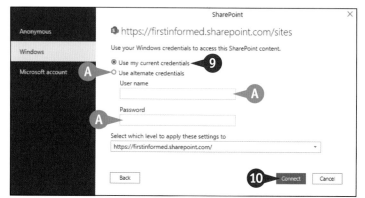

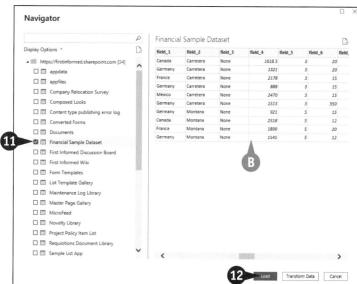

Power BI Desktop displays the data in the Fields pane.

13 Click **Expand** (⟩ changes to ⌄) to the left of the table containing the list you imported.

C The table's tree expands, showing the fields it contains.

14 Click **Save** (🖫).

The Save As dialog box opens.

15 Navigate to the folder in which you want to save the file.

16 Type the filename.

17 Click **Save**.

The Save As dialog box closes.

Power BI Desktop saves the file.

The file is now ready for shaping and cleanup. See Chapter 3.

18 Click **Close** (❎).

The file closes.

Which Microsoft 365 plans include SharePoint?

Two of the business-oriented Microsoft 365 plans, the Microsoft 365 Business Standard plan and the Microsoft 365 Business Premium plan, include SharePoint. Several of the enterprise-oriented Microsoft 365 plans also include SharePoint: Microsoft 365 E3; Microsoft 365 E5; and Microsoft 365 F3, which was formerly known as Microsoft 365 F1.

Implementations vary depending on the company or organization, but Business Standard and Business Premium are plans you might administer yourself. The enterprise-oriented plans would normally be administered by dedicated administrators.

Connect to a SQL Server Database

SQL Server is a relational database management system (RDBMS) developed by Microsoft. SQL Server retrieves and stores data. The data can be stored on a local device, such as your computer; on a server; or on the Internet. SQL Server can work with small to large applications and datasets across various platforms.

To work through this section, you need three things: first, a running instance of SQL Server; second, a database connected to that instance of SQL Server; and third, a means of connecting to SQL Server, such as Microsoft's SQL Server Management Studio tool. See the tips for advice.

Connect to a SQL Server Database

1 In Power BI Desktop, click **Home**.

The Home tab of the ribbon appears.

2 Click **Get data**.

Note: Click the icon part of the Get Data button, not the button's text.

The Get Data dialog box opens.

3 In the left pane, click **Database**.

The Database list appears.

4 Click **SQL Server database** (▥).

5 Click **Connect**.

The Get Data dialog box closes.

The SQL Server Database dialog box opens.

6 Type the server name. This name will vary depending on your computer.

7 Click **Database (optional)** and type the database name. This example uses the database AdventureWorks2019.

8 Click **Advanced options**.

The Advanced Options section expands.

9 Click **Include relationship columns** (☐ changes to ☑).

10 Click **OK**.

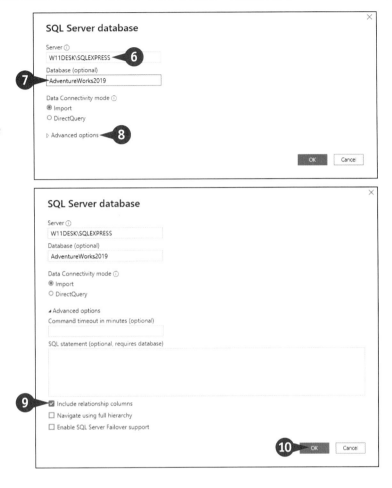

How can I get a SQL Server instance for testing?

Go to www.microsoft.com/en-us/sql-server/sql-server-downloads, locate the Or, Download a Free Specialized Edition section, and then download and install either SQL Server Developer edition or SQL Server Express edition. Both these editions are free. The Developer edition is a full-featured edition for development and testing in nonproduction environments. The Express edition is a somewhat limited edition that Microsoft provides for development and production for desktop, web, and small server applications. You can install either edition on 64-bit versions of Windows 11 or Windows 10 version 1607 or later; you do not need Windows Server.

continued ▶

Connect to a SQL Server Database (continued)

If your company or organization has a SQL Server instance, you will likely want to use that instance. Ask the SQL Server administrator what server name, database name, and credentials to use for the connection.

To work through this section's example directly, download and install SQL Server Management Studio (SMSS) from Microsoft's website, and then install the AdventureWorks2019 database, as explained in the tip.

Connect to a SQL Server Database (continued)

The SQL Server Database dialog box closes.

The SQL Server Database window opens.

11 Click **Use my current credentials** (○ changes to ◉).

12 Click **Connect**.

The SQL Server Database window closes.

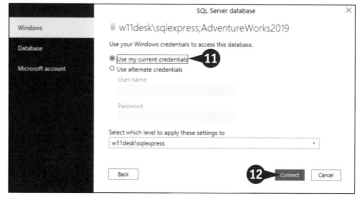

The Navigator dialog box opens.

13 In the left pane, click **HumanResource.vEmployee** (☐ changes to ☑).

A The HumanResource.vEmployee data appears in the right pane.

14 Click **Load**.

The Navigator dialog box closes.

Power BI Desktop displays the data in the Fields pane.

⑮ Click **Expand** (⟩ changes to ⌄) to the left of HumanResources vEmployee.

ⓑ The HumanResources vEmployee tree expands, showing the fields it contains.

⑯ Click **Save** (🖫).

The Save As dialog box opens.

⑰ Navigate to the folder in which you want to save the file.

⑱ Type the filename.

⑲ Click **Save**.

The Save As dialog box closes.

Power BI Desktop saves the file.

You can now work with the connected data.

⑳ When you finish, click **Close** (✖).

The file closes.

TIP

How can I create a SQL Server test environment for working with Power BI?

You can download and install SQL Server Management Studio and a sample database. Microsoft provides SMSS and the sample database for free here: docs.microsoft.com/en-us/sql/samples/adventureworks-install-configure?view=sql-server-ver15&tabs=data-studio#deploy-to-azure-sql-database. You can install SMSS on 64-bit versions of Windows 11 or Windows 10 version 1607 or later; you do not need Windows Server.

Next, import the downloaded database into SQL Server Management Studio. You can then connect from Power BI Desktop as explained in this section.

CHAPTER 3

Cleaning and Shaping Data

In an ideal world, every dataset would be clean, neatly shaped, and ready for use; but in reality, you will likely need to prepare your data carefully before you analyze it. Power BI Desktop enables you to clean and shape data by using Microsoft's Power Query tool, which takes a visual approach to data preparation.

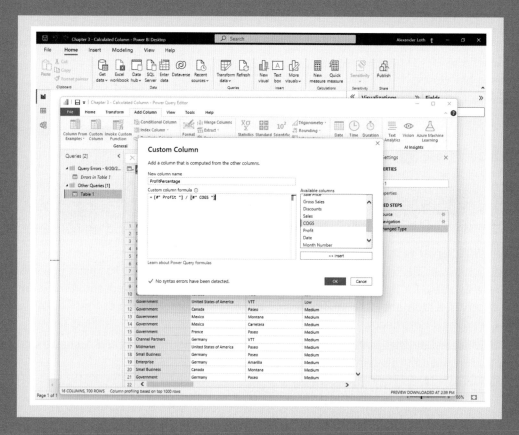

Remove Duplicate Values

When shaping or transforming a dataset, you may discover duplicate records. You can make your data more accurate for your analysis in Power BI by removing all duplicate records. Duplicate records distort your calculations because they contain the same data two or more times. To solve this, you should remove duplicate records.

Power Query Editor's Remove Duplicates feature enables you to remove duplicate values in moments, sparing you hours of tedious manual work. You can use the Remove Duplicates feature either on a single column or on multiple columns at once.

Remove Duplicate Values

Note: This chapter uses the file Chapter 3 - Remove Duplicates.pbix, available at www.wiley.com/go/tyvpowerbi. It also uses the file Financial Sample.xlsx, which you downloaded in Chapter 2. Make sure Financial Sample.xlsx is in the C:\Power BI folder.

1 In Power BI Desktop, open the file Chapter 3 - Remove Duplicates.pbix.

2 Click **Home**.

The Home tab of the ribbon appears.

3 Click **Transform data**.

Note: Click the icon part of the Transform Data button, not the drop-down button (▼).

The Power Query Editor window opens in front of the Power BI Desktop window.

4 Right-click the Segment column heading.

The Segment column becomes selected.

A The Segment column contains many duplicates of "Government."

The contextual menu opens.

5 Click **Remove Duplicates**.

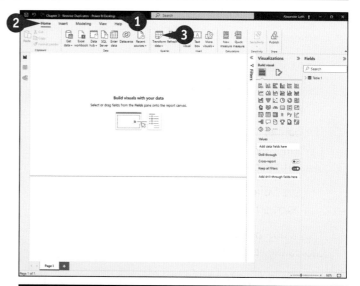

Ⓑ Power Query Editor removes the duplicate values. The Segment column now contains only unique values, such as a single instance of "Government."

Ⓒ The Removed Duplicates step appears in the Applied Steps list.

Ⓓ You can click **Remove** (✖) to remove a step applied to the query.

⑥ Click **Home**.

⑦ Click **Close & Apply** (↑).

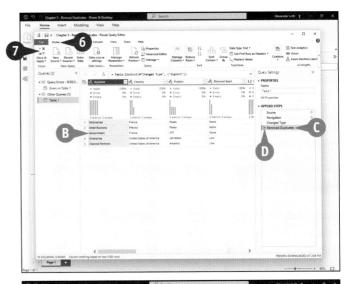

Power Query Editor closes, and the Power BI Desktop window becomes active again.

Ⓔ The banner warns you that your queries contain pending changes that have not been applied.

Ⓕ The Load dialog box appears while Power BI Desktop applies those pending changes.

The dialog box closes automatically, and the banner disappears.

⑧ Click **Save** (💾) to save your changes.

⑨ Click **Close** (✖), and the Chapter 3 - Remove Duplicates.pbix file closes.

TIP

Can I remove duplicate data from multiple columns at the same time?

Yes. Start by selecting the columns. Click the heading of the first column you want to include, and then `Ctrl`+click the heading of each other column you want to include. If all the columns are contiguous, click the first column heading, and then `Shift`+click the last column heading. Right-click any of the selected column headings, and then click **Remove Duplicates** on the contextual menu.

When you select multiple columns, Power Query Editor *concatenates* — joins — the data from the selected columns in each row into a single value. Power Query Editor uses that concatenated value to evaluate the row's uniqueness.

Replace Values in a Column

In many datasets, you will need to replace text, characters, or spaces within the columns when cleaning up the data. Power Query Editor's Replace Values feature enables you to make such replacements easily. The Replace Values feature works in a similar way to Replace features in many apps: You specify the target value in the Value to Find box and the replacement value in the Replace With box. However, you can also search for and fill blank cells, restrict the search to matching entire cell contents, and use special characters in the replacement values.

Replace Values in a Column

Note: This chapter uses the file Chapter 3 - Replace Values.pbix, available at www.wiley.com/go/tyvpowerbi. It also uses the file Financial Sample.xlsx, which you downloaded in Chapter 2. Make sure Financial Sample.xlsx is in the C:\Power BI folder.

1 In Power BI Desktop, open the file Chapter 3 - Replace Values.pbix.

2 Click **Home**.

The Home tab of the ribbon appears.

3 Click **Transform data**.

Note: Click the icon part of the Transform Data button, not the drop-down button (▼).

The Power Query Editor window opens.

4 Click **Home**.

The Home tab of the ribbon appears.

Note: You can also access the Replace Values command in the Any Column group on the Transform tab of the ribbon.

5 Click the heading of the Segment column.

A The Segment column becomes selected.

6 Click **Replace Values**.

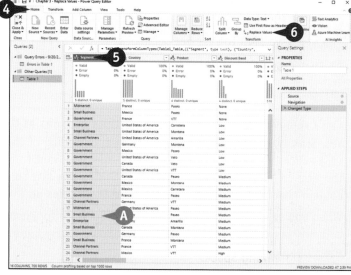

The Replace Values dialog box opens.

7 In the Value to Find box, type the search term. This example uses **Midmarket**.

8 Click **Replace With** and type the replacement text. This example uses **Midmarket changed**.

9 Click **Advanced options** (▷ changes to ◢).

The Advanced Options section appears.

Note: See the first tip to use the Advanced Options controls.

10 Click **OK**.

Power Query Editor replaces all instances of the search term with the replacement text.

Ⓑ The replacement text appears.

Ⓒ The Replaced Value step appears in the Applied Steps list.

11 Click **Close & Apply** (⬆×).

Power Query Editor closes, and the Power BI Desktop window becomes active again.

12 Click **Save** (💾) to save your changes.

13 Click **Close** (✖) to close the file.

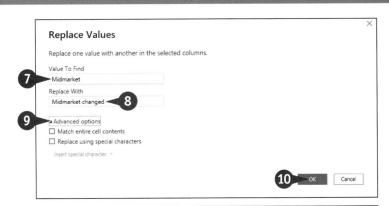

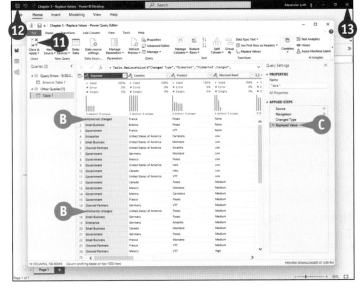

TIPS

How do I use the advanced options in the Replace Values dialog box?
Click **Match entire cell contents** (☐ changes to ☑) to restrict the replacement to when the search term matches the entire cell contents rather than partial cell contents. Click **Replace using special characters** (☐ changes to ☑) if you need to insert tabs, carriage-return characters, line-feed characters, carriage-return-and-line-feed characters, or nonbreaking spaces. Click **Insert special characters** (▼), and then click **Tab**, **Carriage Return**, **Line Feed**, **Carriage Return and Line Feed**, or **Non-breaking Space**.

How do I replace blank cells?
Leave the Value to Find box blank, specify the replacement text in the Replace With box, and then click **OK**.

Split a Column Using a Delimiter

When shaping and forming the data in a dataset, you will often need to split the data contained in a single column. For example, you may need to split a full name into a first name column and a last name column; split a date into day, month, and year columns; or split a text field, as in this example.

Power Query Editor's Split Column feature enables you to split a column's data in six different ways. The Custom setting allows you to use a character, a character combination, or a blank value as the delimiter for the split.

Split a Column Using a Delimiter

Note: This chapter uses the file Chapter 3 - Split Column.pbix, available at www.wiley.com/go/tyvpowerbi. It also uses the file Financial Sample.xlsx, which you downloaded in Chapter 2. Make sure Financial Sample.xlsx is in the C:\Power BI folder.

1. In Power BI Desktop, open the file Chapter 3 - Split Column.pbix.

2. Click **Home**.

   The Home tab of the ribbon appears.

3. Click **Transform data**.

Note: Click the icon part of the Transform Data button, not the drop-down button (▼).

   The Power Query Editor window opens.

4. Right-click the heading of the Segment column.

   Ⓐ The Segment column becomes selected.

   The contextual menu opens.

5. Click or highlight **Split Column**.

   The continuation menu opens.

6. Click **By Delimiter**.

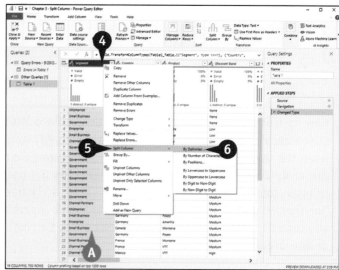

7 In the Split Column by Delimiter dialog box, click **Select or enter delimiter** (▼) and then click the delimiter you want to use. This example uses **Space**.

8 In the Split At area, click the split option you want (○ changes to ◉). This example uses **Each occurrence of the delimiter**.

9 Click **OK**.

Ⓑ Power Query Editor splits all the text entries at the spaces they contain. It renames the original column "Segment.1" and creates a new column named "Segment.2."

Ⓒ The Split Column by Delimiter step and the Changed Type1 step appear in the Applied Steps list.

10 Click **Close & Apply** (⌐×↑).

Power Query Editor closes.

The Power BI Desktop window appears again.

11 Click **Save** (💾).

Power BI Desktop saves your changes.

12 Click **Close** (✕).

The file closes.

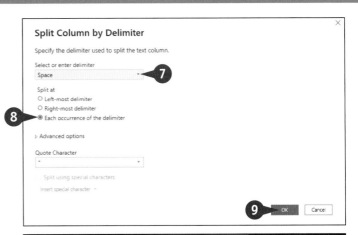

TIP

What other ways can I split a column?

You can split a column by specifying a number of characters. For example, you might move the left 15 characters of the existing column to a new column or split the existing column into three-character groups. You can split a column by specifying the character positions at which to split, such as **0, 3, 8, 12**. You can choose **By Lowercase to Uppercase** or **By Uppercase to Lowercase** to split the column where the case changes. You can choose **By Digit to Non-Digit** or **By Non-Digit to Digit** to split the column where the text changes between digits and other characters.

Group Data

When preparing your dataset for analysis, you may want to group related data into a single item. Power Query Editor enables you to group the same values in one or more columns into a single grouped row. You can either group columns by using an aggregate function or group them by values in a row.

Which group function you use depends on the type of data you are grouping. For example, you can group numeric data by using functions such as SUM, AVERAGE, MAX, and MIN.

Group Data

Note: This chapter uses the file Chapter 3 - Group Data.pbix, available at www.wiley.com/go/tyvpowerbi. It also uses the file Financial Sample.xlsx, which you downloaded in Chapter 2. Make sure Financial Sample.xlsx is in the C:\Power BI folder.

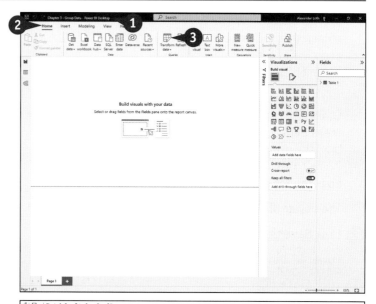

1 In Power BI Desktop, open the file Chapter 3 - Group Data.pbix.

2 Click **Home**.

The Home tab of the ribbon appears.

3 Click **Transform data**.

Note: Click the icon part of the Transform Data button, not the drop-down button (▼).

The Power Query Editor window opens.

4 Right-click the heading of the column by which you want to group. The example uses **Segment**.

A The Segment column becomes selected.

The contextual menu opens.

5 Click **Group By** to open the Group By dialog box.

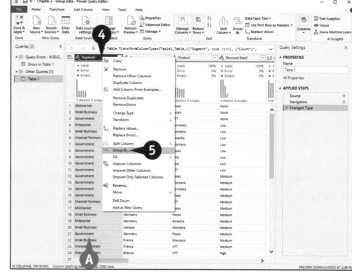

6 Click **Basic** (○ changes to ◉).

7 Verify that the first drop-down list contains the correct column; if not, click ▼ and click the column. This example uses the **Segment** column.

8 Click **New column name** and type the name for the new column. This example uses **COGS by Segment**.

9 Click **Operation** (▼) and then click the operation. This example uses **Sum**.

10 Click **Column** (▼) and then click the column to use. This example uses **COGS**.

11 Click **OK**.

Ⓑ Power Query Editor creates a summary table showing the Segment column and the COGS by Segment column. Power Query Editor removes all other columns from the table.

12 Click **Close & Apply** (⬚).

Power Query Editor closes, and the Power BI Desktop window becomes active again.

13 Click **Save** (▣) to save your changes.

14 Click **Close** (▣) to close the file (not shown).

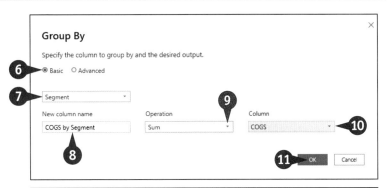

TIP

How do I group by multiple columns?

In the Group By dialog box, click **Advanced** (○ changes to ◉). Make sure the first drop-down list contains the first column you want to use, and then click **Add grouping** to display a second drop-down list. Click ▼ to open this drop-down list, and then click the next column. To add further columns, click **Add grouping** again; lather, rinse, and repeat. Specify the means of aggregation as explained in steps **8** to **10**. To add another grouping, click **Add aggregation** to display another row of controls, and then specify the new column name, the operation, and the column. After making your choices, click **OK**.

Add a Calculated Column

To analyze your datasets effectively, you can leverage Power Query Editor's capability for adding calculated columns. A *calculated column* is a new column that contains the result of a calculation that uses existing columns. This section's example calculates the profit percentage per row of the table using the formula Profit/COGS. This is a simple query in the M language that Power Query uses.

That example is straightforward, but you can also create intelligence-based calculated columns. For example, a calculated column could automatically calculate age, days, months, or years by extracting the data from a Date and Time column.

Add a Calculated Column

Note: This chapter uses the file Chapter 3 - Calculated Column.pbix, available at www.wiley.com/go/tyvpowerbi. It also uses the file Financial Sample.xlsx, which you downloaded in Chapter 2. Make sure Financial Sample.xlsx is in the C:\Power BI folder.

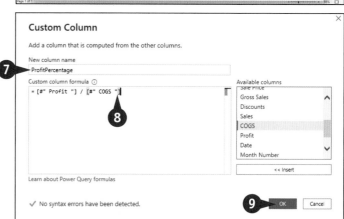

① In Power BI Desktop, open the file Chapter 3 - Calculated Column.pbix.

② Click **Home**.

The Home tab of the ribbon appears.

③ Click **Transform data**.

The Power Query Editor window opens.

④ Click **Add Column**.

The Add Column tab of the ribbon appears.

⑤ Click the Segment column heading.

Ⓐ The Segment column becomes selected.

⑥ Click **Custom Column**.

The Custom Column dialog box opens.

⑦ Type a new column name. This example uses **Profit Percentage**.

⑧ Click after the equal sign, =, in the Custom Column Formula box and type the formula in the M language. This example uses **[#" Profit "] / [#" COGS "]**.

⑨ Click **OK**.

The Custom Column dialog box closes.

Ⓑ Power Query Editor inserts the Profit Percentage column after the last existing column.

Note: Power Query Editor assigns the Any data type to the new column. Usually, you will want to assign a specific data type to the new column to make it show its contents the way you want them to appear.

⑩ Click **Any** (ABC 123).

The drop-down menu opens.

⑪ Click **Percentage** (%).

Ⓒ Power Query Editor changes the data type to Percentage.

⑫ Click **Home**.

The Home tab of the ribbon appears.

⑬ Click **Close & Apply** (⌐×↗).

Power Query Editor closes.

The Power BI Desktop window appears again.

⑭ Click **Save** (💾).

Power BI Desktop saves your changes.

⑮ Click **Close** (✕).

The file closes.

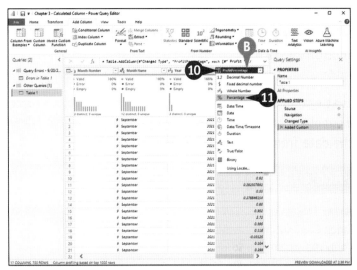

TIP

How do I use the Available Columns list box in the Custom Column dialog box?
Instead of typing the names of the columns you want to use in a formula, you can use the entries in the Available Columns box to insert column names quickly and accurately. Position the insertion point where you want the column name to appear in the formula. Then either click the column name and click **<< Insert**, or simply double-click the column name. Power Query Editor inserts the column name in the required format.

Add an Index Column

When you need to identify every row in a table uniquely, you can add an index column. Index columns are frequently used in transaction tables and can be helpful for selecting, grouping, and sorting data.

Power Query Editor enables you to add an index column to a table quickly and easily. Better still, you can perform the indexing at any point in your transformation steps. Normally, you start the index numbering at 1 and increase it by 1 for each item, but you can start at a different number or use a different increment when you need to.

Add an Index Column

Note: This chapter uses the file Chapter 3 - Index Column.pbix, available at www.wiley.com/go/tyvpowerbi. It also uses the file Financial Sample.xlsx, which you downloaded in Chapter 2. Make sure Financial Sample.xlsx is in the C:\Power BI folder.

1 In Power BI Desktop, open the file Chapter 3 - Index Column.pbix.

2 Click **Home**.

The Home tab of the ribbon appears.

3 Click **Transform data**.

Note: Click the icon part of the Transform Data button, not the drop-down button (▼).

The Power Query Editor window opens.

4 Click **Add Column**.

The Add Column tab of the ribbon appears.

5 Click **Index Column** (▼).

The drop-down menu opens.

6 Click **Custom**.

The Add Index Column dialog box opens.

7 Type the starting value. This example uses **1**.

8 Click in the Increment box and type the increment value. This example uses **1**.

9 Click **OK**.

The Add Index Column dialog box closes.

A Power Query Editor adds an index column after the last column.

B Power Query Editor populates the index column starting at the number you entered and using the increment you specified.

10 Click **Home**.

The Home tab of the ribbon appears.

11 Click **Close & Apply** (⌧).

Power Query Editor closes.

The Power BI Desktop window appears again.

12 Click **Save** (🖫).

Power BI Desktop saves your changes.

13 Click **Close** (⌧).

The file closes.

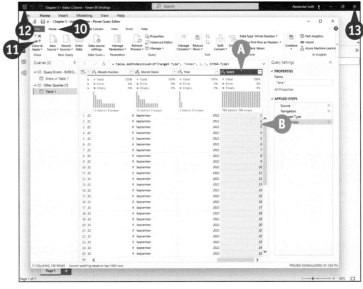

TIP

Why does the Index Column drop-down list give zero as a starting number?

The starting number 0 in the Index Column drop-down list can be useful if you need to map your index numbers directly to computer-style counting, which starts at zero by default. However, if your numbering scheme starts at 1, as is typical for human counting, it usually makes more sense to start your index numbering at 1.

CHAPTER 4

Modeling Data in Model View

Power BI Desktop includes extensive features for performing data modeling on your datasets. In this chapter, you work with Model View, which enables you to work with complex datasets that contain many tables. Model View displays all your model's tables, columns, and relationships, enabling you not only to grasp complex relationships between many tables easily but also to manipulate them.

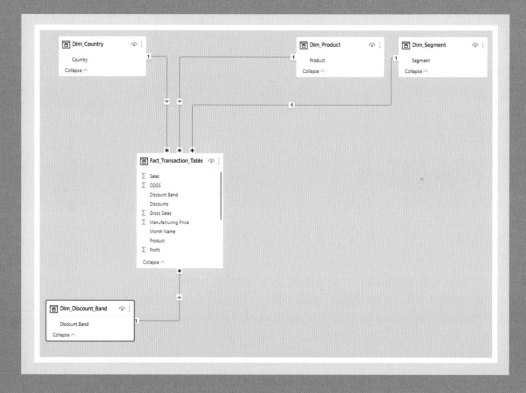

Create Dimension Tables

A dimension table is one of the components of a data warehouse schema, in which the dimension table connects to a fact table. A dimension table contains a key column that acts as a unique identifier for this connection, plus descriptive columns that provide extra data.

In this section, you create four dimension tables by copying an existing table, removing all the columns except one, and then stripping out duplicate values. Later in this chapter, you use these four dimension tables as components of a star schema — see the section "Create a Star Schema."

Create Dimension Tables

Note: This section uses the database Chapter 4 - Dimension Tables.pbix, available at www.wiley.com/go/tyvpowerbi. This database is based on results from Chapter 3.

Create a Dimension Column for Segments

1 In Power BI Desktop, open the database file Chapter 4 - Dimension Tables.pbix.

2 Click **Home**.

The Home tab of the ribbon appears.

3 Click **Transform data**.

Note: Click the icon part of the Transform Data button, not the drop-down button (▼).

The Power Query Editor window opens.

4 Right-click the Table 1 name.

The contextual menu opens.

5 Click **Duplicate**.

Ⓐ Power Query Editor duplicates Table 1 and names the duplicate Table 1 (2).

Power Query Editor selects the duplicate table.

6 Right-click the Segment column heading.

The contextual menu opens.

7 Click **Remove Other Columns**.

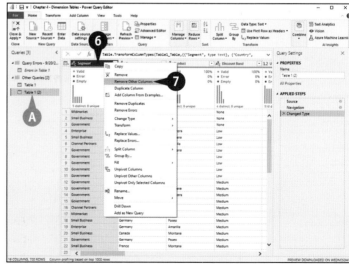

Power Query Editor removes all the other columns, leaving only the Segment column.

8 Right-click the Segment column heading.

The contextual menu opens.

9 Click **Remove Duplicates**.

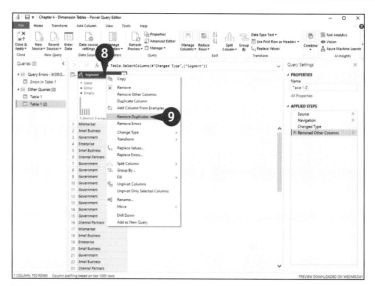

B Power BI removes all duplicate values, leaving only the unique values in the column.

10 Double-click **Table 1 (2)**.

Power Query Editor opens the table name for editing, selecting the existing name so that you can type over it.

11 Type the new name, **Dim_Segment**, and then press Enter.

Power Query Editor applies the new name.

You have created a dimension table.

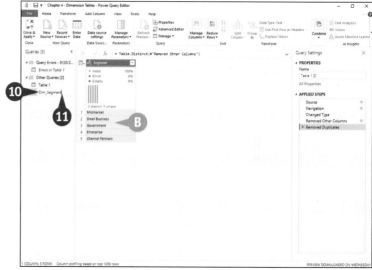

TIP

What naming convention should I use for my tables?

Start the names of your dimension tables with Dim and the names of your fact tables with Fact to enable any user to understand which tables are dimension tables and which are fact tables. After this identifying prefix, use either the convention _Table_Name, separating the initial-capped words with underscores, or simply the convention TableName, using an initial capital to start each word. So a dimension table might be named Dim_Discount_Band or DimDiscountBand, and a fact table might be named Fact_Sales or FactSales.

continued ▶

Create Dimension Tables (continued)

You use dimension tables to describe different aspects of a business process. For example, when determining sales targets, you can store the targets' attributes in a dimension table and refer to the table in your calculations.

The four dimension tables you create in this section have names derived from the table columns that provide their data. The Dim_Segment dimension table draws from the Segment column, the Dim_Country dimension table from the Country column, the Dim_Product dimension table from the Product column, and the Dim_Discount_Band dimension table from the Discount Band column.

Create Dimension Tables (continued)

Create a Dimension Table for Countries

1 Still working in Power Query Editor, right-click **Table 1** in the Queries pane.

The contextual menu opens.

2 Click **Duplicate**.

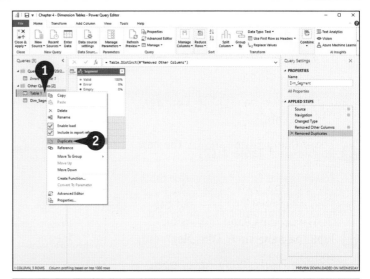

A Power Query Editor creates a duplicate of Table 1, naming it Table 1 (2).

3 Right-click the Country column heading.

B The Country column becomes selected.

The contextual menu opens.

4 Click **Remove Other Columns**.

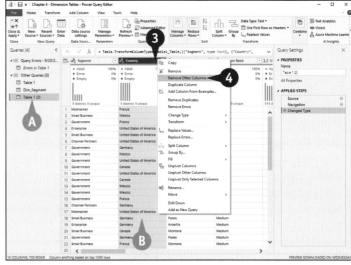

Power Query Editor removes all the other columns, leaving only the Country column.

5 Right-click the Country column heading.

The contextual menu opens.

6 Click **Remove Duplicates**.

C Power Query Editor removes all duplicate values, leaving only the unique values in the column.

7 Double-click **Table 1 (2)**.

Power Query Editor opens the table name for editing.

8 Type the new name, **Dim_Country**, and then press **Enter**.

Power Query Editor applies the new name.

You can now create the Dim_Product dimension table and the Dim_Discount_Band dimension table. See the tip for details.

Note: Leave Power Query Editor open so you can continue with the next section, "Create Relationships Between Tables."

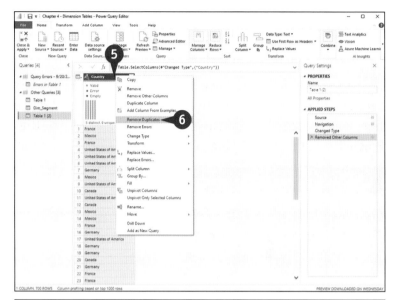

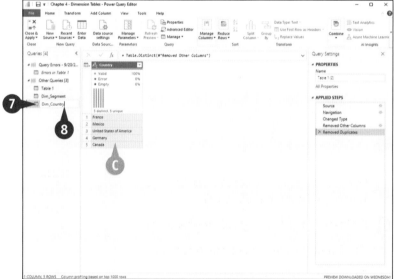

TIP

How do I create the Dim_Product and Dim_Discount_Band dimension tables?

To create the Dim_Product dimension table, repeat steps **1** to **8** in the subsection "Create a Dimension Table for Countries." This time, use the Product column instead of the Country column, and name the dimension table **Dim_Product** rather than Dim_Country.

Create the Dim_Discount_Band dimension table in the same way, by following steps **1** to **8** in the subsection "Create a Dimension Table for Countries." Use the Discount Band column and name the dimension table **Dim_Discount_Band**.

Create Relationships Between Tables

To create a star schema or snowflake schema, you need a fact table and at least one dimension table. Once you have these tables, you can create a relationship between the fact table and each dimension table that will connect to it in the schema.

In this section, you work with the four dimension tables you created in the previous section: Dim_Segment, Dim_Country, Dim_Product, and Dim_Discount_Band. You create a fact table named Fact_Transaction_Table and then connect the dimension tables to it by establishing relationships using Model View in Power BI Desktop.

Create Relationships Between Tables

Note: Start this section in Power Query Editor after completing the previous section and creating the four dimension tables.

1 Double-click the Table 1 name in the Queries pane.

Power Query Editor opens the name for editing.

2 Type the new name, **Fact_Transaction_Table**, and press Enter.

Power Query Editor applies the new name, creating a fact table. You now have four dimension tables and one fact table.

3 Click **Home**.

The Home tab of the ribbon appears.

4 Click **Close & Apply**.

Power Query Editor saves your changes and closes.

The Power BI Desktop window becomes active.

5 Click **Model View** (⊞).

Power BI Desktop switches to Model View.

A Power BI Desktop automatically creates a data model with active relationships.

6 Right-click a relationship line.

7 In the contextual menu, click **Delete**.

8 In the Delete Relationship dialog box, click **Yes**.

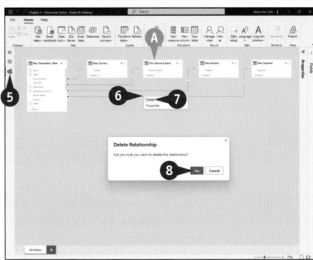

Power BI Desktop deletes the relationship line.

9 Repeat steps **6** to **8** for the remaining three relationship lines, deleting each one.

10 In the Fact_Transaction_Table table, scroll down as far as needed to make the Country column and the Segment column appear in the columns shown.

11 Click **Segment** in the Dim_Segment table, drag it to the Segment column in the Fact_ Transaction_Table table, and drop it there.

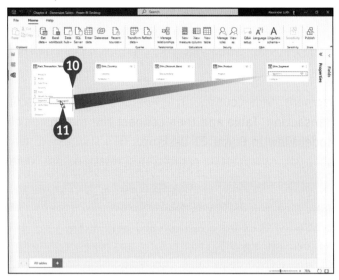

B Power BI creates a one-to-many relationship between the Dim_Segment table to the Fact_Transaction_Table table.

C The arrow (◀) indicates that the relationship has a single directional filter capability.

D The 1 icon (1) indicates One.

E The * icon (*) indicates Many.

12 Click **Country** in the Dim_Country table, drag it to the Country column in the Fact_ Transaction_Table table, and drop it there.

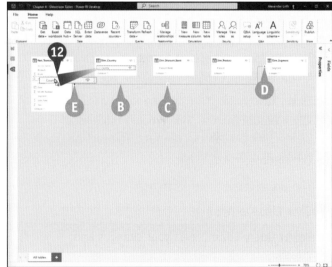

TIP

What does the Properties item on the contextual menu for a relationship line do?

Right-click a relationship line to open the contextual menu, and then click **Properties** to display the Edit Relationship dialog box, which enables you to configure the relationship's details, including its cardinality and the direction of the filtering applied to the relationship. In databases, *cardinality* describes the type of relationship between two objects, such as tables. The three most widely used cardinalities are one-to-one, one-to-many, and many-to-many.

continued ▶

Power BI not only enables you to build your data model by specifying the relationships between your various data tables but also can automatically detect relationship cardinality and suggest a data model. While Power BI's detection capabilities are impressive, you should always review and test the relationships in a suggested data model before moving on to analytics. Even after beginning your data analysis, you should periodically review your data model to ensure it is delivering optimal performance.

In this section, you delete Power BI's suggested relationships not because they are wrong but so that you can practice establishing relationships manually.

Create Relationships Between Tables (continued)

A Power BI creates a one-to-many relationship between the Dim_Country table and the Fact_Transaction_Table table. This relationship has a single directional filter capability, as indicated by the arrow (◄).

13 In the Fact_Transaction_Table table, scroll up as far as needed to make the Discount Band column and the Product column appear in the columns shown.

14 Click **Product** in the Dim_Product table, drag it to the Product column in the Fact_Transaction_Table table, and drop it there.

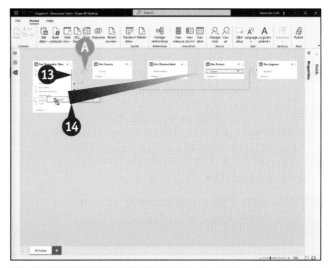

B Power BI creates a one-to-many relationship between the Dim_Product table and the Fact_Transaction_Table table. This relationship has a single directional filter capability, as indicated by the arrow (◄).

15 Click **Discount Band** in the Dim_Discount_Band table, drag it to the Discount Band column in the Fact_Transaction_Table table, and drop it there.

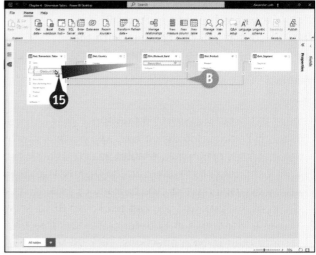

C Power BI creates a one-to-many relationship between the Dim_Discount_Band table and the Fact_Transaction_Table table. This relationship has a single directional filter capability, as indicated by the arrow (◀).

16 Click **Manage Relationships**.

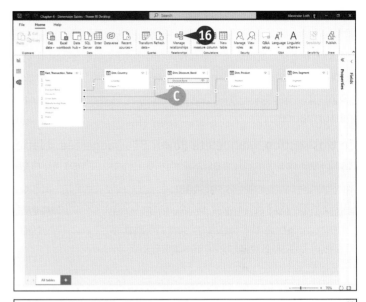

The Manage Relationships dialog box opens, showing the relationships in the data model.

D You can click the check box (☑ changes to ☐) to make a relationship inactive.

E You can click **Edit** to edit the selected relationship.

F You can click **Delete** to delete the selected relationship.

17 When you finish reviewing and editing the relationships, click **Close**.

The Manage Relationships dialog box closes.

Note: Leave the file open in Power BI Desktop so that you can continue with the next section, "Create a Star Schema."

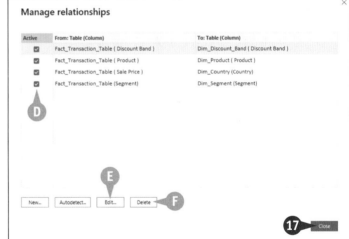

TIP

What edits can I make to a relationship?

The Edit Relationship dialog box, which opens when you click **Edit** for a selected link in the Manage Relationships dialog box, enables you to make wide-ranging changes to a relationship. You can change the tables and columns involved in the relationship. You can change the cardinality of the relationship — for example, changing from one-to-many cardinality to one-to-one cardinality. You can make the relationship active or inactive, and you can tell Power BI to assume referential integrity for the relationship. You can choose either Single or Both for cross-filter direction; if you choose both, you can make Power BI apply a security filter in both directions. Click **OK** when you finish making changes.

Create a Star Schema

ow that you have established the relationships between your fact table and your four dimension tables, you can organize the five tables into a star schema. A *star schema* is a structure for organizing a database suitably for data warehousing or business intelligence using a single fact table and one or more dimension tables.

The term *star schema* is derived from the logical shape of the data model, in which the fact table sits at the center of the star with the dimension tables arranged around it, each on a separate arm consisting of a relationship line.

Create a Star Schema

Note: Start this section in Power BI Desktop after completing the previous section and creating the relationships between the fact table and the four dimension tables.

1. Verify that Power BI Desktop is using Model View. If not, click **Model view** (⊞) to switch to Model View.

2. Click the title bar of the Fact_Transaction_ Table table and drag the table to the middle of the window.

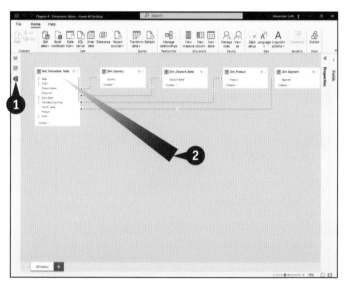

Ⓐ The Fact_Transaction_Table table appears in its new position.

Ⓑ Power BI Desktop redraws the relationship lines to suit the table's new position.

3. Click the title bar of the Dim_Discount_ Band table and drag the table to the lower-left corner.

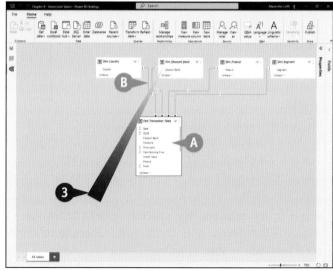

C The Dim_Discount_Band table appears in its new position.

D Power BI Desktop redraws the relationship lines to reflect the table's new position.

4 Click the title bar of the Dim_Segment table and drag the table to the lower-right corner.

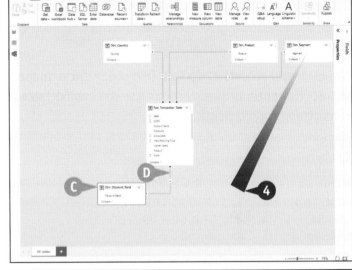

E The Dim_Segment table appears in its new position.

F Again, Power BI Desktop redraws the relationship lines appropriately.

You now have a four-pointed star schema. The center of the star is the fact table, and each of the four points is a dimension table.

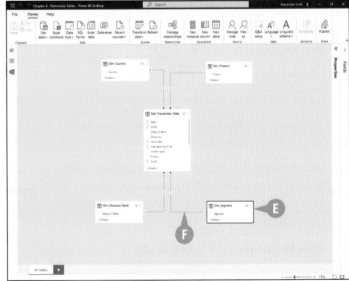

TIP

What is the star schema good for?

The star schema is optimized for querying large datasets and is best used for historical data. Users can filter and group these aggregations by dimensions, "slicing and dicing" the data to locate information that interests them.

For technical reasons, the Power BI engine generally works best with a star schema. So if you are trying to decide which type of schema to create, start by evaluating a star schema to see if it meets your company's or organization's needs.

Create a Hierarchical Schema

Astar schema, such as the one you created in the previous section, "Create a Star Schema," is useful for various data models. But Power BI Desktop also enables you to create hierarchical schemas, which can give better performance when your data model draws data from multiple isolated systems.

A *hierarchical schema* has a tree-like organizational structure in which a root directory stores data as records that link to subdirectories. The root directory is considered the *parent* directory, and the subdirectories are *child* directories. For example, if your company has a Country-based Product category, Country is the parent directory and Product is the child directory.

Create a Hierarchical Schema

Note: This section uses the Chapter 4 - Hierarchical Schema.pbix file, available at www.wiley.com/go/tyvpowerbi.

Lay Out the Tables for a Parent-Child Hierarchical Schema

1 Open the Chapter 4 - Hierarchical Schema.pbix file.

2 Click **Model view** (▦).

Power BI Desktop switches to Model View.

Note: Collapse the Properties pane and the Fields pane if you need more space.

3 Click the title bar of the Fact_Transaction_Table table and drag the table to the lower-right corner, freeing up space in the upper-left corner.

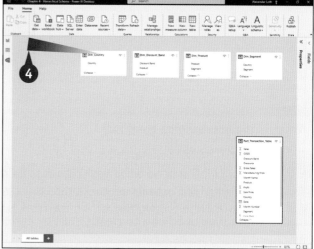

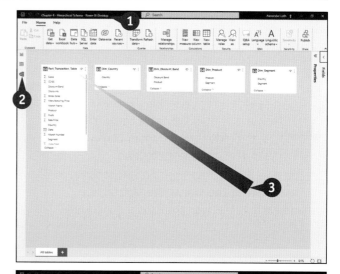

4 Click the title bar of the Dim_Country table and drag the table to the upper-left corner.

5 Click the title bar of the Dim_Segment table and drag the table to the right of the Dim_Country table, placing it slightly lower as if creating steps on a staircase.

6 Click the title bar of the Dim_Product table and drag the table to the right of the Dim_Segment table, again placing it slightly lower as if one step down.

7 Click the title bar of the Dim_Discount_ Band table and drag the table to the right of the Dim_Product table, again placing it slightly lower as if one step down.

You have now arranged the four dimension tables and one fact table in the basis of a simple parent–child hierarchical schema.

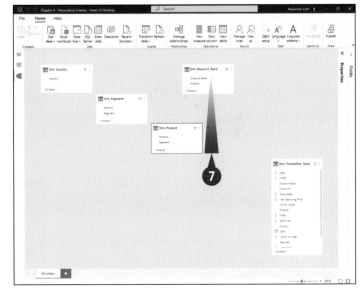

TIP

When should I create a hierarchical schema?
Create a hierarchical schema when your data model draws data from multiple isolated systems. Because the tables in a hierarchical schema are separated from physical storage structures, you can quickly add or delete information without affecting the rest of the database. As a result, the data model is fast and responsive.

continued ▶

To create a hierarchical schema, you need dimension tables configured differently from the dimension tables you created for the star schema. Each dimension table for a hierarchical schema must have a parent column and a child column for that column. You can create these dimension tables from the Fact_Transaction_Table table by using the SUMMARIZE function; see the tip for an outline of the process.

Because creating these dimension tables is peripheral to this book's focus, the Chapter 4 - Hierarchical Schema.pbix file contains ready-to-use dimension tables, so you need not create them yourself.

Create a Hierarchical Schema (continued)

Create the Relationships Between the Tables

1 Click the Country column in the Dim_Country table and drag it to the Country column in the Dim_Segment table.

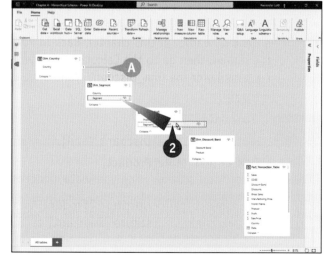

A Power BI Desktop creates a one-to-many link between the Dim_Country table and the Dim_Segment table.

2 Click the Segment column in the Dim_Segment table and drag it to the Segment column in the Dim_Product table.

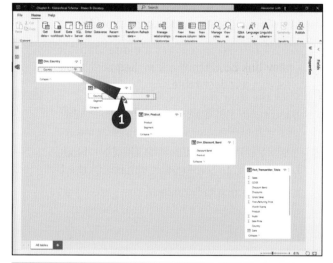

The Create Relationship dialog box opens.

3 Verify that the Cardinality drop-down menu shows Many to Many.

4 Verify that the Cross Filter Direction drop-down menu shows Both.

5 Click **OK**.

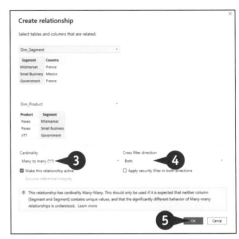

The Create Relationship dialog box closes.

B Power BI Desktop creates a bidirectional many-to-many link between the Dim_Segment table and the Dim_Product table.

C The double-arrow icon (◆▶) indicates that the link is bidirectional.

6 Click the Product column in the Dim_Product table and drag it to the Product column in the Dim_Discount_Band table.

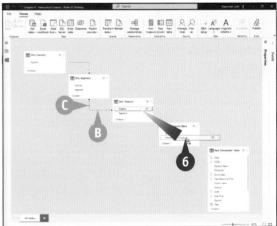

TIP

How would I create the dimension tables for the hierarchical schema?

Create the Fact_Transaction_Table table as explained at the start of the section "Create Relationships Between Tables," earlier in this chapter. Back in Power BI Editor, click **Modeling** to display the Modeling tab of the ribbon; then go to the Calculations group and click **New table**. In the Formula bar, enter the following formula for the Dim_Discount_Band dimension table:

= SUMMARIZE (

    Fact_Transaction_Table,

    Fact_Transaction_Table[Discount Band],

    Fact_Transaction_Table[Product]

)

For the Dim_Product table, substitute **[Product]** on the third line and **[Segment]** on the fourth line. For the Dim_Segment table, substitute **[Segment]** on the third line and **[Country]** on the fourth line.

continued ▶

Once you have the right type of dimension tables for the hierarchical schema, you can create the schema by dragging the dimension tables and the fact table to suitable places on the workspace and establishing relationships between them. To establish a relationship, you drag the parent column in a table to the child column in the table to which you want to link it. Power BI Desktop automatically detects the appropriate relationship type. If Power BI Desktop detects a many-to-many relationship, it displays the Create Relationship dialog box so that you can easily configure the relationship.

Create a Hierarchical Schema (continued)

The Create Relationship dialog box opens again.

7 Verify that the Cardinality drop-down menu shows Many to Many.

8 Verify that the Cross Filter Direction drop-down menu shows Both.

9 Click **OK**.

The Create Relationship dialog box closes.

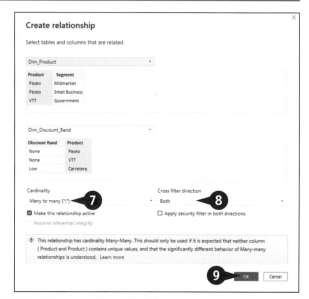

A Power BI Desktop creates a bidirectional many-to-many link between the Dim_Product table and the Dim_Discount_Band table.

10 Click the Discount_Band column in the Dim_Discount_Band table and drag it to the Discount_Band column in the Fact_Transaction_Table table.

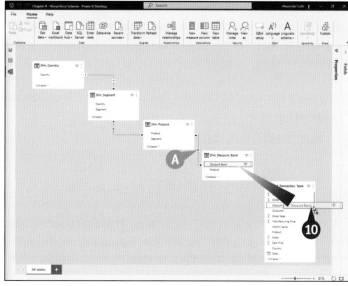

The Create Relationship dialog box opens once more.

⑪ Verify that the Cardinality drop-down menu shows Many to Many.

⑫ Verify that the Cross Filter Direction drop-down menu shows Both.

⑬ Click **OK**.

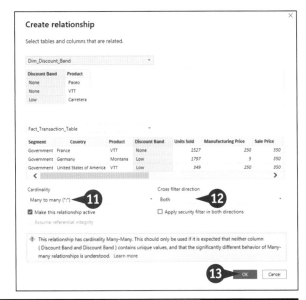

The Create Relationship dialog box closes.

Ⓑ Power BI Desktop creates a bidirectional many-to-many link between the Dim_ Discount_Band table and the Fact_ Transaction_Table table.

Note: Leave the Power BI database file open so that you can work through the next section, "Using the Properties Pane."

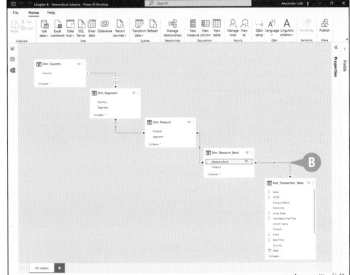

TIP

How do I change a relationship created using the wrong type?
Double-click the relationship line to open the Edit Relationship dialog box, which is essentially the Create Relationship dialog box under a different name. You can then change the relationship's cardinality or cross-filter direction; make the relationship active or inactive, as needed; and set Power BI Desktop to assume referential integrity for the relationship. If you set Both in the Cross Filter Direction drop-down list, you can choose whether to apply the security filter in both directions.

Using the Properties Pane

Power BI Desktop's Model View includes the Properties pane and the Fields pane. The Properties pane enables you to view and change the properties of individual objects in your model. The Fields pane provides a way to navigate the tables, columns, and measures in your model, enabling you to select the object you want to inspect or configure. If the Fields pane is hidden, click **Show** (**<**) to display it. If the Properties pane is collapsed, click **Expand** (**«**) to expand it.

Configure Table Properties

Ⓐ Fields Pane

Click a table here to display its properties in the Properties pane. Click **Expand** (**>**) to show the table's contents.

Ⓑ Properties Pane

This pane displays the properties of the selected object.

Ⓒ Name

View or change the table name.

Ⓓ Description

View or change the table's description, which should explain its purpose.

Ⓔ Synonyms

View or change synonyms used by DAX calculation references.

Ⓕ Row Label

Select the row that best represents the table.

Ⓖ Key Column

Select the column for connecting the table to another table.

Ⓗ Is Hidden

Set this switch to On (○— changes to —●) to hide the table from the report view.

Ⓘ Is Featured Table

Set this switch to On (○— changes to —●) to mark the table as featured, which makes its data discoverable in connected products.

Ⓙ Storage Mode

In this drop-down list, choose the storage mode: Direct Query, Import, or Dual.

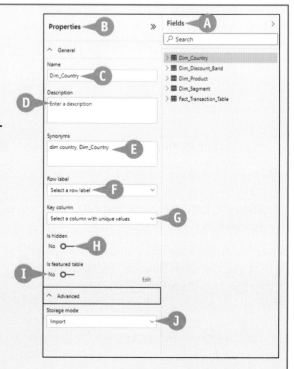

Configure Column Properties

Ⓐ Column in the Fields Pane

Click the column whose properties you want to display.

Ⓑ Name

View or change the column name.

Ⓒ Description

View or change the column's description, which should make clear its purpose.

Ⓓ Synonyms

View or change synonyms used by DAX calculation references.

Ⓔ Display Folder

Optionally create a folder for grouping the column, enabling you to organize your data more neatly.

Ⓕ Is Hidden

Set this switch to On (○— changes to —●) to hide the column from the report view.

Ⓖ Data Type

In this drop-down list, select the column's data type, such as Text, True/False, or Whole Number.

Ⓗ Format

In this drop-down list, specify any format needed for the column's data, such as Currency or Percentage.

Ⓘ Sort by Column

In this drop-down list, select the column used to sort the table.

Ⓙ Data Category

In this drop-down list, select the column's data category, such as Address, Longitude, or Web URL.

Summarize By

Use the scroll bar to scroll down and continue viewing properties. In the Summarize By drop-down list, set the function by which to summarize the column, such as Sum, Max, or Average.

Is Nullable

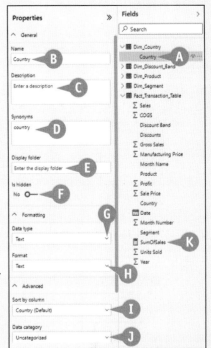

Use the scroll bar to scroll down and continue viewing properties. Set the Is Nullable switch to On (—●) to permit null cells in the column; set it to Off (○—) to ban null cells.

Ⓚ Measures

In the Fields pane, click a measure, such as SumOfSales in the Fact_Transaction_Table table, to display its properties. The Name, Description, Synonyms, Display Folder, Is Hidden, Format, and Data Category settings work as for the equivalent column properties. Other settings include Home Table, which lets you specify the table containing the measure; and Percentage Format, Thousands Separator, and Decimal Place, which enable you to configure the display of the measure's numbers.

CHAPTER 5

Creating Basic Visualizations

Visualizations, also known as *visuals* or *charts*, allow you to see your data as pictures instead of numbers. Visualizations help you to grasp, understand, and gain insights from your data faster. Power BI includes a wide range of visualizations, including waterfall, ribbon, pie, scatter, and gauge. You can slice, filter, highlight, modify, and even drill into the visualizations.

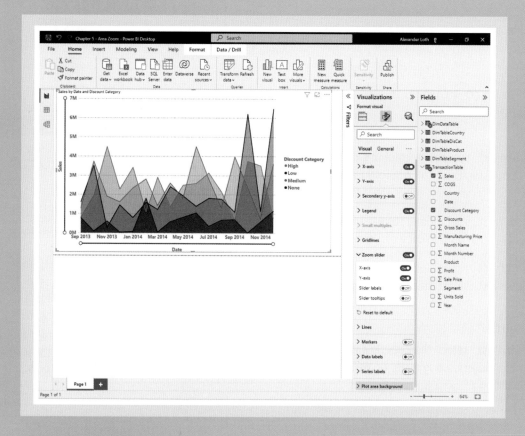

Create a Bar Chart

A bar chart is one of the most basic types of visual, but it is also one of the most useful tools for exploring and understanding your data. A *bar chart*, also called a *bar graph* or a *column chart*, represents numeric values for different categories as a series of bars. The numeric values are plotted on one axis of the chart, with the individual categories on the other axis.

Because the length of each bar indicates its value, and because the bars are plotted on a common baseline, you can easily compare the values. Power BI automatically sorts the bar chart from largest value to smallest value.

Create a Bar Chart

Note: This section uses the Chapter 5 - Bar Chart.pbix database, available at www.wiley.com/go/tyvpowerbi.

1 In Power BI Desktop, open the Chapter 5 - Bar Chart.pbix database file.

Note: If the Fields pane and the Visualizations pane are collapsed, expand them.

2 Click **Build Visual** (▦).

The Build Visual controls appear in the Visualizations pane.

3 Click **Clustered bar chart** (▤).

A A visual placeholder appears.

4 Click **Expand** (⟩ changes to ⌄) to the left of TransactionTable.

The TransactionTable section expands.

5 Click **Country** (☐ changes to ☑).

B The Country field appears in the visual placeholder.

6 Click **Sales** (☐ changes to ☑).

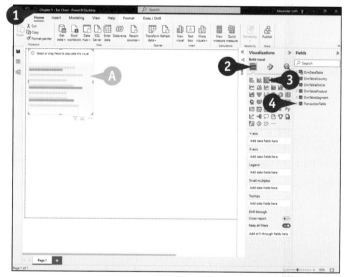

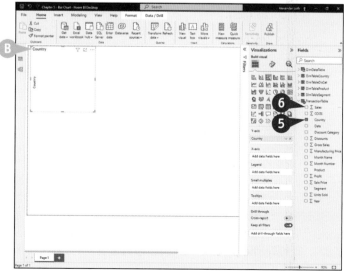

The Sales field's data appears in the visual placeholder, creating the bar chart.

Note: By default, Power BI Desktop displays the Sales field's data as a SUM aggregate. You can choose from various aggregate options.

7 Drag the lower-right frame handle down and to the right.

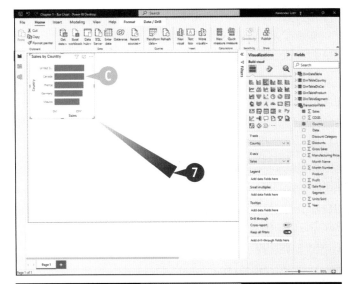

The visual expands, making space for its labels to appear in full instead of truncated and enabling you to see the results more easily.

Note: Drag a corner handle to resize the visual in both dimensions. Drag a side handle to change the visual's width without affecting its height. Drag the top handle or bottom handle to change the visual's height without changing its width.

8 Click **Save** ().

Power BI Desktop saves your changes.

9 Click **Close** (⊠).

The file closes.

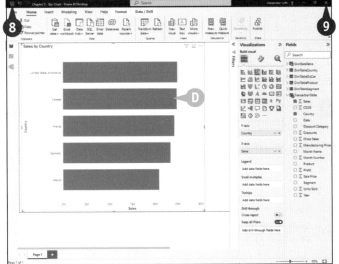

TIP

How do I reposition a visual?

To reposition a visual quickly, move the pointer over the visual, click, and then drag the visual to where you want it.

To reposition a visual more precisely, go to the top of the Visualizations pane and click **Format Visual** (🏠) to display the Format Visual tab. Below the Search box, click **General** to display the General subtab. Click **Properties** to expand the Properties section. Click **Position** to expand the Position section. You can then click **Horizontal** and specify the horizontal position in pixels or click **Vertical** and specify the vertical position in pixels. To control the size, click **Size** to expand the Size section. You can then click **Height** and specify the precise height in pixels or click **Width** and specify the precise width in pixels.

Apply Filters to Visuals

Power BI Desktop enables you to filter your data to display only particular fields or only particular values within fields. For example, if your dataset includes sales figures, you can filter out the sales territories you do not need, letting you create a report on the remaining territories.

Power BI Desktop lets you create filters in two ways. The first way, which you use in this section, is by using the Filter pane to filter visuals. The second way is to use a *slicer*, a visual control that enables you to dynamically filter data on a dashboard.

Apply Filters to Visuals

Note: This section uses the Chapter 5 - Apply Filters.pbix database, available at www.wiley.com/go/tyvpowerbi.

Apply a Filter

1 Open the Chapter 5 - Apply Filters.pbix file.

2 Click the bar chart.

Selection handles appear.

Note: If the Fields pane is collapsed, expand it.

3 Click **Collapse** (≫) to collapse the Visualizations pane.

4 Click **Expand** (≪) to expand the Filters pane.

Ⓐ The Filters on This Visual section shows the filters currently available — one for each field in the visual.

Ⓑ Each filter is set to *is (All)*, which makes all the field's data appear — in other words, no filtering is applied.

Ⓒ The Filters on This Page section shows the filters applied to all visuals on this page — none.

Ⓓ The Filters on All Pages shows the filters applied to all pages — again, none.

5 Click **Country** and drag it to the Add Data Fields Here box in the Filters on This Visual section.

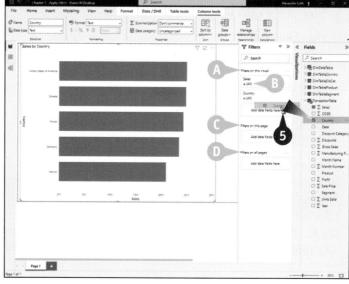

E A second Country filter appears, with its box expanded.

6 Click **Canada** (☐ changes to ☑).

7 Click **France** (☐ changes to ☑).

8 Click **United States of America** (☐ changes to ☑).

F The visual now shows only data that you have specified in your filter.

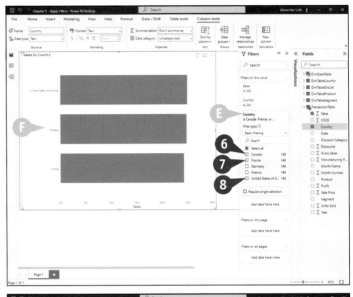

Remove a Filter

1 Move the pointer over the box of the filter you want to remove.

Controls appear at the top of the filter's box.

G You can click **Lock Filter** (🔓 changes to 🔒) to lock the filter against changes.

Note: You cannot remove the filters that Power BI Desktop adds automatically.

2 Click **Remove Filter** (✕).

Power BI removes the filter, and your visual shows the unfiltered data.

3 Click **Save** (💾).

4 Click **Close** (✕).

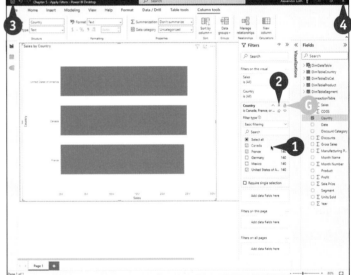

TIP

How do I apply a filter to more than one visual at a time?

You can apply a filter to a single visual, as in the main text; to all the visuals on a page in the report; or to all the visuals on all the pages in a report.

To apply a filter to all the visuals on a page, click the field in the Fields list and drag it to the Add Data Fields Here box in the Filters on This Page section of the Filters pane.

To apply a filter to all the visuals in a report, click the field in the Fields list and drag it to the Add Data Fields Here box in the Filters on All Pages section of the Filters pane.

Format the Y-Axis of a Bar Chart

ower BI Desktop enables you to customize many elements of a visual. Different visual types have different customizable elements, so the best way to learn how to use the formatting options is simply to try them. Most of the formatting options are on the Format Visual tab of the Visualizations pane, which you can display by clicking the visual, clicking **Expand** (≪), and then clicking **Format Visual** (🖋).

The axes are often a good place to start your customization. In this section, you customize the Y-axis of the bar chart.

Format the Y-Axis of a Bar Chart

Note: This section uses the Chapter 5 - Format Y-Axis.pbix database, available at www.wiley.com/go/tyvpowerbi.

1 Open the Chapter 5 - Format Y-Axis.pbix file.

2 Click the bar chart.

Selection handles appear.

Note: If the Visualizations pane is collapsed, expand it.

3 Click **Format Visual** (🖋).

4 Click **Visual**.

5 Click **Y-axis** to expand the Y-Axis section.

6 Click **Values** to expand the Values section.

7 Click **Font** (∨) and select the font.

8 Click **Font Size** (◇) and specify the font size.

Note: You can either type the font size or click **Increase** (⌃) or **Decrease** (⌄).

9 Click **Color** (∨) and select the color.

Ⓐ The Y-axis values labels change to show the choices you made.

10 Click **Switch axis position** (●Off) changes to (On●).

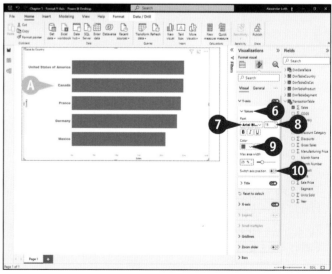

B Power BI Desktop moves the Y-axis title and values labels from the left of the chart to the right of the chart.

11 Click **Title**.

The Title section expands.

12 Click **Font** (∨), and then click the font.

13 Click **Font Size** (○), and specify the font size.

14 Click **Color** (∨), and select the color.

C The Y-axis label changes to show the choices you made.

D You can click **Reset to default** (↺) to reset all the settings in the Y-axis section of the Visual subtab of the Format Visual tab of the Visualizations pane to their defaults.

15 Click **Save** (💾).

Power BI Desktop saves your changes.

16 Click **Close** (✖).

The file closes.

How can I use color and other formatting options effectively in my dashboards?

When designing a dashboard, aim for a consistent look that enables users to identify each element swiftly and easily without being distracted by unnecessary variation. Choose colors carefully to provide visual differentiation and — if appropriate — to mesh with your company's or organization's brand.

Given that Power BI Desktop provides each visual with a wealth of configurable properties, you can benefit from developing documentation that clearly explains the values used in your dashboards. For example, having a quick-reference chart for the properties of Title elements can help you apply consistent formatting swiftly and accurately.

Format the X-Axis of a Bar Chart

ower BI Desktop enables you to format the X-axis title and values as well as the Y-axis titles and values. For the bar chart used as an example here, you can also adjust the range and values used for the X-axis.

By default, Power BI Desktop uses the full range of values in the visual's fields. You can limit the range by specifying a minimum value or maximum value manually. You can apply a logarithmic scale instead of the default linear scale. You can invert the range and set the display units and the number of decimal places.

Format the X-Axis of a Bar Chart

Note: This section uses the Chapter 5 - Format X-Axis.pbix database, available at www.wiley.com/go/tyvpowerbi.

1 Open the Chapter 5 - Format X-Axis.pbix file.

2 Click the bar chart.

Selection handles appear.

Note: If the Visualizations pane is collapsed, expand it.

3 Click **Format Visual** (🖉).

4 Click **Visual**.

5 Click **X-axis** to expand the X-Axis section.

6 Click **Range** to expand the Range section.

Ⓐ You can click **Minimum** and enter the minimum value.

Ⓑ You can click **Maximum** and enter the maximum value.

Ⓒ You can click **Logarithmic scale** (●Off changes to On●) to use a logarithmic scale instead of a linear scale — see the first tip.

Ⓓ You can click **Invert range** (●Off changes to On●) to invert the range, making it run from large values to small.

7 Click **Values**.

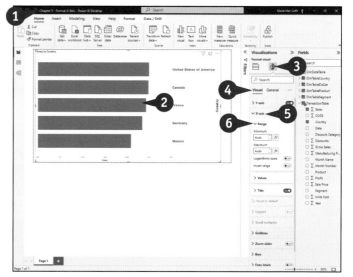

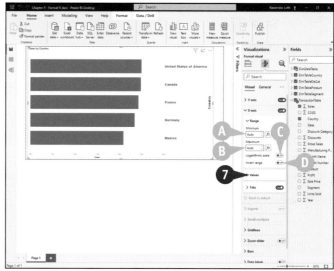

8 In the Values section, click **Font** (∨) and select the font.

9 Click **Font Size** (○) and specify the font size.

10 Click **Color** (∨), and then click the font color.

E You can click **Display Units** (∨) and then click the unit, such as **Thousands**.

F You can click **Value decimal places** (○) and specify the number of decimal places.

11 Click **Title** to expand the Title section.

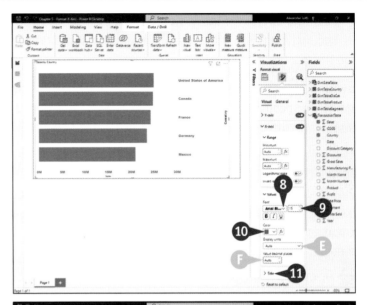

12 Click **Font** (∨) and select the font.

13 Click **Font Size** (○) and specify the font size.

14 Click **Color** (∨), and then click the font color.

G You can click **Bold** (**B**), **Italic** (*I*), or **Underline** (U) to apply additional formatting.

H The X-axis shows the changes you made.

15 Click **Save** (▣).

16 Click **Close** (✕).

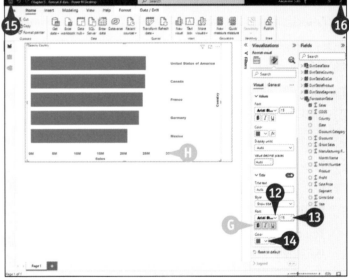

When would I use a logarithmic scale for a chart?

You might use a logarithmic scale to chart a wide range of values in an easy-to-grasp manner. For example, say your company's share price has increased greatly since its foundation at the turn of the millennium. By using a logarithmic scale, you could make the early price movements of a few cents clear on the chart even while including recent price swings of many dollars that would render the early movements indecipherable on a linear scale.

Add and Format the Data Category of a Bar Chart

Having a single category along the X-axis can work well for some visuals, but for other visuals, you will want to add a data category to subdivide the data column and add depth.

Power BI Desktop makes it easy to add a legend to a visual. As with other visual elements, you have a wide range of formatting choices for a legend. You can customize the legend's font, font size, and color; reposition the legend to the most convenient area of the visual; and simply turn off the display of the legend when you do not need to show it.

Add and Format the Data Category of a Bar Chart

Note: This section uses the Chapter 5 - Data Category.pbix database, available at www.wiley.com/go/tyvpowerbi.

1 Open the Chapter 5 - Data Category.pbix file.

2 Click the bar chart.

Selection handles appear.

Note: If the Fields pane and the Visualizations pane are collapsed, expand them.

3 Click **Build Visual** (▤).

4 In the Fields pane, click the appropriate field and drag it to the Legend field in the Visualizations pane. This example uses the Discount Category field.

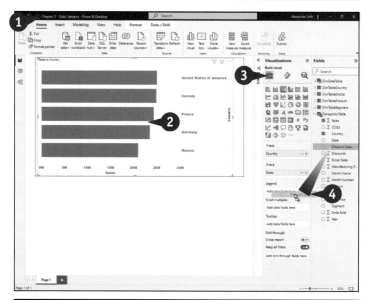

Ⓐ Power BI Desktop applies the field to the visual.

Ⓑ In this case, adding the Discount Category field makes the bar chart show sales by country and discount category.

Ⓒ The field's check box becomes selected (☐ changes to ☑).

5 Click **Format Visual** (🖌).

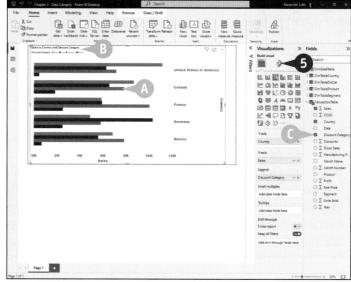

The Format Visual tab appears in the Visualizations pane.

6 Click **Visual**.

The Visual subtab appears.

7 Verify that the Legend switch is set to On (On●). If not, click the **Legend** switch (●Off changes to On●).

D The legend appears near the top of the visual.

8 Click **Legend**.

The Legend section expands.

9 Click **Text**.

The Text section expands.

10 Click **Font** (⌄) and click the font you want.

11 Click **Font Size** (⌃) and specify the font size.

12 Click **Color** (⌄) and select a color.

E The legend values take on the font, size, and color you specified.

13 Click **Save** (🖫).

14 Click **Close** (✖).

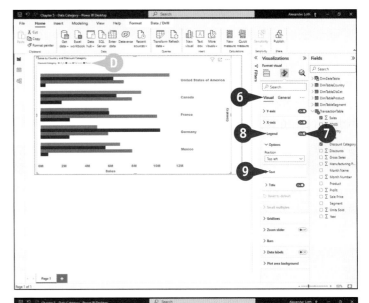

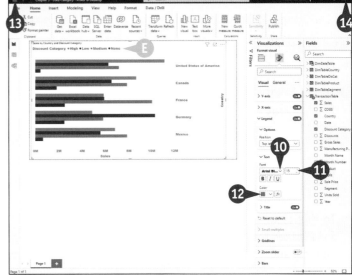

How can I use different colors for my visuals?

The Theme Colors list and the Recent Colors list in the Color panel are handy, but you can also choose any other color you can specify. To get a custom color, click **Color** (⌄), click **More colors** (🎨), and then work in the resulting Colors pane. Here, you can type a hexadecimal value such as #E66C37 in the Hex box or specify a value in the 0–255 range in the Red box, the Green box, and the Blue box. Once you have applied a custom color, it appears in the Recent Colors list, from which you can apply it quickly to another element.

Move a Bar Chart's Legend and Add Gridlines

After you add a legend to a visual, you may need to reposition the legend, either to make it easier to locate or to make it match your personal preferences or your company's or organization's house style. Power BI Desktop makes it easy to move the legend to various positions in the visual that contains it.

You may also want to add gridlines to a visual to help the reader determine exactly where data points fall on the X-axis and Y-axis. Power BI Desktop lets you not only add gridlines but also add fixed lines to mark baselines or targets.

Move a Bar Chart's Legend and Add Gridlines

Note: This section uses the Chapter 5 - Bar Legend.pbix database, available at www.wiley.com/go/tyvpowerbi.

Move the Legend

1. Open the Chapter 5 - Bar Legend.pbix file.

2. Click the bar chart.

   Selection handles appear.

Note: If the Visualizations pane is collapsed, expand it.

3. Click **Format Visual** (🖋).

4. Click **Visual**.

5. Verify that the Legend switch is set to On (On●). If not, click the switch ((●Off) changes to (On●)).

6. Click **Legend**.

7. In the Legend section, click **Options**.

8. In the Options section, click **Position** (∨), and then click the position, such as Top Left, Top Right Stacked, or Bottom Right. This example uses **Center right**.

Ⓐ Power BI Desktop moves the legend to the position you specified.

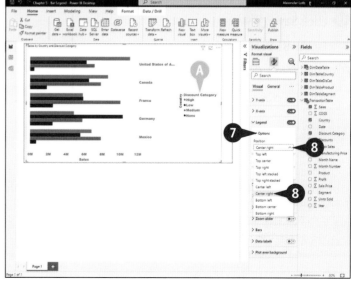

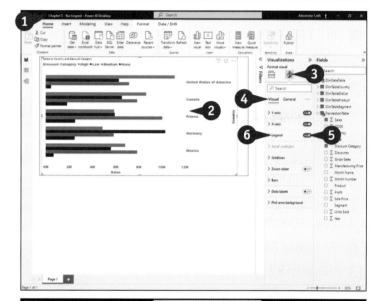

Add Gridlines

1 Click the bar chart.

Selection handles appear around the bar chart.

2 Click **Format Visual** (🖌).

The Format Visual tab appears.

3 Click **Visual**.

The Visual subtab appears.

4 Click **Gridlines**.

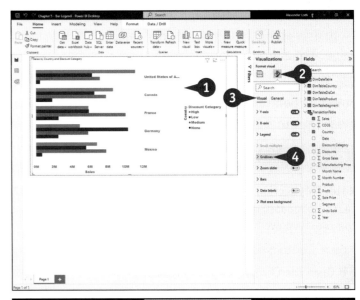

The Gridlines section expands.

5 Verify that the Vertical switch is set to On (On●). If not, click the switch ((●Off) changes to On●).

6 Click **Style** (˅), and then click Dashed, Solid, or Dotted. This example uses **Solid**.

7 Click **Color** (˅), and then click the color.

8 Click **Width** (◌), and enter the width.

Ⓑ The visual displays the updated gridlines.

9 Click **Save** (💾).

Power BI Desktop saves your changes.

10 Click **Close** (✖).

The file closes.

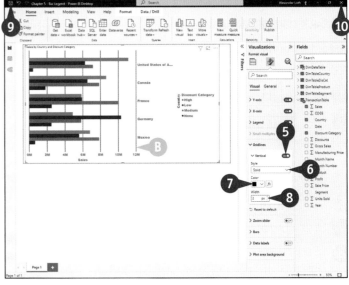

TIPS

What controls the spacing between the gridlines?

The spacing between the gridlines depends on the number of categories displayed on the axis. To decrease the spacing between the gridlines, increase the number of category values.

How can I change the text shown for a legend?

In the Visualizations pane, click **Format Visual** (🖌) to display the Format Visual tab, and then click **Visual** to display the Visual subtab. Click **Legend** to expand the Legend section, click **Title** to expand the Title section, and then click the **Title text** box and type the legend title you want.

Add a Zoom Slider and Update Bar Colors

To make a visual easier for the user to navigate, you can add a zoom slider to it. A zoom slider is particularly helpful when there is a large difference between the minimum value and the maximum value. The zoom slider enables the user to zoom in on the range of data that interests them and to identify minor variations or differences.

Power BI Desktop also enables you to change the look of the bars in a bar chart. You can change both the bar colors for the high, low, and medium values and the bar width.

Add a Zoom Slider and Update Bar Colors

Note: This section uses the Chapter 5 - Zoom Colors.pbix database, available at www.wiley.com/go/tyvpowerbi.

Add a Zoom Slider

1 Open the Chapter 5 - Zoom Colors.pbix file.

Note: If the Fields pane is collapsed, expand it.

2 Click the bar chart.

Selection handles appear.

3 Click **Format Visual** (🖌).

4 Click **Visual**.

5 Click **Zoom slider** to expand the Zoom Slider section.

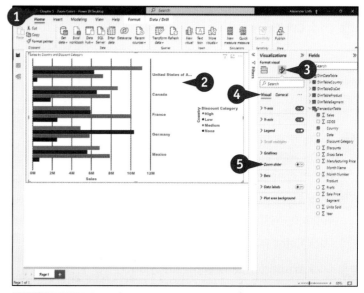

6 On the Zoom Slider heading, click the switch (●Off changes to On●).

Ⓐ Power BI Desktop adds a zoom slider to the visual.

Ⓑ You can click the Slider Labels switch (●Off changes to On●) to display labels below the slider.

Ⓒ You can click the Slider Tooltips switch (●Off changes to On●) to display a tooltip of the current value as you drag the slider.

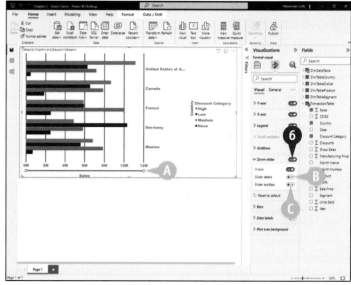

Update Bar Colors

1 Click the bar chart.

Selection handles appear.

2 Click **Format Visual** (✎).

3 Click **Visual**.

4 Click **Bars** to expand the Bars section.

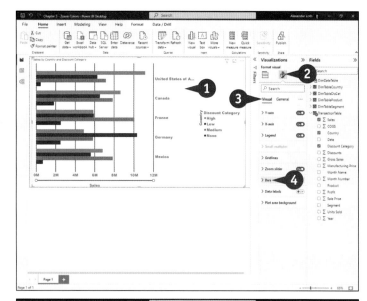

5 Click **Colors** to expand the Colors section.

6 Click **High** (⌄), and then click the color for the High category.

7 Click **Low** (⌄), and then click the color for the Low category.

8 Click **Medium** (⌄), and then click the color for the Medium category.

9 Click **None** (⌄), and then click the color for the None category.

D The category bars and legend take on the colors you chose.

10 Click **Save** (▥).

Power BI Desktop saves your changes.

11 Click **Close** (✕).

The file closes.

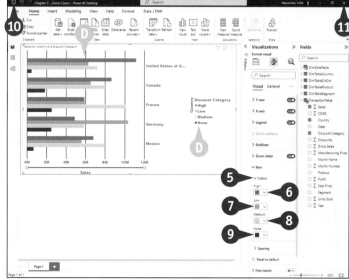

TIPS

Why would I change the color of the bars?
You may want to change the colors for various reasons, such as to increase the differentiation between the colors — especially if you may need to print the visual in grayscale — or to make your dashboard conform to a corporate color theme.

Should I add labels to my zoom slider?
Labels can be helpful, but more so for some types of visuals than for others. In a bar chart, the zoom slider appears directly below the X-axis labels, so those labels provide a convenient reference point. If you add slider labels, they appear below the slider and are largely redundant.

Add Data Labels to a Bar Chart

As well as the labels that mark axes and legends, Power BI Desktop enables you to add data labels to your visuals to help readers understand them. *Data labels* are text that show the values of data points in the visual or provide other explanatory data. When you turn on data labels, Power BI Desktop displays default data labels, but you can customize them extensively. Your options include specifying which series have labels; changing the label position; formatting the font, size, and color; controlling the display units and decimal places; and adjusting the background color and transparency to improve readability.

Add Data Labels to a Bar Chart

Note: This section uses the Chapter 5 - Data Labels.pbix database, available at www.wiley.com/go/tyvpowerbi.

1 Open the Chapter 5 - Data Labels.pbix file.

Note: If the Visualizations pane is collapsed, expand it.

2 Click the bar chart.

Selection handles appear.

3 Click **Format Visual** ().

4 Click **Visual**.

5 On the Data Labels heading, click the switch (Off changes to On).

A Power BI Desktop displays default data labels.

6 Click **Data labels**.

7 Click **Apply settings to**.

8 Click **Series** (ν), and then click the series to affect: All, High, Low, Medium, or None. This example uses **All**.

9 Click **Options**.

10 Click **Position** (ν), and then click the position, such as Auto, Inside End, or Inside Base. This example uses **Auto**.

11 Click **Values**.

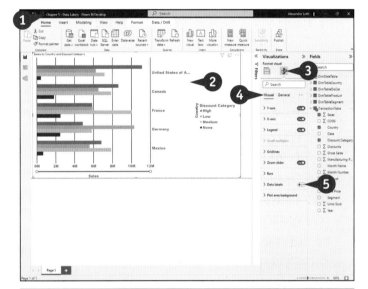

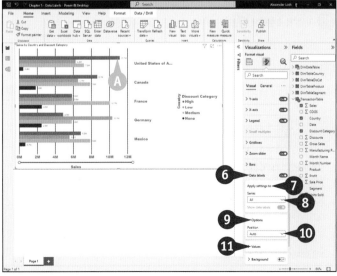

12 Click **Font** (∨), and then click the font.

13 Click **Size** (◇), and then click the size.

14 Click **Color** (∨), and then click the color.

Ⓑ You can click **Display units** (∨) and change the units displayed.

Ⓒ You can click **Value decimal places** (◇) and change the number of decimal places.

15 Click the **Overflow text** switch (⬤Off changes to On⬤) if you want data labels to appear in full even if they overflow the space available.

16 Click **Background**.

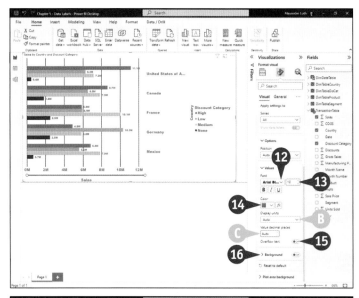

17 Click the **Background** switch (⬤Off changes to On⬤).

18 Click **Color** (∨) and click the background color to apply.

19 Click **Transparency** (◇) and set the transparency percentage.

Ⓓ The data labels take on the new formatting.

20 Click **Save** (💾).

21 Click **Close** (✖).

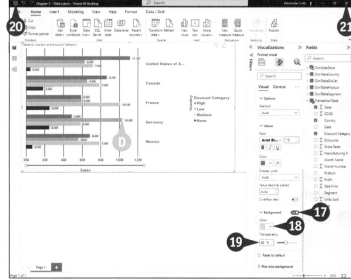

TIPS

How can I use data labels most effectively?
Display data labels only when they will enhance the viewer's understanding of a visual. For example, a visual that compares sales figures for different territories will likely benefit from data labels, but data labels may detract from the message of a visual that illustrates broad trends. Format your data labels consistently so that readers can easily identify them.

Why should I adjust the background color and transparency of data labels?
Adjust the background color and transparency to make the data labels suitably visible on the visual. Using a low transparency value, such as 20 percent, makes the labels highly visible. But if the data labels appear obtrusive, set a higher transparency value to make them less visible.

Add an Image to the Plot Area Background

ower BI Desktop lets you add an image to the plot area background for a visual. Adding an image can be an effective way of customizing the visual thematically, for branding purposes, or even for asset protection.

Adding an image can greatly improve the look of a visual, but you must make sure that the image does not overpower the visual. You can adjust the image's impact by increasing or decreasing its transparency. A high transparency value, such as 80 percent, makes the image mostly see-through, whereas a low transparency value, such as 20 percent, makes it mostly opaque.

Add an Image to the Plot Area Background

Note: This section uses the Chapter 5 - Plot Image.pbix database, available at www.wiley.com/go/tyvpowerbi.

1 Open the Chapter 5 - Plot Image.pbix file.

Note: If the Visualizations pane is collapsed, expand it.

2 Click the bar chart.

Selection handles appear around the bar chart.

3 Click **Format Visual** (🖌).

The Format Visual tab appears.

4 Click **Visual**.

The Visual subtab appears.

5 Click **Plot area background**.

The Plot Area Background section appears.

6 Click **Browse** (🖾).

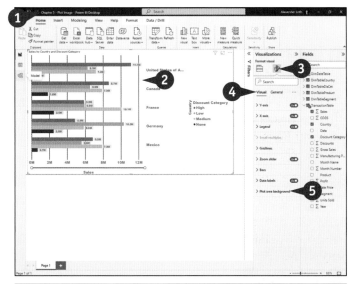

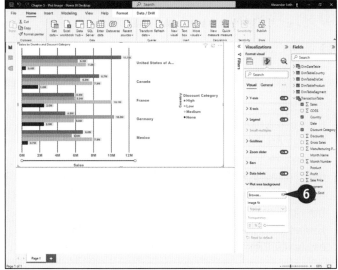

The Open dialog box appears.

7 Navigate to the folder that contains the image file.

8 Click the image file.

9 Click **Open**.

The Open dialog box closes.

A The image appears in the background of the visual.

10 Click **Image fit** (⌄), and click the fit you want: Normal, Fit, or Fill. This example uses **Fit**.

11 Click **Transparency** (◌), and set the transparency percentage.

Note: Alternatively, you can drag the Transparency slider to set the transparency percentage.

12 Click **Save** (🖫).

Power BI Desktop saves your changes.

13 Click **Close** (✖).

The file closes.

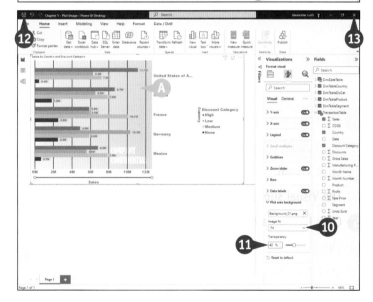

How would I use a picture background for asset protection?

You can place an image as a kind of watermark on a visual to show that the visual was created by your company. For example, you might use an image containing your company's name and a copyright notice. By using high transparency, you could make the image just visible but not obtrusive.

What types of image files can I use?

You can insert a wide variety of image file types, including BMP, JPEG, GIF, TIFF, and PNG formats. If the image file you want to use has different file formats available, PNG is often a sensible choice, as it provides high quality with a relatively compact file size.

Create a Line Chart or Area Chart

hen you need to measure a trend over a period, such as months or years, you can use a line chart. A *line chart* uses a line to connect a series of data points that represent the values in a category. A line chart can have a single category or multiple categories.

Power BI Desktop also enables you to create area charts, which are often used to represent quantitative graphical data. An *area chart* builds on a line chart by filling the area between the axis and the lines with colors, textures, or patterns, making clear how much each category contributes.

Create a Line Chart or Area Chart

Note: This section uses the Chapter 5 - Area Chart.pbix database, available at www.wiley.com/go/tyvpowerbi.

1. In Power BI Desktop, open the Chapter 5 - Area Chart.pbix database file.

Note: If the Fields pane and the Visualizations pane are collapsed, expand them.

2. Click **Build Visual** (▦).

3. Click **Area chart** (◭).

Ⓐ A visual placeholder appears.

4. Click **Expand** (❯ changes to ⌄) to the left of DimDateTable.

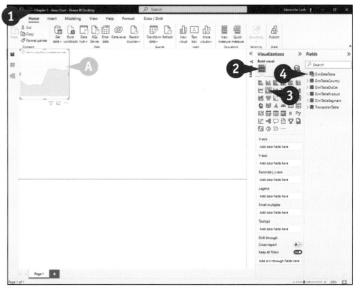

5. In the DimDateTable section, click **Date** and drag it to the visual placeholder.

Ⓑ The Year label appears in the visual placeholder.

Ⓒ The Date data appears in the X-axis box.

6. Click **Date** (⌄).

7. Click **Date**.

The Date label replaces the Year label in the visual placeholder.

8. Click **Expand** (❯ changes to ⌄) to the left of TransactionTable.

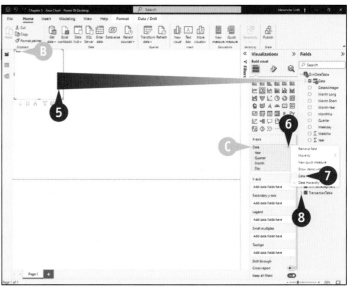

The TransactionTable section expands.

9 Click **Sales** (☐ changes to ☑).

D The sales data appears in the visual, creating an area chart.

10 Click the lower-right corner handle and drag it down and to the right.

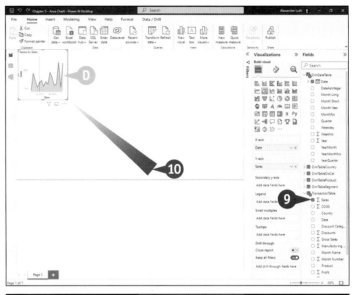

The visual expands, enabling you to see its contents more clearly.

11 Click **Save** (💾).

Power BI Desktop saves your changes.

12 Click **Close** (✖).

The file closes.

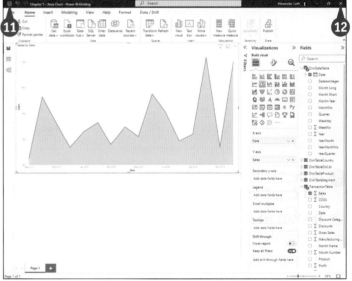

TIP

How do I drill down through the date hierarchy?

On the Build Visual tab of the Visualizations pane, go to the X-Axis box, click **Date** (∨), and then click **Date hierarchy** on the drop-down menu. You can then click **Drill down** (↓ changes to ⬤) at the top of the visual to activate the Drill Down feature and then click the data point to which you want to drill down. You drill down first from years to quarters, then from quarters to months, and then from months to days. Click **Drill up** (↑) to drill back up. Click **Drill down** (⬤ changes to ↓) when you are ready to deactivate the Drill Down feature.

Format the Axes of a Line or Area Chart

To help make a line chart or area chat deliver its information effectively, you will often need to format its axes. Power BI Desktop provides a wealth of formatting options, enabling you to customize everything from the range of values shown to the display units used and the number of decimal places. In this section, you adjust the font, font size, and font color of the X-axis and Y-axis.

Format the Axes of a Line or Area Chart

Note: This section uses the Chapter 5 - Area Axes.pbix database, available at www.wiley.com/go/tyvpowerbi.

1. Open the Chapter 5 - Area Axes.pbix file.

2. Click the area chart.

   Selection handles appear.

Note: If the Visualizations pane is collapsed, expand it.

3. Click **Format Visual** (🖋).

4. Click **Visual**.

5. Click **X-axis**.

6. Verify that the X-Axis switch is set to On (**On ●**). If not, click the switch (**● Off** changes to **On ●**).

7. Click **Values**.

8. Click **Font** (⌄) and select the font.

9. Click **Font Size** (◌) and specify the font size.

Note: You can either type the font size or click **Increase** (⌃) or **Decrease** (⌄).

10. Click **Color** (⌄) and select the color.

    Ⓐ The X-axis values labels change to show the choices you made.

11. Click **Title**.

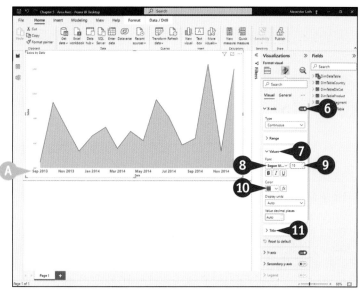

12 Click **Font** (⌄), and then click the font.

13 Click **Font Size** (↕), and specify the font size.

14 Click **Color** (⌄), and select the color.

Ⓑ The X-axis title changes to show the choices you made.

15 Verify that the Y-Axis switch is set to On (On ●). If not, click the switch (● Off changes to On ●).

16 Click **Y-axis**.

17 Click **Values**.

The Values section expands.

18 Click **Font** (⌄), and then click the font.

19 Click **Font Size** (↕), and specify the font size.

20 Click **Color** (⌄), and select the color.

21 Click **Title**.

22 Repeat steps **18** to **20** to format the title text.

Ⓒ The Y-axis title and values change to show the choices you made.

23 Click **Save** (💾).

24 Click **Close** (✖).

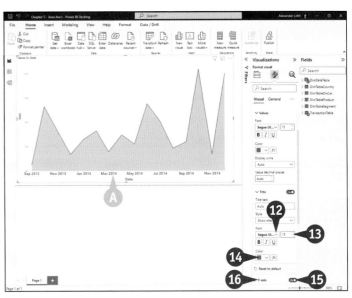

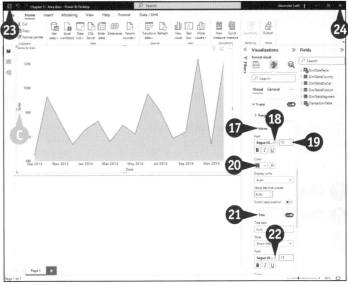

When should I use a line chart or area chart?

Use a line chart or area chart when you need to show changes across a period of time. Choose a line chart when you need either to show a single data series or to compare several data series that do not have a part-to-whole relationship. For example, you might use a line chart to show how the prices of two items changed over time.

Choose an area chart when the data series are related or have a summation relationship. For example, if your company sells three products, you could use an area chart to show the products' relative contributions to the company's bottom line.

Add a Legend to a Line or Area Chart

ower BI Desktop enables you to add a legend to a line chart or an area chart and to format the legend so that it looks the way you need. A legend helps the viewer to identify the data in the visual, so adding a legend is usually beneficial. In a line chart, the legends are formatted to form individual series of lines that represent categorical data, displaying a trend showing how the data changes over a period or sequence.

Add a Legend to a Line or Area Chart

Note: This section uses the Chapter 5 - Area Legend.pbix database, available at www.wiley.com/go/tyvpowerbi.

Add a Legend

1 Open the Chapter 5 - Area Legend. pbix file.

Note: If the Visualizations pane is collapsed, expand it.

2 Click the area chart.

Selection handles appear around the area chart.

3 Click **Build Visual** (▦).

The Build Visual tab appears.

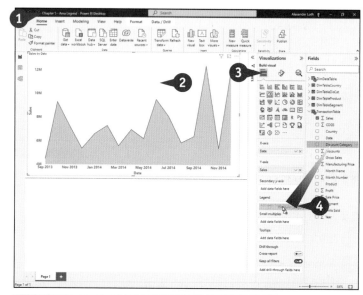

4 Click the appropriate field and drag it to the Legend field in the Visualizations pane. This example uses the Discount Category field.

A Power BI Desktop applies the field to the visual.

B The visual's title changes to *Sales by Date and Discount Category*.

C The legend appears in the upper-left corner of the visual.

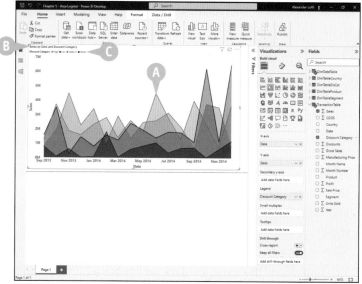

Format a Legend

1 Click the area chart.

Selection handles appear around the area chart.

2 Click **Format Visual** (🖦).

The Format Visual tab appears in the Visualizations pane.

3 Click **Visual**.

The Visual subtab appears.

4 Click **Legend**.

The Legend section expands.

5 Click **Text**.

The Text section expands.

6 Click **Font** (∨), and click the font you want.

7 Click **Font Size** (◌), and specify the font size.

8 Click **Color** (∨), and select a color.

Ⓓ The legend values take on the font, size, and color you specified.

9 Click **Save** (🖫).

Power BI Desktop saves your changes.

10 Click **Close** (❎).

The file closes.

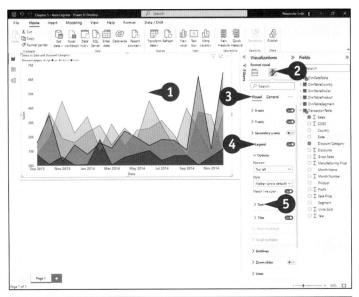

TIP

How does the legend in a line chart or area chart differ from the legend in a bar chart?
The legend in a line chart or area chart produces lines of different colors. These lines demonstrate the changes of every single category across time. A bar chart shows different-size bars separated by categories. In a line chart, the category data points are all linked together to form a line.

Move the Legend and Add Gridlines to a Line or Area Chart

After adding a legend to a line chart or area chart, you can move it to a different position on the chart. For example, you might want to move the legend to where the visual has more free space or to the position your company's house style mandates. Power BI Desktop lets you quickly move the legend to different positions.

To make the line chart or area chart easier to read, you may want to add gridlines to it. Gridlines help the reader see precisely where data points are located on the X-axis and Y-axis.

Move the Legend and Add Gridlines to a Line or Area Chart

Note: This section uses the Chapter 5 - Area Gridlines.pbix database, available at www. wiley.com/go/tyvpowerbi.

Move the Legend

1 Open the Chapter 5 - Area Gridlines.pbix file.

Note: If the Visualizations pane is collapsed, expand it.

2 Click the area chart.

Selection handles appear.

3 Click **Format Visual** (✏️).

4 Click **Visual.**

5 Verify that the Legend switch is set to On (On ●).

6 Click **Legend.**

7 Click **Options.**

8 Click **Position** (⌄), and then click the position, such as Top Center, Top Left Stacked, or Bottom Left. This example uses **Center right.**

Ⓐ Power BI Desktop moves the legend to the position you specified.

Ⓑ You can click **Style** (⌄) and then click the legend style you want: Marker (Circle Default), Marker, Line, or Line and Markers.

Ⓒ You can click **Title** and then type a different legend title in the Title Text box.

Add Gridlines

1 Click the area chart.

Selection handles appear around the area chart.

2 Click **Format Visual** (✐).

The Format Visual tab appears.

3 Click **Visual**.

The Visual subtab appears.

4 Click **Gridlines**.

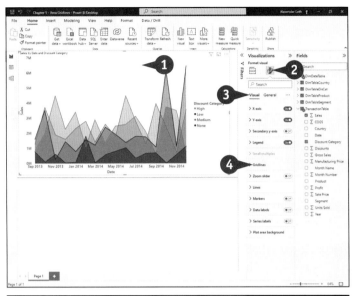

The Gridlines section expands.

5 Verify that the Horizontal switch is set to On (On ●). If not, click the switch (● Off) changes to On ●).

6 Click **Style** (∨), and then click Dashed, Solid, or Dotted. This example uses **Dotted**.

7 Click **Color** (∨) and then click the color.

8 Click **Width** (◇) and enter the width.

Note: You can either type the width or click **Increase** (∧) or click **Decrease** (∨).

Ⓓ The visual displays the updated gridlines.

9 Click **Save** (💾).

10 Click **Close** (❎).

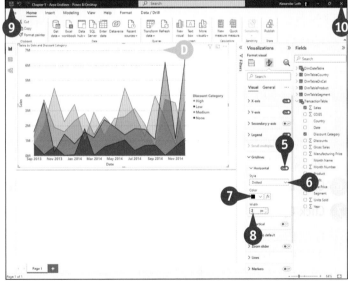

What does the fx button to the right of the Color selector do?

The fx button enables you to apply conditional formatting — formatting that changes depending on conditions you specify. For example, you may want to display gridlines in a different color if a particular field has an unusually high or low value. Click **fx** (fx) to display the Line Color – Gridlines dialog box, which provides controls for applying conditional formatting.

Add a Zoom Slider and Steps to a Line or Area Chart

When your chart's data has a large range between its minimum and maximum, you can add a zoom slider for easier navigation. The zoom slider lets the viewer zoom in on a small range of data without having to apply a filter to the chart.

You can also change a line chart or area chart from a sharp lines chart to stepped lines. Sharp lines follow the data series faithfully, whereas stepped lines create steps between data points.

Add a Zoom Slider and Steps to a Line or Area Chart

Note: This section uses the Chapter 5 - Area Zoom.pbix database, available at www.wiley.com/go/tyvpowerbi.

Add a Zoom Slider

1 Open the Chapter 5 - Area Zoom.pbix file.

Note: If the Visualizations pane is collapsed, expand it.

2 Click the area chart.

Selection handles appear.

3 Click **Format Visual** (✐).

4 Click **Visual**.

5 Click **Zoom slider** to expand the Zoom Slider section.

6 On the Zoom Slider heading, click the switch (⬤Off) changes to On⬤).

A Power BI Desktop adds horizontal and vertical zoom sliders to the visual.

B You can click the Slider Labels switch (⬤Off) changes to On⬤) to display labels below the slider.

C You can click the Slider Tooltips switch (⬤Off) changes to On⬤) to display a tooltip of the current value as you drag the slider.

Add Steps to a Line Chart or Area Chart

1 Click the area chart.

Selection handles appear around the area chart.

2 Click **Format Visual** (✏️).

The Format Visual tab appears.

3 Click **Visual**.

The Visual subtab appears.

4 Click **Lines**.

The Lines section expands.

5 Click **Line style** (⌄) and then click Dashed, Solid, or Dotted. This example uses **Solid**.

6 Click **Join type** (⌄) and then click Miter, Round, or Bevel. This example uses **Round**.

7 Click **Stroke width** (⌃) and specify the width.

8 Click the **Stepped** switch (⊙Off changes to On⊙).

Ⓓ Power BI Desktop applies your changes. In this case, it changes the area chart to a stepped chart.

9 Click **Save** (💾).

10 Click **Close** (❌).

To which chart types can I add a zoom slider?

Power BI Desktop enables you to add a zoom slider to any Cartesian chart — any chart, that is, that includes a horizontal axis and a vertical axis.

What would I use a stepped line graph for?

A stepped line graph is often useful for showing changes that occur at irregular intervals, such as the changes in the price of a commodity — for example, gasoline. Rather than changing in a sharp line between two data points, the price might be at one level for two weeks, move down a step to another level for a week, move up again, and so on.

Add Data Markers and Labels to a Line or Area Chart

Power BI Desktop enables you to add data markers to a line chart or area chart to help the viewer pinpoint where data points fall. Power BI Desktop offers various shapes of data markers, such as squares, bullets, triangles, and X symbols. You can also customize the size and color of the data markers to make them easy to identify.

To make the value of data points clear, you can also display data labels on a line chart or area chart.

Add Data Markers and Labels to a Line or Area Chart

Note: This section uses the Chapter 5 - Area Markers.pbix database, available at www.wiley.com/go/tyvpowerbi.

Add Data Markers

1 Open the Chapter 5 - Area Markers.pbix file.

Note: If the Visualizations pane is collapsed, expand it.

2 Click the area chart.

Selection handles appear.

3 Click **Format Visual** (✋).

4 Click **Visual**.

5 Click **Markers**.

6 On the Markers heading, click the switch (Off changes to On).

Power BI Desktop enables the controls in the Markers section.

7 Click **Type** (⌄), and then click the marker type, such as ▲ or ◆. This example uses ■.

8 Click **Size** (◌), and enter the marker size.

9 Click **Colors**.

10 Click **Default** (⌄), and then click the color.

Ⓐ The markers take on the formatting you specified.

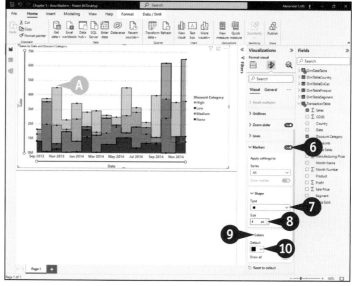

Add Data Labels

1 Click the area chart.

Selection handles appear around the area chart.

2 Click **Format Visual** (✍).

The Format Visual tab appears.

3 Click **Visual**.

The Visual subtab appears.

4 Click **Data labels**.

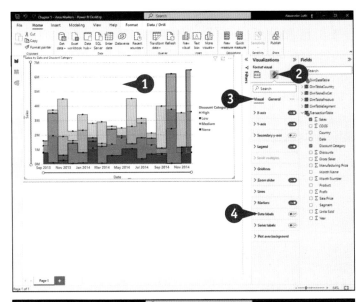

The Data Labels section expands.

5 On the Data Labels heading, click the switch (●Off) changes to (On●).

Ⓑ The data labels appear.

6 Click **Save** (💾).

Power BI Desktop saves your changes.

7 Click **Close** (✖).

The file closes.

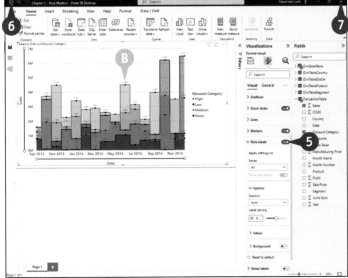

TIP

How do I control the display units for data labels?

Click the visual, and then click **Format Visual** (✍) in the Visualizations pane to display the Format Visual tab. Click **Visual** to display the Visual subtab. Click **Data labels** to expand the Data Labels section, and then click **Values** to expand the Values section. Click **Display units** (⌄), and then click the unit, such as Thousands, Millions, or Billions. If you need to adjust the number of decimal places displayed, click **Value decimal places** (◌), and then specify the number of decimal places.

Format the Data Labels of a Line or Area Chart

When you add data labels to a line chart or area chart, as explained in the previous section, "Add Data Markers and Labels to a Line or Area Chart," Power BI Desktop gives the data labels their default format. To make the labels appear easy to read and to match your company's branding, you can format the data labels' font, font size, and color. You can also apply a background to the labels if needed.

Format the Data Labels of a Line or Area Chart

Note: This section uses the Chapter 5 - Area Labels.pbix database, available at www.wiley.com/go/tyvpowerbi.

1 Open the Chapter 5 - Area Labels.pbix file.

Note: If the Visualizations pane is collapsed, expand it.

2 Click the area chart.

Selection handles appear around the area chart.

3 Click **Format Visual** (🖌).

The Format Visual tab appears.

4 Click **Visual**.

The Visual subtab appears.

5 Click **Data labels**.

The Data Labels section expands.

Note: Scroll down if needed to see the different parts of the Data Labels section.

6 Click **Values**.

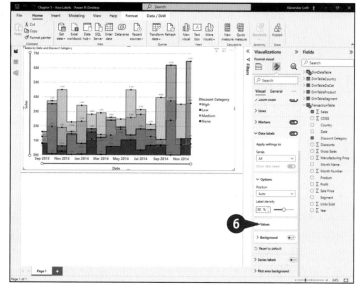

The Values section expands.

7 Click **Font** (∨), and select the font you want.

8 Click **Font Size** (◌), and specify the font size.

Note: You can either type the font size or click **Increase** (⌃) or **Decrease** (∨).

9 Click **Color** (∨), and select the color.

Ⓐ The data labels take on the formatting you specified.

10 Click **Background**.

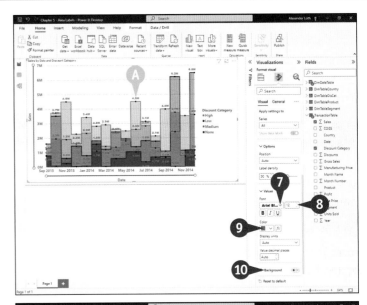

The Background section expands.

11 On the Background heading, click the switch (●Off changes to On●).

Power BI Desktop displays the background for the data labels.

12 Click **Color** (∨), and select the color.

13 Click **Transparency** (◌), and specify the transparency percentage.

Ⓑ The data labels' background and transparency takes effect.

14 Click **Save** (🖫).

15 Click **Close** (✕).

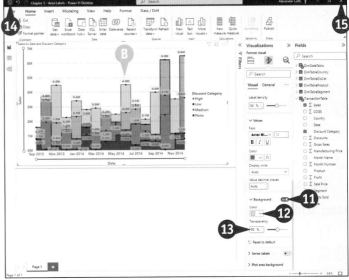

TIP

How do I display data labels for only some series in a visual?
Click the visual, and then click **Format Visual** (🖌) in the Visualizations pane to display the Format Visual tab. Click **Visual** to display the Visual subtab. Click **Data labels** to expand the Data Labels section, and then go to the Apply Settings To box at the top of the section. Click **Series** (∨); click the series you want to remove, such as **Low**; and then click the **Show data labels** switch (On● changes to ●Off). Power BI Desktop removes the data labels for that series. You can then click **Series** (∨) again and configure another series, as needed.

CHAPTER 6

Creating Advanced Data Visualizations

In today's world, most companies and organizations are eager to analyze their own business data to identify trends and data patterns so that they can streamline their operations and improve performance in the future. Power BI includes many advanced visualizations that enable you to analyze data and identify trends efficiently.

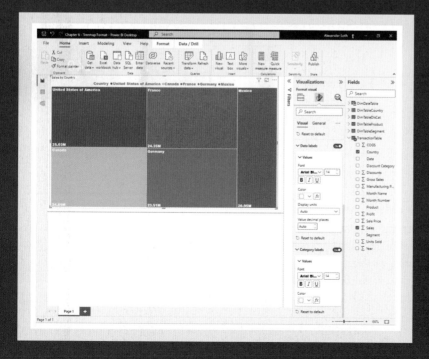

Create and Format a Gauge Chart

When you need to track how your business is performing compared to your goals, you can use a gauge chart. A *gauge chart* has a semicircular arc that displays a single value that measures progress toward a goal. A gauge chart also called a *level indicator*, *speedometer*, or *scale*.

A gauge chart requires a minimum value, a maximum value, and a target value. The target, which is known as a *key performance indicator* (KPI), is represented by a line or needle. The shaded arc represents progress toward that target.

Create and Format a Gauge Chart

Note: This section uses the Chapter 6 - Gauge. pbix database, available at www.wiley.com/go/tyvpowerbi.

1 Open the Chapter 6 - Gauge.pbix database file.

Note: If the Fields pane and the Visualizations pane are collapsed, expand them.

2 Click **Build visual** (▤).

3 Click **Gauge** (⌒).

A Power BI adds a gauge visual to the canvas.

4 Click **Expand** (❯ changes to ⌄) to the left of TransactionTable.

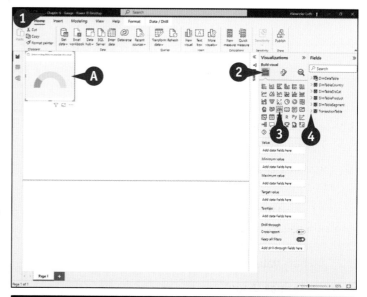

The TransactionTable listing expands.

5 Click **Sales** (☐ changes to ☑).

B The Sales field appears in the Value box.

C The Sales data appears in the visual.

6 Drag the lower-right handle down and to the right to enlarge the visual.

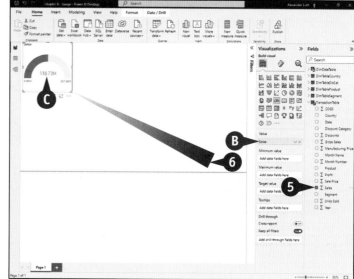

The visual appears at the larger size.

7 Click **Manufacturing Price** (☐ changes to ☑).

D The Manufacturing Price field appears in the Minimum Value box.

E Power BI adds a minimum value to the visual.

8 Click **Gross Sales** (☐ changes to ☑).

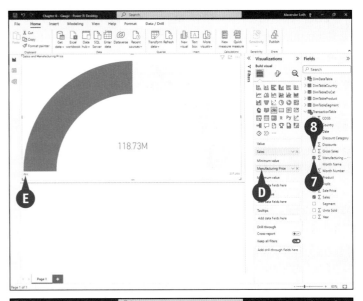

F The Gross Sales field appears in the Maximum Value box.

G The visual changes to show the maximum value.

Note: After adding both the minimum and maximum values, you can see the position of the data column in relation to the maximum and minimum values.

9 Click **Format Visual** (✏️).

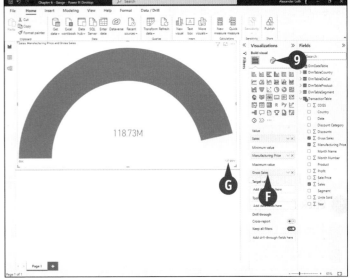

TIP

How do I provide the target value for a gauge chart?

You can provide the target value for a gauge chart either by using a field or by entering a set value. To use a field, go to the Visualizations pane and click **Build visual** (▦) to display the Build Visual tab. Then go to the Fields pane, expand the table that contains the field you want to use, and drag the field to the Target Value box on the Build Visual tab.

If you want to enter a set value for the target, work as explained later in the main text of this section.

continued ▶

Gauge charts can be useful for comparing values between variables. To make the comparison clear, you can either use multiple needles on the same gauge or use multiple gauges with a single needle apiece.

Power BI enables you to format a gauge chart in a wide variety of ways. You can format the axes, the colors, the levels, and the minimum and maximum ranges. You can also change the chart's width and the inner and outer radii; add or remove the grid lines; and deploy colors to add depth to the display.

Create and Format a Gauge Chart (continued)

The Format Visual tab appears.

10 Click **Visual**.

The Visual subtab appears.

11 Click **Gauge axis**.

The Gauge Axis section expands.

12 Click **Target** (○) and set the target value. This example uses **100000000**, or 100 million.

Ⓐ Power BI Desktop adds a target marker to the visual. The target marker signifies the KPI that you set in step **12**.

13 Click **Colors**.

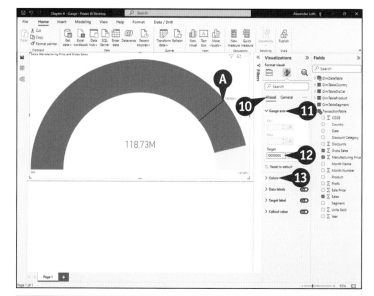

The Colors section expands.

14 Click **Fill color** (∨), and then click the fill color. This example uses lime green.

15 Click **Target color** (∨), and then click the target color. This example uses magenta.

Ⓑ The gauge visual takes on the colors you selected.

16 Set the switch on the Data Labels heading to On (On●).

17 Click **Data labels** to expand the Data Labels section.

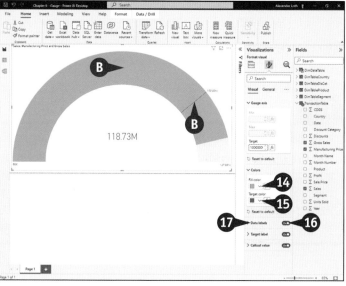

18 Click **Font** (∨), and select a font.

19 Click **Font size** (◇), and specify the font size.

20 Click **Color** (∨), and then click the text color.

C The data labels take on the formatting you chose.

21 Set the switch on the Target Label heading to On (On●).

22 Click **Target label** to expand the Target Label section.

23 In the Values section, repeat steps **18** to **20** to specify the font, font size, and color for the target label.

D The target label takes on the formatting you chose.

24 Set the switch on the Callout Value heading to On (On●).

25 In the Values section, repeat steps **18** to **20** to specify the font and color for the callout value.

E The callout value takes on the formatting you chose.

26 Click **Save** (🖫).

27 Click **Close** (✖).

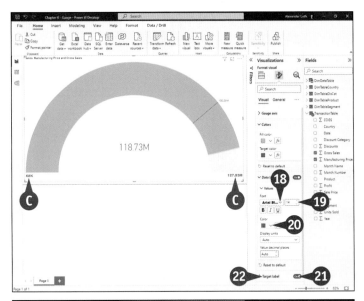

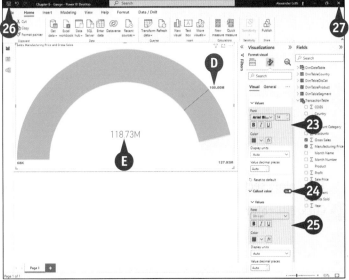

TIP

How do I change the display units for a gauge chart?
Power BI Desktop enables you to set the display units, such as thousands or millions, for data labels, the target label, and the callout value in a gauge chart. In the Visualizations pane, click **Format visual** (🖌) to display the Format Visual tab, and then click **Visual** to display the Visual subtab. Next, click **Data labels**, **Target label**, or **Callout value** to expand the section for the item you want to affect. Click **Display units** (∨), and then click **Auto**, **None**, **Thousands**, **Millions**, **Billions**, or **Trillions**, as needed.

Create and Format a KPI Visual

Power BI Desktop enables you to create your own KPI visuals that highlight individual performance indicators. The *key performance indicator* is a visual tool that shows progress toward a measurable goal. You can use a KPI visual when your data contains both actual performance details and target values attached to a time series — for example, a salesperson's monthly sales figures and the target figures for those months.

The KPI visual displays a single number showing the current value overlaid on an area chart showing the trend over a period of time.

Create a KPI Visual

Note: This section uses the Chapter 6 - KPI.pbix database, available at www.wiley.com/go/tyvpowerbi.

1 Open the Chapter 6 - KPI.pbix database file.

Note: If the Fields pane and the Visualizations pane are collapsed, expand them.

2 Click **Build visual** (▦).

3 Click **KPI** (◢).

A Power BI adds a KPI visual to the canvas.

4 Click **Expand** (⟩ changes to ⌄) to the left of TransactionTable.

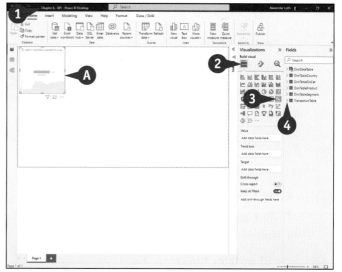

5 Click **Gross Sales** (☐ changes to ☑).

B The Gross Sales field appears in the Value box.

6 Click **Sales**.

C The Sales field appears in the Target box.

D "Gross Sales and Sales" appears in the visual's title.

7 Click **Expand** (⟩ changes to ⌄) to the left of DimDateTable.

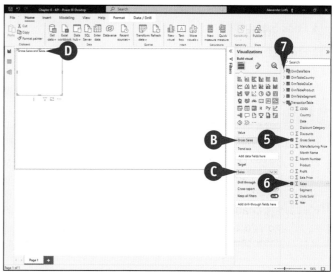

The DimDateTable listing expands.

8 Click **Date** (☐ changes to ☑).

E The Date field appears in the Trend Axis box.

F The Date data appears in the visual.

G The visual's title becomes "Gross Sales and Sales by Date."

9 Drag the lower-right handle down and to the right.

The visual appears at the larger size.

10 Click **Format visual** (🖌).

The Format Visual tab appears.

11 Click **Visual**.

The Visual subtab appears.

12 Click **Callout value**.

The Callout Value section expands.

13 Click **Font** (∨), and select a font.

14 Click **Font size** (◌), and specify the font size.

H Power BI updates the color, font, and size of the callout value.

15 Click **Icons**.

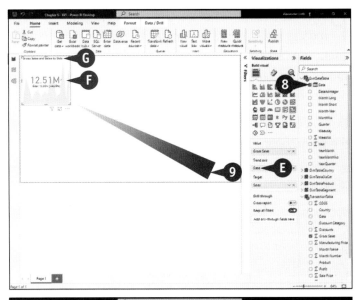

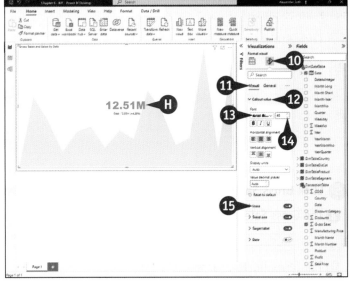

TIP

How can I make the example KPI visual show a bad result?

If the visual is not already selected, click to select it. In the Visualizations pane, click **Build visual** (▦) to display the Build Visual pane. Go to the Value box and click **Remove** (✕) to remove the Gross Sales field, and then go to the Target box and click **Remove** (✕) to remove the Sales field. In the Fields pane, click **Sales** (☐ changes to ☑) to add the Sales field to the Value box, and then click **Gross Sales** (☐ changes to ☑) to add the Gross Sales field to the Target box.

continued ▶

Power BI Desktop lets you format KPI visuals to catch or please the eye, as needed. When you specify a field that provides a target for the KPI, you should go to the Trend Axis section of the Visual subtab of the Format Visual tab and use the Good Color controls, the Neutral Color controls, and the Bad Color controls to specify the colors Power BI Desktop should apply when the KPI is good, neutral, or bad. You can also adjust the transparency level for the area chart, format the callout label and the target label, and format the date.

Create and Format a KPI Visual (continued)

Ⓐ If you do not want the visual to display the icon, click the switch on the Icons heading (On changes to Off).

⓰ Click **Icon size** (↕), and then specify the icon size.

Ⓑ The icon changes to that size.

Note: The icon is a check mark for good performance and an exclamation point for bad performance.

⓱ Click **Trend axis**.

⓲ Click **Direction** (∨), and then click **High is good** or **Low is good**, as needed, to tell Power BI Desktop how to interpret the Value figures and Target figures.

⓳ Click **Good Color** (∨), and then click the color for good performance.

⓴ Click **Neutral Color** (∨), and then click the color for neutral performance.

㉑ Click **Bad Color** (∨), and then click the color for bad performance.

㉒ Click **Transparency** (↕), and then set the transparency percentage for the area chart.

㉓ Click **Target label**.

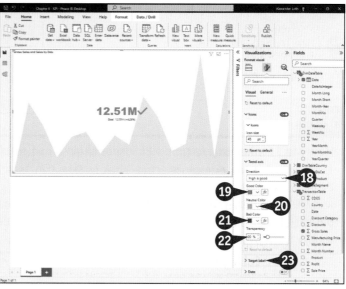

114

㉔ Click **Font** (⌄), and then click the font.

㉕ Click **Font size** (◌), and then specify the font size.

㉖ Click **Font color** (⌄), and then click the color.

Ⓒ You can click **Label** and type a label other than the default, Goal.

㉗ Click **Distance to goal.**

㉘ Click **Style** (⌄), and then click **Value, Percent,** or **Both.**

㉙ Click **Distance direction** (⌄), and then click **Increasing is positive** or **Decreasing is positive.**

Note: The Distance from Goal section automatically picks up the font formatting from the Values section.

㉚ To include the date, click the switch on the Date heading (●Off changes to On●).

㉛ Click **Date.**

㉜ Repeat steps **24** to **26** to specify the font formatting for the date.

Ⓓ The chart takes on the formatting you specified.

㉝ Click **Save** (🖫).

㉞ Click **Close** (✕).

TIP

How can I format the callout value font color?

You can format the callout value color manually only when you do not specify a field containing target values for the KPI visual. When this is the case, the Font Color swatch appears in the Callout Value section of the Visual subtab of the Format Visual tab in the Visualizations pane, and you can click **Font color** (⌄) and select the color you want.

When you specify a field containing target values, the callout value appears in the Good Color, Neutral Color, or Bad Color you have set in the Trend Axis section, depending on the current value.

Create a Matrix Visual

Power BI Desktop enables you to create a matrix visual, a tabular layout that enables you to pivot the data it contains and drill down through the layers of a data hierarchy. A matrix visual shows the relationship between two or more variables in a data set.

A matrix visual needs at least two variables, because it must have at least two dimensions. But it can have further variables to create further dimensions — including a third variable adds a third dimension, a fourth variable adds a fourth dimension, and so on.

Create a Matrix Visual

Note: This section uses the Chapter 6 - Matrix. pbix database, available at www.wiley.com/go/ tyvpowerbi.

1 Open the Chapter 6 - Matrix.pbix database file.

Note: If the Fields pane and the Visualizations pane are collapsed, expand them.

2 Click **Build Visual** (▦).

The Build Visual pane appears.

3 Click **Matrix** (▦).

Ⓐ Power BI Desktop creates a matrix visual.

4 Click **Expand** (⟩ changes to ⌄) to the left of TransactionTable.

The TransactionTable listing expands.

5 Click **Sales** (☐ changes to ☑).

Ⓑ The Sales field appears in the Values box.

Ⓒ The Sales data appears in the visual.

Note: By default, the matrix visual displays the sum of the Sales column.

6 Click **Country** (☐ changes to ☑).

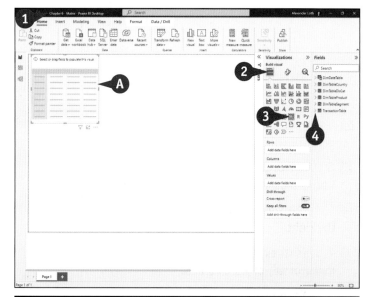

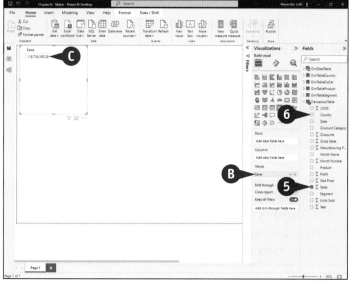

D The Country field appears in the Rows box.

E The Country data appears in the matrix visual, creating a two-column table showing sales by country.

7 Click **Product** (☐ changes to ☑).

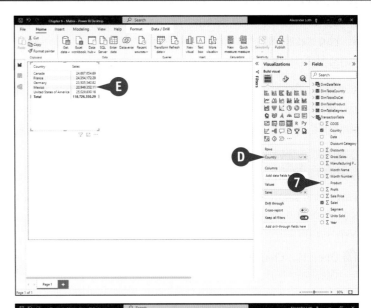

F The Product field appears in the Columns box.

G The Product data appears in the matrix visual, expanding the table to eight columns.

8 Drag the lower-right handle down and to the right.

The visual expands, enabling you to see more, or all, of its columns.

9 Click **Save** (🖫).

Power BI Desktop saves your changes.

10 Click **Close** (✕).

The file closes.

TIP

How do I drill down through a matrix visual?
To drill down through a matrix visual, you first need to have two or more fields in the Rows box on the Build Visual tab of the Visualizations pane. If you are working from the example matrix, which has a single field in the Rows box, add one or more fields by expanding the appropriate table in the Fields pane and then dragging the field or fields to the Rows box. Drag the fields into the order in which you want them to appear. Next, click **Drill Down** (↓ changes to ●) below the matrix to enable Drill Mode. You can then click the data point from which you want to drill down.

Format a Matrix Visual

You can quickly format a matrix visual by applying one of nine preset styles, such as Minimal, Contrast Alternating Rows, or Condensed. If the preset looks good enough, you can leave it as is; if not, you can customize it as needed.

Power BI Desktop lets you choose whether to display horizontal and vertical gridlines and, if you do, format their color and width. You can also adjust the *row padding*, the amount of blank space between rows in the matrix, to make the table more or less compact or make it easier to read.

Format a Matrix Visual

Note: This section uses the Chapter 6 - Matrix Format.pbix database, available at www.wiley.com/go/tyvpowerbi.

1. Open the Chapter 6 - Matrix Format.pbix database file.

Note: If the Visualizations pane is collapsed, expand it.

2. Click the matrix visual.

   Selection handles appear around the visual.

3. Click **Format Visual** (🖋).

4. Click **Visual**.

5. Click **Style presets**.

6. Click the drop-down list (⌄), and then click the preset you want. This example uses **Minimal**.

Ⓐ The matrix visual takes on the style preset's formatting.

7. Click **Grid**.

8. Set the switch on the Horizontal Gridlines heading to On (On).

9. Set the switch on the Vertical Gridlines heading to On (On).

Ⓑ The visual displays the gridlines you specified.

10. Click **Border** to expand the Border section.

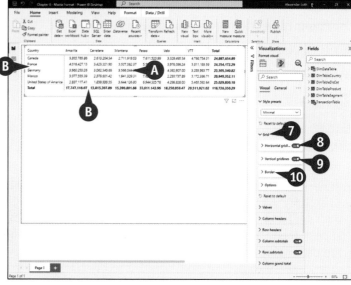

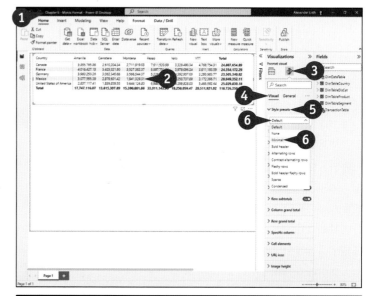

⑪ Click **Section** (⌄), and then click the visual section you want to affect: All, Column Header, Row Headers, or Values Section. This example uses **Row headers**.

⑫ In the Border Position list, select (☑) **Top**, **Bottom**, **Left**, or **Right** to specify which borders to display for that section.

⑬ Click **Color** (⌄), and then click the border color.

⑭ Click **Width** (◌) and specify the border width.

⑮ Repeat steps **11** to **14** to apply any other border formatting you want (not shown).

⑯ Click **Options**.

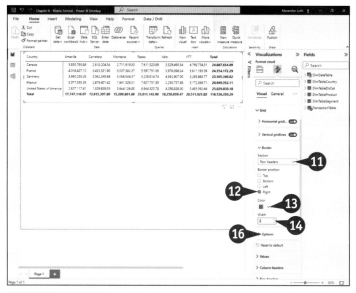

⑰ Click **Row padding** (◌) and set the amount of space between lines. See the tip for advice.

⑱ Click **Global font size** (◌) and specify the font size for all column headers, row headers, and cell elements.

⑲ Click **Save** (▣).

⑳ Click **Close** (✕).

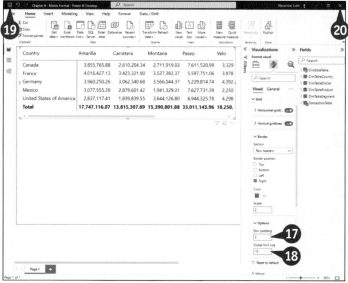

TIP

How much row padding should I add to a matrix visual?
How much padding a matrix visual needs varies greatly depending on the information the matrix is presenting and the way you are presenting it. Use a setting of 0 when you want the most compact layout possible, even at the expense of some readability. For general use, a setting in the 3–5 range produces a comfortably readable matrix, but you may want to try greater amounts of padding for complex matrices or for audiences with older eyes.

Format the Values and Column Headers of a Matrix Visual

Power BI Desktop enables you to format the values and the column headers in a matrix visual to convey your message more effectively. You can change the font, font size, and font color of the text and specify the background color against which the text appears.

To improve the readability of a matrix visual, you can apply alternate-row formatting — that is, use different formatting for the odd-numbered rows than for the even numbered rows. To apply alternate-row formatting in Power BI Desktop, you specify an alternate text color and, optionally, an alternate background color.

Format the Values and Column Headers of a Matrix Visual

Note: This section uses the Chapter 6 - Matrix Values.pbix database, available at www.wiley.com/go/tyvpowerbi.

1 Open the Chapter 6 - Matrix Values.pbix database file.

Note: If the Visualizations pane is collapsed, expand it.

2 Click the matrix visual.

3 Click **Format Visual** (🖌).

4 Click **Visual**.

5 Click **Values**.

6 Click **Font** (⌄), and then click the font.

7 Click **Font size** (◌), and then click the font size.

8 Click **Text color** (⌄), and then click the text color.

9 Click **Background color** (⌄), and then click the color.

10 Click **Alternate text color** (⌄), and then click the color.

11 Click **Alternate background color** (⌄), and then click the color.

12 Set the **Text wrap** switch to On (On ●) to allow values text to wrap.

13 Click **Column headers**.

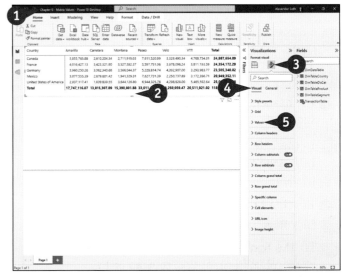

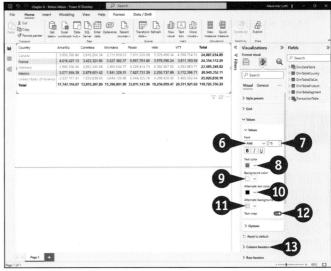

14 Click **Font** (∨), and then click the font.

15 Click **Font size** (◯), and then click the font size.

16 Click **Text color** (∨), and then click the text color.

17 Click **Background color** (∨), and then click the background color.

18 In the Header Alignment area, click **Left** (▤), **Center** (▤), or **Right** (▤), as needed.

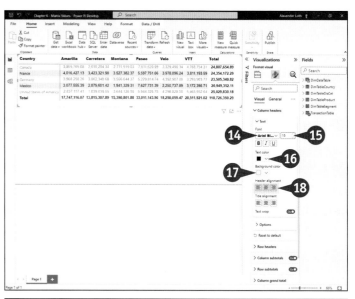

A The headers take on the alignment you specified.

19 In the Title Alignment area, click **Left** (▤), **Center** (▤), or **Right** (▤), as needed.

B The title takes on the alignment you specified.

20 Set the **Text wrap** switch to On (On ●) to allow column header text to wrap or to Off (● Off) to prevent column header text from wrapping.

21 Click **Save** (▤).

22 Click **Close** (✕).

TIP

How can I turn off alternate-row formatting?
Power BI Desktop does not offer a setting for turning off alternate-row formatting, but you can simply format the alternate rows the same as the other rows to remove any differentiation. Click **Alternate text color** (∨), and choose the same color you specified for the Text Color setting. Then click **Alternate background color** (∨) and select the same color you used for the Background Color setting.

Format the Row Headers of a Matrix Visual

Power BI Desktop allows you to format the row headers, the labels in the leftmost column that identify the rows of a matrix visual. You can specify the font, font size, text color, and background color to control how the row headers appear. You can also control whether the row header text takes on the banded row color you specified as the alternate row color for the rows text.

Power BI Desktop also lets you format the column subtotals. You can apply this formatting either to all column subtotals or to a particular column's subtotal.

Format the Row Headers of a Matrix Visual

Note: This section uses the Chapter 6 - Matrix Rows.pbix database, available at www.wiley.com/go/tyvpowerbi.

1. Open the Chapter 6 - Matrix Rows.pbix database file.

Note: If the Visualizations pane is collapsed, expand it.

2. Click the matrix visual.

3. Click **Format Visual** (✍).

4. Click **Visual**.

5. Click **Row headers**.

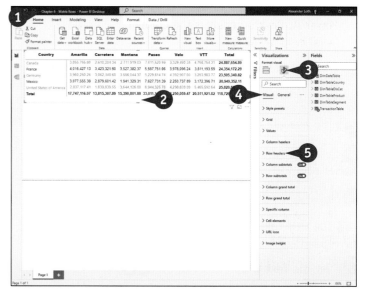

6. Click **Font** (⌄), and then click the font.

7. Click **Font size** (⟐), and then click the font size.

8. Click **Text color** (⌄), and then click the text color.

9. Click **Background color** (⌄), and then click the background color.

10. Set the **Banded row color** switch to On (On●).

11. In the Header Alignment area, click **Left** (▤), **Center** (▤), or **Right** (▤), as needed.

Ⓐ The row headers take on the formatting.

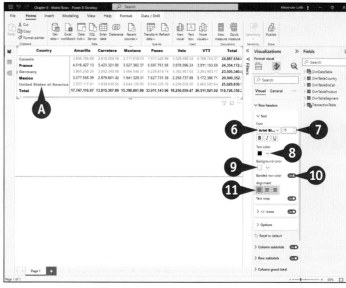

12 Set the **Text wrap** switch to On (On●) to allow row header text to wrap or to Off (●Off) to prevent row header text from wrapping.

13 Set the switch on the Column Subtotals heading to On (On●).

14 Click **Column subtotals**.

15 Click the **Per column level** switch (●Off changes to On●).

Power BI Desktop enables the Column Level drop-down list.

16 Click **Column level** (⌄), and then click **All** or the column you want to format.

17 Click **Columns**.

18 Set the **Show subtotal** switch to On (On●).

19 Optionally, click the **Subtotal label** text box and type a different label.

20 Click **Values**.

21 Repeat steps **6** to **9** to format the values.

Ⓑ The matrix visual takes on the formatting.

22 Click **Save** (🖫).

23 Click **Close** (✖).

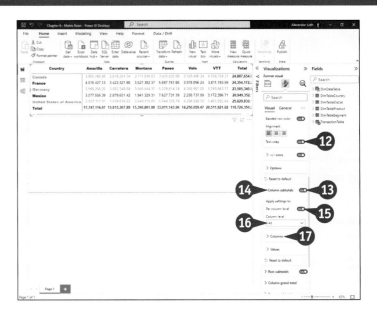

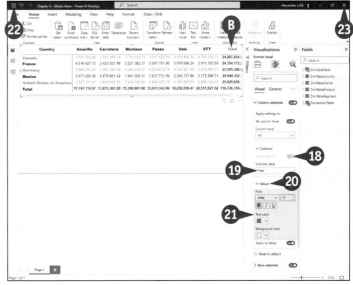

TIP

What do the +/- Icons controls in the Row Headers box do?
When you add two or more fields to the Rows box on the Build Visual tab of the Visualizations pane, Power BI Desktop can display Expand (⊞) and Collapse (⊟) icons next to the fields in the matrix's first column. Click **Expand** (⊞) to expand the hidden rows; click **Collapse** (⊟) to collapse them again. If you do not want to have these icons displayed, set the switch on the +/- Icons heading to Off (●Off). If you do display them, you can click **Color** (⌄) to control their color and click **Size** (◌) to adjust their size.

Format the Row Subtotals and Grand Totals of a Matrix Visual

Power BI Desktop lets you decide whether to display row subtotals in your matrix visuals that contain nested category data. If you do display row subtotals, you can format them as needed. You can choose whether to format row subtotals individually or as a group.

Power BI Desktop automatically displays the row grand total for the matrix. You can format the font, font size, text color, and background color of the row grand total.

Format the Row Subtotals and Grand Totals of a Matrix Visual

Note: This section uses the Chapter 6 - Matrix Totals.pbix database, available at www.wiley.com/go/tyvpowerbi.

1 Open the Chapter 6 - Matrix Totals.pbix database file.

Note: If the Visualizations pane is collapsed, expand it.

2 Click the matrix visual.

3 Click **Format Visual** (🖌).

4 Click **Visual**.

5 Set the switch on the Row Subtotals heading to On (On●).

6 Click **Row subtotals**.

7 Click the **Per row level** switch (●Off) changes to (On●).

8 Click **Row Level** (⌄), and then click **All** or the row level you want to affect.

9 Click **Rows**.

10 Set the **Show subtotal** switch to On (On●).

11 Click the **Subtotal label** text box and type a label.

12 Click **Position** (⌄), and then click **Top** or **Bottom**, as needed.

13 Click **Values**.

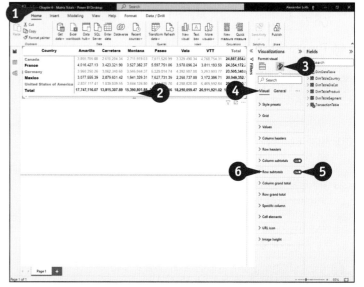

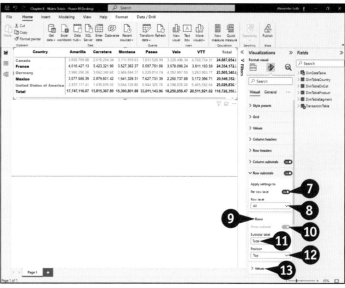

14 Click **Font** (∨), and then click the font.

15 Click **Font size** (○), and then click the font size.

16 Click **Text color** (∨), and then click the text color.

17 Click **Background color** (∨), and then click the background color.

18 Set the **Apply to labels** switch to On (On).

Ⓐ The label takes on the formatting.

19 Click **Column grand total** to expand the Column Grand Total section.

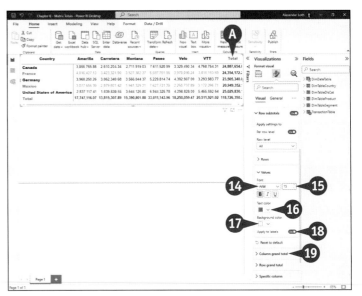

20 Repeat steps **14** to **18** to apply formatting to the column grand totals.

21 Click **Row grand total** to expand the Row Grand Total section.

22 Repeat steps **14** to **18** to apply formatting to the row grand totals.

Ⓑ The column grand totals and row grand totals take on the formatting.

23 Click **Save** (🖫).

24 Click **Close** (✖).

TIP

How do I remove the subtotal values from the matrix visual?

Click the matrix visual to select it, click **Format Visual** (🖌) to display the Format Visual tab of the Visualizations pane, and then click **Visual** to display the Visual subtab. To hide the column subtotals, set the switch on the Column Subtotals heading to Off (Off). Similarly, to hide the row subtotals, set the switch on the Row Subtotals heading to Off (Off).

Format the Specific Column and Cell Elements of a Matrix Visual

Power BI Desktop enables you to format specific columns in a matrix visual and to add elements such as data bars and icons to cells. In the Apply Settings To subsection of the Specific Column section, you can specify which of the column's components — the header, the subtotals, the total, and the values — receive the formatting you set.

Similarly, in the Apply Settings To subsection of the Cell Elements section, you can specify which elements — the background color, the font color, the data bars, the icons, and the web URL — to display in the cells.

Format the Specific Column and Cell Elements of a Matrix Visual

Note: This section uses the Chapter 6 - Matrix Elements.pbix database, available at www.wiley.com/go/tyvpowerbi.

1 Open the Chapter 6 - Matrix Elements.pbix database file.

Note: If the Visualizations pane is collapsed, expand it.

2 Click the matrix visual.

3 Click **Format Visual** (✏️).

4 Click **Visual**.

5 Click **Specific column**.

6 Click **Series** (⌄), and then click the column to format.

7 Set the **Apply to header** switch to On (On●) or Off (●Off)

8 Set the **Apply to subtotals** switch to On (On●) or Off (●Off).

9 Set the **Apply to total** switch to On (On●) or Off (●Off).

10 Set the **Apply to values** switch to On (On●) or Off (●Off).

11 Click **Values**.

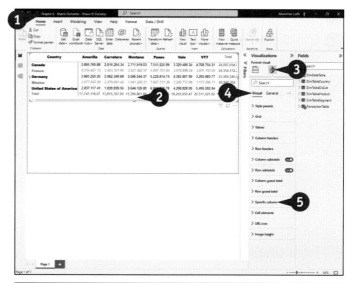

12 Click **Text color** ($\vee$), and then click the text color.

13 Click **Background color** ($\vee$), and then click the background color.

14 Click **Left** (▤), **Center** (▤), or **Right** (▤) for alignment.

15 Click **Display units** ($\vee$), and then click the units, such as **Thousands**.

Ⓐ The visual takes on the formatting.

16 Click **Cell elements**.

17 Click **Series** ($\vee$), and then click the column to format.

18 Set the **Background color** switch to On (On●) or Off (●Off).

19 Set the Font Color switch to On (On●) or Off (●Off).

20 Set the **Data bars** switch to On (On●) or Off (●Off).

21 Set the **Icons** switch to On (On●) or Off (●Off).

22 Set the **Web URL** switch to On (On●) or Off (●Off).

Ⓑ The visual takes on the formatting.

23 Click **Save** (🖫).

24 Click **Close** (✕).

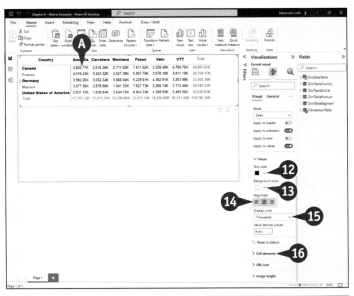

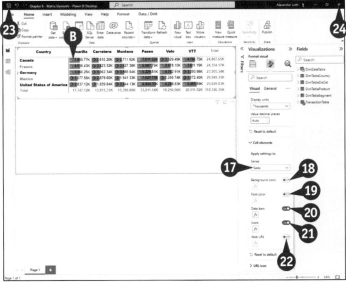

TIP

What are the data bars and the icons for matrix visuals?

Set the **Data bars** switch to On (On●) to display a shaded data bar on the left side of each value cell showing how the cell's value compares to others in its series.

Set the **Icons** switch to On (On●) to display a color- and shape-coded icon on the left side of each value cell to show how the cell's value compares to others in its series. The default icon set shows ◆ for the lower third, ▲ for the middle third, and ● for the upper third. Click 𝑓𝑥 to customize the icon set or to choose a different icon set.

Create a Waterfall Chart

You can use a waterfall chart, a type of bar graph, to demonstrate the net change in value between two points. A *waterfall chart* shows how the initial values gradually increase and decrease over a series of values to reach the final value. The chart breaks down all the individual components that contribute to the net change in value and shows them individually.

Waterfall charts are sometimes called *bridge charts*. This is because the initial-value column and the final-value column typically touch the X-axis, with the intermediate values floating between these columns and forming a span.

Create a Waterfall Chart

Note: This section uses the Chapter 6 - Waterfall.pbix database, available at www. wiley.com/go/tyvpowerbi.

1 Open the Chapter 6 - Waterfall.pbix database file.

Note: If the Fields pane and the Visualizations pane are collapsed, expand them.

2 Click **Build visual** (▦).

3 Click **Waterfall chart** (▮▮▮).

A Power BI adds a waterfall chart visual to the canvas.

4 Click **Expand** (❯ changes to ❮) to the left of DimDateTable.

The DimDateTable listing expands.

5 Click **Date** (☐ changes to ☑).

B The Date field hierarchy appears in the Category box.

C The Date field appears in the waterfall chart visual.

6 Click **Date** (❮).

The drop-down list opens.

7 Click **Date**.

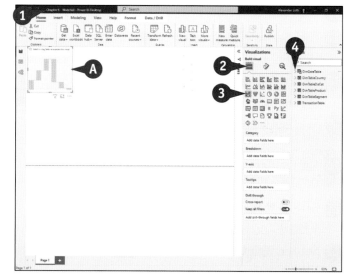

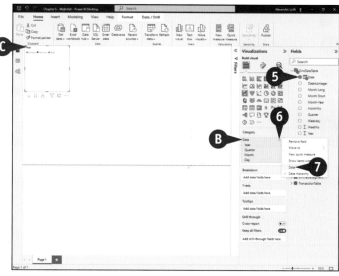

D The Date field from the hierarchy appears in the Category box, rather than the Date hierarchy as a whole appearing.

8 Drag the lower-right handle down and to the right to enlarge the visual.

9 Click **Expand** (> changes to ∨) to the left of TransactionTable.

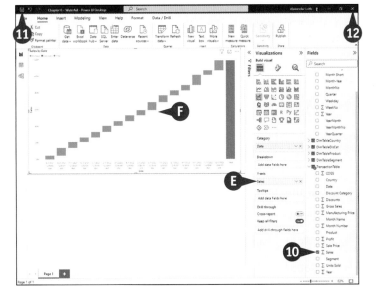

The TransactionTable listing expands.

10 Click **Sales** (☐ changes to ☑).

E The Sales field appears in the Y-Axis box.

F The data appears in the waterfall chart.

11 Click **Save** (💾).

Power BI Desktop saves your changes.

12 Click **Close** (☒).

The file closes.

TIP

What is a good use of a waterfall chart?

Create a waterfall chart when you need to illustrate visually how a starting value changes, through intermediate additions and subtractions, to a final value. For example, you might use a waterfall chart to show gross sales and net income within the same month, or the difference in net income between last year and this year, and the factors responsible for this change.

Format a Waterfall Chart

Power BI Desktop provides a good range of visual formatting options for waterfall charts. You can choose whether to display the X-axis, the Y-axis, and the legend; if you do display them, you can format their text and background as needed.

This section explains how to format the Y-axis of a waterfall chart. The following section covers formatting the X-axis and legend.

Format a Waterfall Chart

Note: This section uses the Chapter 6 - Waterfall Format.pbix database, available at www.wiley.com/go/tyvpowerbi.

1 Open the Chapter 6 - Waterfall Format.pbix database file.

Note: If the Visualizations pane is collapsed, expand it.

2 Click the waterfall chart visual.

3 Click **Format Visual** (✍).

4 Click **Visual**.

5 Set the switch on the Y-Axis heading to On (On ●).

6 Click **Y-axis**.

The Y-Axis section expands.

7 Click **Values**.

The Values section expands.

8 Click **Font** (∨), and then click the font.

9 Click **Font size** (◌), and then specify the size.

10 Click **Color** (∨), and then click the color.

Ⓐ The Y-axis values take on the formatting.

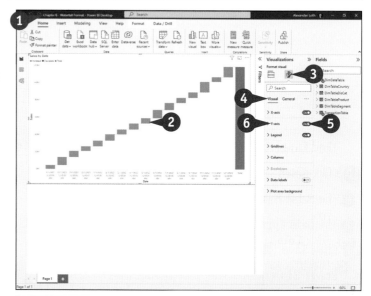

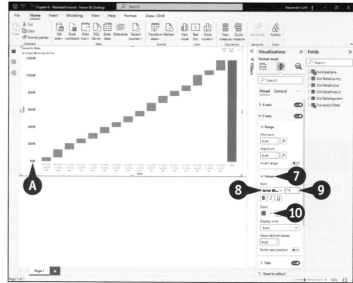

130

11 Click the **Switch axis position** switch (⬤Off changes to On⬤).

B The Y-axis moves from the left of the visual to the right.

12 Click **Title**.

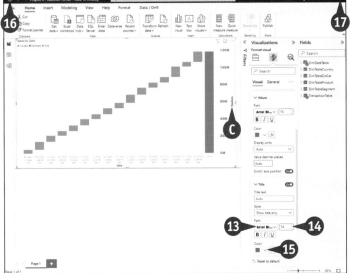

The Title section expands.

13 Click **Font** (⌄), and then click the font.

14 Click **Font size** (⌃), and then specify the size.

15 Click **Color** (⌄), and then click the color.

C The title takes on the formatting.

16 Click **Save** (💾).

Power BI Desktop saves your changes.

17 Click **Close** (❌).

The file closes.

TIP

What other changes can I make to the Y-axis?

First, you can change the axis title from its default — the name of the field supplying the values — to text of your choosing; simply click in the **Title text** box and type the text you want in place of the Auto value, which inserts the field name. Second, you can specify the title style by clicking **Style** (⌄) to open the Style drop-down list and then clicking **Show title only**, **Show unit only**, or **Show both**, as needed.

Format the X-Axis and Legend of a Waterfall Chart

Power BI Desktop enables you to format the X-axis and the legend of a waterfall chart. The X-axis controls the order in which the values on the Y-axis change, so getting the X-axis order and format right is essential to having your data appear correctly in the waterfall chart.

You can choose a position for the legend to best fit the pattern of the chart. For example, you might place the legend in the center-left area if that is where a suitable amount of space is vacant.

Format the X-Axis and Legend a Waterfall Chart

Note: This section uses the Chapter 6 - Waterfall Legend.pbix database, available at www.wiley.com/go/tyvpowerbi.

1 Open the Chapter 6 - Waterfall Legend. pbix database file.

Note: If the Visualizations pane is collapsed, expand it.

2 Click the waterfall chart visual.

3 Click **Format Visual** (🖌️).

The Format Visual tab appears.

4 Click **Visual**.

5 Set the switch on the X-Axis heading to On (On⬤).

6 Click **X-axis** to expand the Title section.

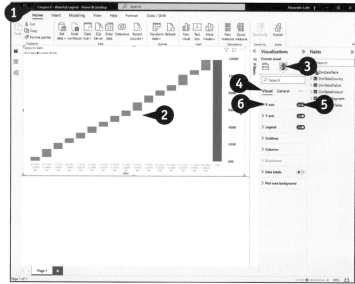

7 Click **Font** (∨), and then click the font.

8 Click **Font size** (◌), and then specify the font size.

9 Click **Text color** (∨), and then click the text color.

10 Click **Title** to expand the Title section.

11 Repeat steps **7** to **9** to format the title.

Ⓐ The values and title take on the formatting.

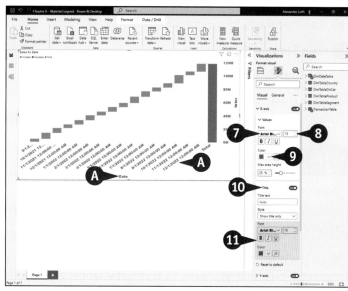

⑫ Scroll down and click **Legend**.

The Legend section expands.

⑬ Click **Options**.

The Options section expands.

⑭ Click **Position** (⌄), and then click the position, such as **Top center** or **Bottom left**. This example uses **Center right**.

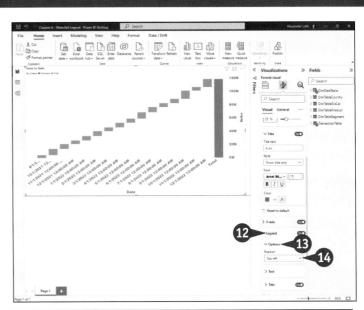

Ⓑ The legend moves to the position you specified.

⑮ Click **Text**.

The Text section expands.

⑯ Click **Font** (⌄), and then click the font.

⑰ Click **Font size** (○), and then specify the font size.

⑱ Click **Text color** (⌄), and then click the text color.

Ⓒ The legend takes on the formatting.

⑲ Click **Save** (🖫).

Power BI Desktop saves your changes.

⑳ Click **Close** (✕).

The file closes.

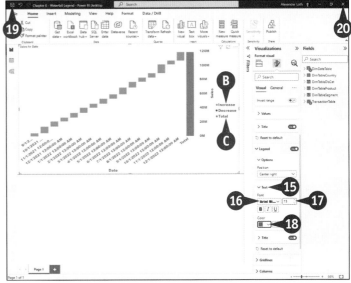

TIP

How do I change the range for a waterfall chart?

Click the waterfall chart, click **Format Visual** (🗗) to display the Format Visual tab of the Visualizations pane, and then click **Visual** to display the Visual subtab. Make sure the switch on the Y-Axis heading is set to On (On●), click **Y-axis** to expand the Y-Axis section, and then click **Range** to expand the Range section. Click **Minimum** (○) and specify the minimum value for the range; then click **Maximum** (○) and specify the maximum value. If you want to invert the range, click the **Invert range** switch (●Off changes to On●).

Add and Format Breakdowns in a Waterfall Chart

After creating a waterfall chart, you can add a breakdown field to analyze the chart's data more closely. The breakdown field breaks down each data point by subcategories, enabling you to see more clearly what contributes to each value. You can adjust the number of breakdowns between 1 and the number of subcategories the breakdown field provides.

Adding breakdowns can be most helpful for analyzing some datasets but less helpful for others. Usually, it is well worth trying. If adding the breakdown field turns out not to be helpful, you can remove it in moments, as in this section's example.

Add and Format Breakdowns in a Waterfall Chart

Note: This section uses the Chapter 6 - Waterfall Breakdown.pbix database, available at www.wiley.com/go/tyvpowerbi.

1 Open the Chapter 6 - Waterfall Breakdown. pbix database file.

Note: If the Fields pane and the Visualizations pane are collapsed, expand them.

2 Click the visual.

3 Click **Build Visual** (▤).

4 Click **Expand** (﹥ changes to ﹀) to the left of TransactionTable to expand the listing.

5 Click **Discount Category** (☐ changes to ☑).

Ⓐ The Discount Category field appears in the Breakdown box.

Ⓑ The High, Medium, Low, and None subcategories appear for each month on the X-axis.

Note: High, Medium, Low, and None are the four discount categories.

Ⓒ Each subcategory has a separate bar that shows its result for the month.

6 Click **Format Visual** (🖌).

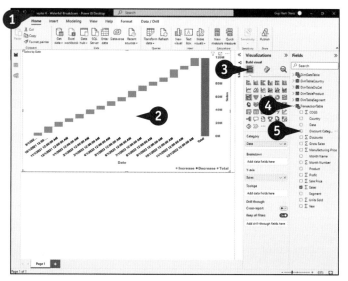

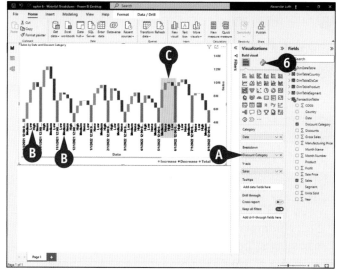

The Format Visual tab appears.

7 Click **Visual**.

The Visual subtab appears.

8 Click **Breakdown**.

The Breakdown section expands.

9 Click **Maximum breakdowns** (◡) and specify **2**.

D Each month now shows three columns: one column for each of the two largest subcategories for that month, plus the Other column, which wraps up the remaining subcategories.

Note: Specifying 1 for the Maximum Breakdowns setting displays two columns: one for the largest subcategory, plus the Other column.

10 Click **Discount Category** (☑ changes to ☐).

E Power BI Desktop removes the Discount Category field from the Breakdown box.

F The waterfall chart reverts to its previous form.

11 Click **Save** (💾).

Power BI Desktop saves your changes.

12 Click **Close** (✖).

The file closes.

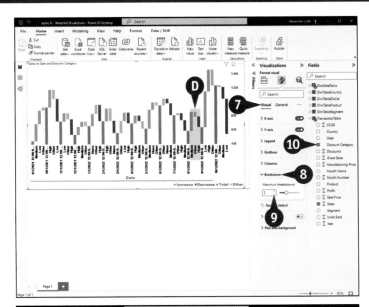

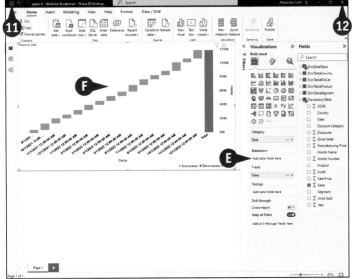

How do I change the column colors and widths in the breakdown?
Click the waterfall chart visual, click **Format Visual** (🖌), and then click **Visual** to display the Visual subtab. Click **Columns** to expand the Columns section. In the Colors section, click **Increase** (⌄), **Decrease** (⌄), **Other** (⌄), and **Total** (⌄) in turn, and click the color you want for each category. Then click **Spacing** to expand the Spacing section. Click **Maximum category width** (◡) and specify the maximum width in pixels. Then click **Inner padding** (◡) and specify the number of pixels to leave between columns.

Create, Format, and Label a Funnel Chart

Power BI Desktop enables you to create funnel charts, which are often used to illustrate the flow of business processes. A *funnel chart* displays categorical information arranged from the largest value to the smallest value, giving a distinctive funnel shape. You can display either all the categories or a number of the top categories — such as the top five categories.

For example, you might create a funnel chart to show how individual sales reps transitioned prospects from one stage of the sales process to another. The top-ranking sales rep would appear at the top of the funnel chart.

Create, Format, and Label a Funnel Chart

Note: This section uses the Chapter 6 - Funnel. pbix database, available at www.wiley.com/go/ tyvpowerbi.

1 Open the Chapter 6 - Funnel.pbix database file.

Note: If the Fields pane and the Visualizations pane are collapsed, expand them.

2 Click **Build Visual** (▦).

The Build Visual tab appears.

3 Click **Funnel** (⌂).

Ⓐ Power BI adds a funnel visual to the canvas.

4 Click **Expand** (❯ changes to ⌄) to the left of TransactionTable.

The TransactionTable listing expands.

5 Click **Country** (☐ changes to ✅).

Ⓑ The Country field appears in the Category box.

Ⓒ The Country data appears in the funnel visual.

6 Drag the lower-right handle down and to the right.

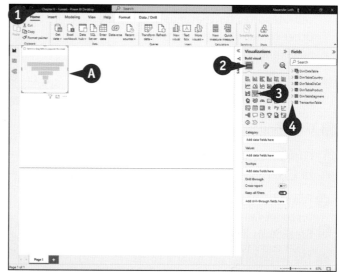

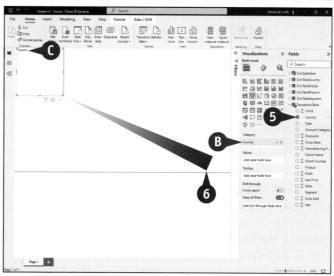

The funnel visual expands.

7 Click **Sales**.

D The Sales field appears in the Values box.

E The Sales data appears in the funnel visual, ranked from largest to smallest.

8 Click **Format Visual** (🖌).

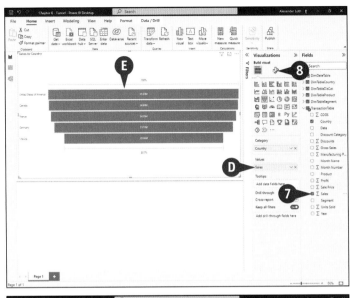

The Format Visual tab appears.

9 Click **Visual**.

The Visual subtab appears.

10 Click **Colors**.

The Colors section expands.

F By default, the funnel visual uses the same color for all the bars.

Note: If you want to use a different single color for all the bars in the funnel visual, click **Default** (∨), and then click the color.

11 Click the **Show all** switch (●Off) changes to (On●).

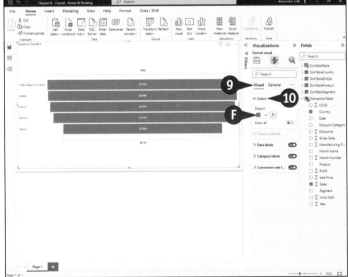

TIP

How do I use a function other than Sum for the Values field in my funnel chart?
Click the funnel chart to select it, and then click **Build Visual** (▦) to display the Build Visual tab of the Visualizations pane. Right-click the field in the Values box to open the contextual menu, and then click the function you want to use. Apart from Sum, your choices are Average, Minimum, Maximum, Count (Distinct), Count, Standard Deviation, Variance, and Median.

continued ▶

By default, Power BI Desktop uses the same color for each bar in the funnel chart, giving it a uniform look. You can change this single color, as needed; you can also specify what color to use for each bar if you want.

Power BI Desktop provides three types of labels for funnel charts: data labels that show the values or contribution of each category, category labels that identify the categories, and conversion labels that show the conversion percentages. You can format all three types of labels to look the way you prefer.

Create, Format, and Label a Funnel Chart (continued)

Ⓐ A drop-down list appears for each item in the data series, arranged from largest to smallest, like the funnel.

12 Click each drop-down list and select the color.

Ⓑ The funnel takes on the colors.

13 Set the switch on the Data Labels heading to On (On⬤).

14 Click **Data labels**.

The Data Labels section expands.

15 Click **Values**.

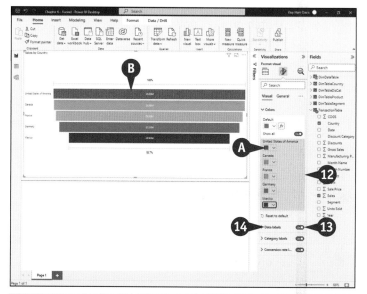

The Values section expands.

16 Click **Font** (⌄) and then click the font.

17 Click **Font size** (◌) and then specify the font size.

18 Click **Color** (⌄) and then click the color.

Ⓒ You can click **Display units** (⌄) and select a specific unit, such as **Thousands** or **Millions**, instead of **Auto**, which displays default units suited to the values.

Ⓓ The data labels take on the formatting.

19 Click **Category labels**.

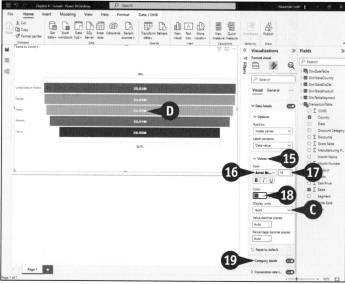

The Category Labels section expands.

20 Set the switch on the Category Labels heading to On (On).

21 Click **Font** (∨), and then click the font.

22 Click **Font size** (⌃), and then specify the font size.

23 Click **Color** (∨), and then click the color.

E The category labels take on the formatting.

24 Set the switch on the Conversion Rate Labels heading to On (On).

25 Click **Conversion rate labels**.

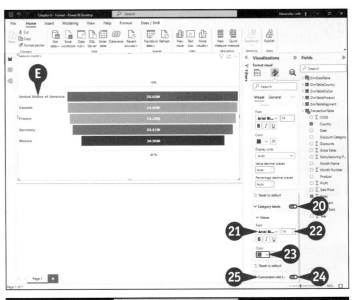

The Conversion Rate Labels section expands.

26 Click **Font** (∨), and then click the font.

27 Click **Font size** (⌃), and then specify the font size.

28 Click **Color** (∨), and then click the color.

F The category labels take on the formatting.

29 Click **Save** (▤).

30 Click **Close** (☒).

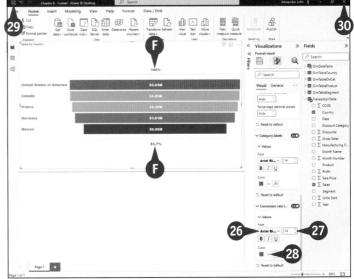

How do I make a funnel chart show percentages on its bars?

Click the funnel chart to select it, click **Format Visual** (⊡) to display the Format Visual tab of the Visualizations pane, and then click **Visual** to display the Visual subtab. Click **Data labels** to expand the Data Labels section, and then click **Options** to expand the Options section if it is collapsed. Click **Label contents** (∨) to open the Label Contents drop-down list, and then click **Percent of first**, **Percent of previous**, **Data value, percent of first**, or **Data value, percent of previous**.

Create a Pie Chart or Donut Chart

When you need to show the proportional relationship of segments in your data to the whole, you can create a pie chart or donut chart. A *pie chart* is a circular statistical graph divided into sections that represent the different segments. A *donut chart* is similar to a pie chart but consists of a ring with a hole in the center — hence the name.

Each slice of a pie chart or donut chart represents a percentage, and the sum of all parts should equal 100 percent. Pie charts and donut charts are normally used to show the same category of data.

Create a Pie Chart or Donut Chart

Note: This section uses the Chapter 6 - Pie. pbix database, available at www.wiley.com/go/tyvpowerbi.

1. Open the Chapter 6 - Pie.pbix database file.

Note: If the Fields pane and the Visualizations pane are collapsed, expand them.

2. Click **Build Visual** (▦).

   The Build Visual tab appears.

3. Click **Pie chart** (◔).

   Ⓐ Alternatively, you can click **Donut Chart** (◎) to create a donut chart.

   Ⓑ Power BI adds a pie chart visual to the canvas.

4. Click **Expand** (⟩ changes to ⌄) to the left of TransactionTable.

   The TransactionTable listing expands.

5. Click **Sales** (☐ changes to ☑).

   Ⓒ The Sales field appears in the Values box.

   Ⓓ The Sales data appears in the visual, creating an unsliced pie.

6. Drag the lower-right handle down and to the right.

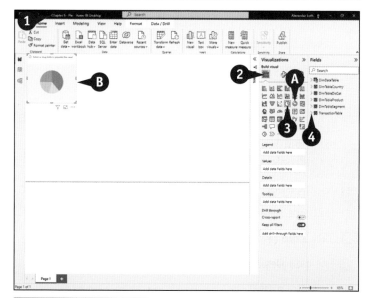

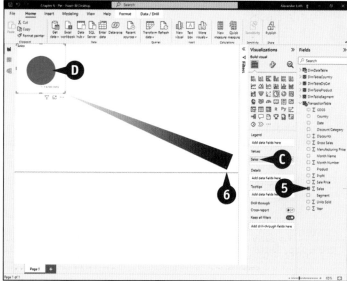

The pie chart visual expands.

7 Click **Country** (☐ changes to ☑).

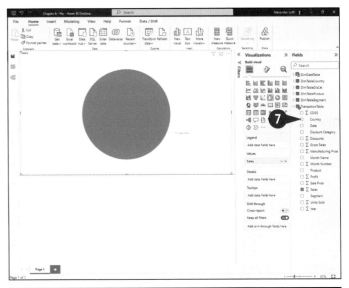

E The Country field appears in the Details box.

F The Country data appears in the pie chart, creating slices.

G Default labels appear.

H A default legend appears.

8 Click **Save** (⊟).

Power BI Desktop saves your changes.

9 Click **Close** (☒).

The file closes.

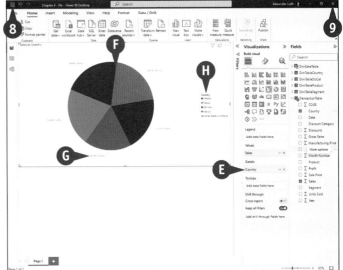

TIP

When should I use a pie chart and when a donut chart?

Choosing between a pie chart and a donut chart in Power BI can be difficult. Both charts allow you to have only a single data series and enable you to show how the parts of that data series contribute to the whole. While some charting tools enable you to create donut charts with multiple data series, Power BI's built-in tools do not.

In many cases, a pie chart is the better choice, because the size differences of pie slices are easier to identify visually than the differences in donut segments. But if you need to place extra data at the center of a confection chart, choose a donut rather than a pie.

Format a Pie Chart or Donut Chart

A fter creating a pie chart or donut chart, you can take advantage of the formatting options that Power BI Desktop provides for making the chart look appealing and easy to read. You can customize the colors of the pie slices or donut arcs. You can choose whether to include a legend, data labels, or both; and if you include them, you can specify their position and their formatting. You can also rotate the pie or donut to help draw attention to the slices or arcs that most merit it.

Format a Pie Chart or Donut Chart

Note: This section uses the Chapter 6 - Pie Format.pbix database, available at www.wiley.com/go/tyvpowerbi.

1 Open the Chapter 6 - Pie Format.pbix database file.

Note: If the Visualizations pane is collapsed, expand it.

2 Click the pie chart visual.

Selection handles appear around the visual.

3 Click **Format Visual** ( ).

The Format Visual tab appears.

4 Click **Visual**.

5 Set the switch on the Legend heading to On (On).

6 Click **Legend**.

7 Click **Text**.

8 Click **Font** (∨), and then click the font.

9 Click **Font size** (↕), and then specify the font size.

10 Click **Color** (∨), and then click the text color.

A The legend takes on the formatting.

11 Click **Position** (∨), and then click a different position, such as **Top right**. This example uses **Bottom center**.

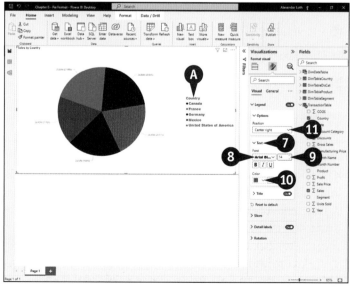

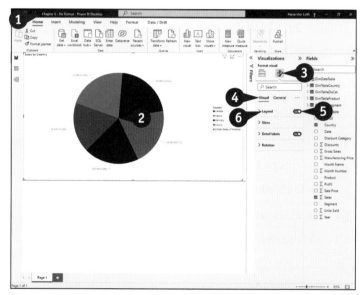

The legend moves to that position.

12 Click **Slices** to expand the Slices section.

13 In the Colors area, click each drop-down list, and then click the color to apply.

Ⓑ The slices take on those colors.

14 Set the switch on the Detail Labels heading to On (⬤).

15 Click **Detail labels**.

16 Click **Position** (⌄), and then click **Inside**.

17 Click **Label contents** (⌄), and then click **All-detail labels**.

Ⓒ The labels move inside and display all details.

18 Click **Values** to expand the Values section.

19 Repeat steps **8** to **10** to format the values.

Ⓓ The values take on the formatting.

20 Click **Rotation** to expand the Rotation section.

21 Drag the Rotation slider to rotate the visual as far as you want.

Ⓔ The visual rotates.

22 Click **Save** (💾).

23 Click **Close** (❎).

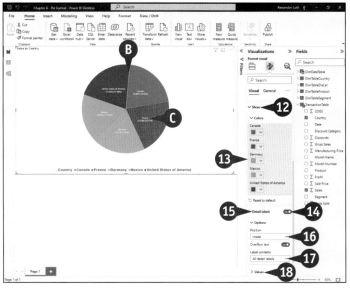

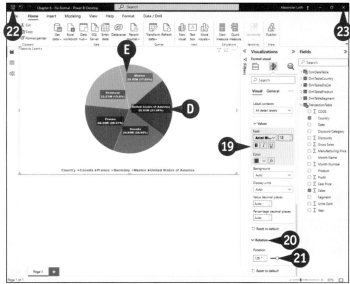

TIP

What other options are there for pie or donut labels?
Apart from All-Detail Labels, you can display the category names, such as Canada and France in the example; the data value, such as 24.35M; the percentage of the total, such as 20.51%; or combinations of the three. Click **Label contents** (⌄), and then click any of the following, as needed: the **Category** item, the **Data value** item, the **Percent of total** item, the **Category, data value** item, the **Category, percent of total** item, or the **Data value, percent of total** item.

Create a Treemap Chart

Power BI Desktop enables you to create treemap charts to visualize your data. A *treemap* is a visual that represents the categories in a dataset as colored rectangles arranged within a larger rectangle that portrays the entire data set. The size of the rectangles varies to indicate their data values. Within the larger rectangle, Power BI Desktop arranges the category rectangles in descending order of size from top left to bottom right.

Create a Treemap Chart

Note: This section uses the Chapter 6 - Treemap.pbix database, available at www.wiley.com/go/tyvpowerbi.

1 Open the Chapter 6 - Treemap.pbix database file.

Note: If the Fields pane and the Visualizations pane are collapsed, expand them.

2 Click **Build Visual** (⊞).

The Build Visual tab appears.

3 Click **Treemap** (⊞).

Ⓐ Power BI adds a treemap visual to the canvas.

4 Click **Expand** (⟩ changes to ⌄) to the left of TransactionTable.

The TransactionTable listing expands.

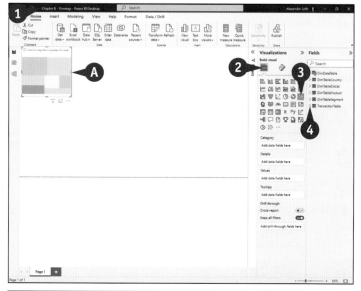

5 Click **Sales** (☐ changes to ☑).

Ⓐ The Sales field appears in the Values box.

Ⓑ The Sales data appears in the treemap visual as a blue rectangle.

6 Drag the lower-right handle down and to the right to enlarge the visual.

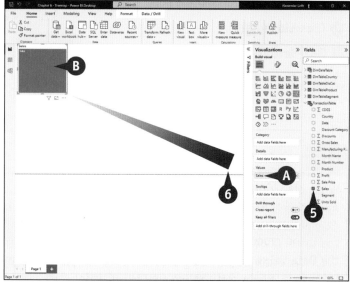

The visual appears at the larger size.

7 Click **Country** (☐ changes to ☑).

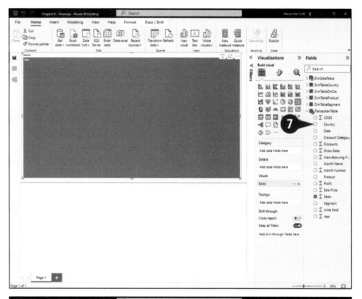

C The Country field appears in the Category box.

D The Country data appears in the treemap visual, creating a separate rectangle for each of the five countries in the category.

8 Click **Save** (💾).

Power BI Desktop saves your changes.

9 Click **Close** (✖).

The file closes.

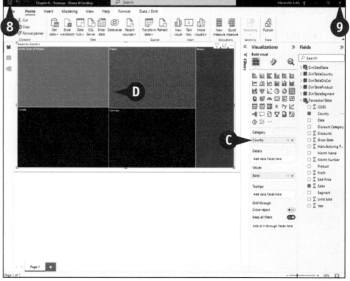

Format a Treemap Chart

After creating a treemap visual, you can format it for readability and impact. Your first choice is whether to display a legend and, if you do, where to position it in relation to the visual. Second, you can specify what color Power BI Desktop uses for each category in the visual. Third, you can decide whether to display data labels in the categories showing their values. Fourth, you can choose whether to display category labels, which are labels that show the category names. You can format the font, size, and color of the legend; the data labels; and the category labels.

Format a Treemap Chart

Note: This section uses the Chapter 6 - Treemap Format.pbix database, available at www.wiley.com/go/tyvpowerbi.

1. Open the Chapter 6 - Treemap Format.pbix database file.

Note: If the Visualizations pane is collapsed, expand it.

2. Click the treemap visual.

3. Click **Format Visual** (🖌).

4. Click **Visual**.

5. Set the switch on the Legend heading to On (**On ●**).

Ⓐ The legend appears.

6. Click **Legend**.

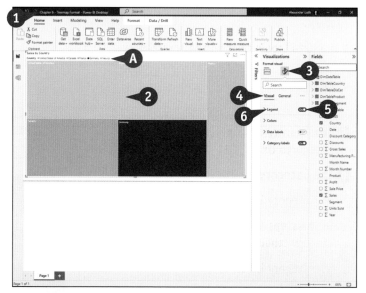

7. Click **Position** (∨), and then click the position, such as **Top right** or **Bottom left**. This example uses **Top center**.

8. Click **Text**.

9. Click **Font** (∨), and then click the font.

10. Click **Font size** (○), and then specify the font size.

11. Click **Color** (∨), and then click the color.

Ⓑ The legend takes on the position and formatting.

12. Click **Colors**.

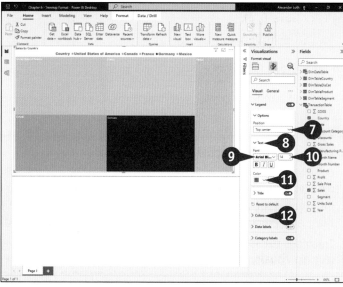

The Colors section expands.

⑬ Click each category (∨), and then click the color.

⑭ Set the switch on the Data Labels heading to On (On●).

⑮ Click **Data labels**.

The Data Labels section expands.

⑯ Repeat steps **9** to **11** to format the data labels.

Ⓒ The data labels take on the formatting.

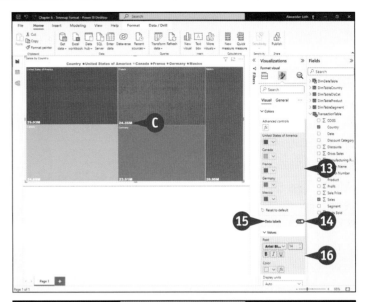

⑰ Set the switch on the Category Labels heading to On (On●).

⑱ Click **Category labels**.

The Category Labels section expands.

⑲ Repeat steps **9** to **11** to format the category labels.

Ⓓ The category labels take on the formatting.

⑳ Click **Save** (🖫).

Power BI Desktop saves your changes.

㉑ Click **Close** (✕).

The file closes.

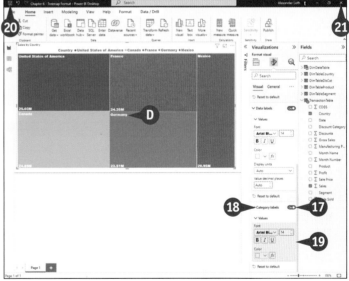

TIP

Is it better to use a legend or category labels to identify the categories in a treemap visual?
There is no hard-and-fast answer to this question. A legend on its own works well for a simple treemap containing only a few categories. For a treemap containing more than, say, a half-dozen categories, category labels become more important. Category labels are especially helpful for a treemap containing enough colors that some colors look similar to each other or for audience members with color vision deficiency. For many treemap visuals, including both a legend and category labels is helpful and not distracting.

CHAPTER 7

Showing Geographic Data on Maps

Power BI Desktop enables you to create a wide range of different map types with your data. Maps can be a great tool for identifying regional dependencies and displaying localized trends, enabling you to spot regional correlations that would be difficult to infer from a tabular view of the same data.

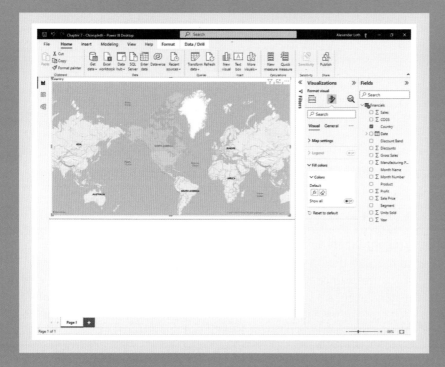

Create a Proportional Symbol Map

A *proportional symbol map* is a thematic map that uses different-size symbols to represent quantities. If your data contains geographic information, you can create a proportional symbol map visualization in seconds by adding a geographic field, selecting a check box, and then adding any key figure.

In the sample Power BI dataset, the Country field is already marked as a geographic field. If you select the Country check box and add a field such as Profit, Power BI Desktop creates a world map that shows you the profit in each country using different-size bubbles.

Create a Proportional Symbol Map

Note: This section uses the Chapter 7 - Proportional.pbix database, available at www. wiley.com/go/tyvpowerbi.

1 In Power BI Desktop, open the file Chapter 7 - Proportional.pbix.

Note: If the Fields pane and the Visualizations pane are collapsed, expand them.

2 Click **Build visual** (▤).

The Build Visual pane appears.

3 Click **Map** (◉).

Ⓐ A visual placeholder appears on the canvas.

4 Click **Expand** (❯ changes to ⌄) to the left of Financials.

The Financials hierarchy expands.

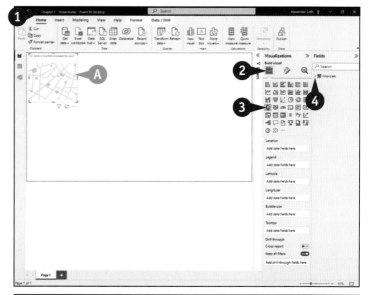

5 Click **Country** (☐ changes to ☑).

Ⓑ The Country field appears in the Location box.

Ⓒ The visual displays the Country data.

6 Drag the lower-right handle down and to the right.

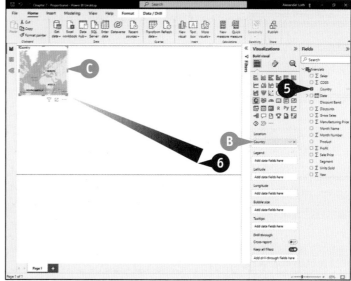

The visual expands.

D The blue circles indicate the countries in the dataset.

Note: The blue circles are all the same size at this point, because you have not yet applied a data field that will differentiate them.

7 Click **Sales** (☐ changes to ✓)

Power BI Desktop adds the sales data to the visual.

The map becomes a proportional symbol map.

E The blue circles change size to indicate the proportion of sales for each country.

F You can hold the pointer over a blue circle to display the sales data.

8 Click **Save** (🖫).

Power BI Desktop saves your changes.

9 Click **Close** (✕).

The file closes.

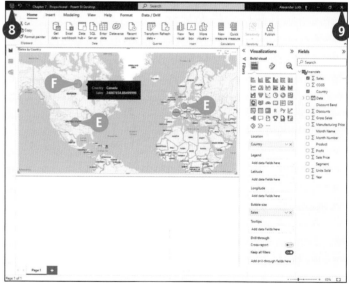

TIP

What technical requirements do you need to meet in order to display maps in Power BI?
Power BI draws map data from Microsoft's Bing service, so your PC running Power BI Desktop must have an Internet connection to create map visuals. You do not need an additional license to use Bing's map visualizations in Power BI; Bing map visualizations are part of Power BI, even if you use the free Power BI license.

Create a Choropleth Map

Power BI Desktop enables you to create *choropleth maps*, maps in which the various regions appear as different-colored areas. Choropleth maps, also called filled maps, are a long-standing staple for data visualization and are often used to illustrate how a key figure differs between regions.

Choropleth maps can be a great tool for exploring your data. A choropleth map uses different color shades to encode the information for defined areas, such as countries, provinces, or states. You can also use choropleth maps to show the distribution of discrete categories, such as the leading party per constituency in an election.

Create a Choropleth Map

Note: This section uses the Chapter 7 - Choropleth.pbix database, available at www.wiley.com/go/tyvpowerbi.

1 In Power BI Desktop, open the file Chapter 7 - Choropleth.pbix.

Note: If the Fields pane and the Visualizations pane are collapsed, expand them.

2 Click **Build visual** (▦).

The Build Visual pane appears.

3 Click **Filled map** (▧).

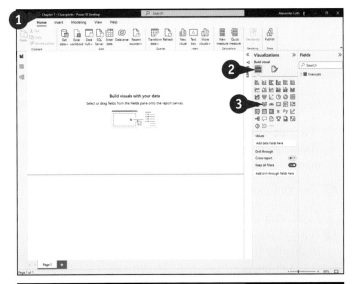

Ⓐ A visual placeholder appears on the canvas.

4 Click **Expand** (⟩ changes to ⌄) to the left of Financials.

The Financials hierarchy expands.

5 Click **Country** (☐ changes to ☑).

B The Country field appears in the Location box.

C The visual displays the Country data.

6 Drag the lower-right handle down and to the right.

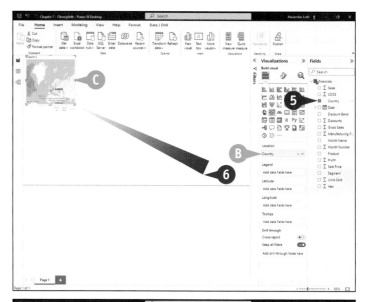

The visual expands.

D The blue-shaded areas indicate the countries in the dataset.

E You can move the pointer over a shaded area to display its name.

7 Click **Save** (💾).

Power BI Desktop saves your changes.

Note: Leave the file open so that you can work through the next task, "Add Conditional Formatting to a Choropleth Map."

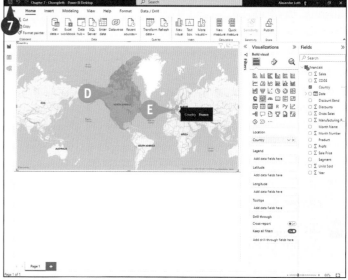

What should I know about projection when using choropleth maps?
Keep two main points in mind. First, most countries and states have irregular boundaries, which can make it hard to compare their size visually. Second, and more seriously, be aware that the *Mercator projection* of the round surface of Earth onto a two-dimensional map causes massive distortion near the polar regions, causing land masses near the poles to appear disproportionately large. You can see an extreme example in this section's choropleth map, where Greenland — to the northeast of North America — appears larger than Africa. In reality, Africa is 14 times larger than Greenland.

Add Conditional Formatting to a Choropleth Map

ower BI Desktop enables you to add conditional formatting to a choropleth map to display continuous data with different shades of color. This is especially useful if you want to draw attention to regional differences in figures such as sales, profit, or gross domestic product, GDP.

In this section, you add a color scale to color the map's countries according to their profit levels. The color scale makes Germany and France appear in shades of blue, indicating that these countries deliver above-average profits. In North America, by contrast, the profit is below average, as indicated by the shades of orange.

Add Conditional Formatting to a Choropleth Map

Note: This section uses the Chapter 7 - Choropleth.pbix database, available at www.wiley.com/go/tyvpowerbi. It assumes you have completed the previous section, "Create a Choropleth Map."

1 In the file Chapter 7 - Choropleth.pbix, click the choropleth visual.

Selection handles appear around the visual.

Note: If the Fields pane is collapsed, expand it.

2 Click **Format visual** (🖾).

The Format Visual tab appears.

3 Click **Visual**.

The Visual subtab appears.

4 Click **Fill colors**.

The Fill Colors section expands.

5 Click **Conditional formatting** (𝑓𝑥).

The Default Color - Fill Colors dialog box opens.

6 Click **What field should we base this on?** (⌄).

The drop-down menu opens.

7 Click the field you want to use. This example uses **Profit**.

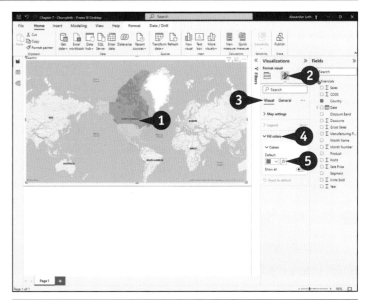

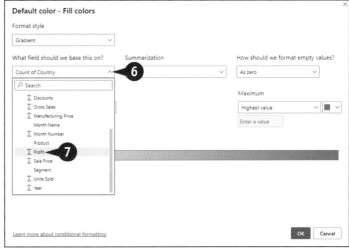

154

8 Click the Minimum color swatch (∨), and then click the color to use for minimum profit.

9 Click the Maximum color swatch (∨), and then click the color to use for maximum profit.

10 Click **Add a middle color** (☐ changes to ☑).

Ⓐ The Center controls appear.

11 Click the Center color swatch (∨), and then click the color for the middle of the scale.

12 Click **OK**.

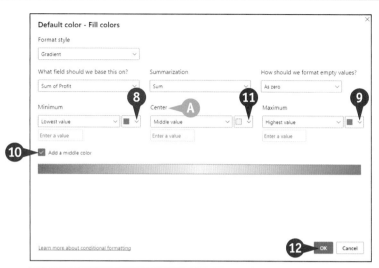

The Default Color - Fill Colors dialog box closes.

Ⓑ The countries in the dataset take on the colors to indicate their relative profitability.

13 Click **Save** (💾).

Power BI Desktop saves your changes.

14 Click **Close** (✖).

The file closes.

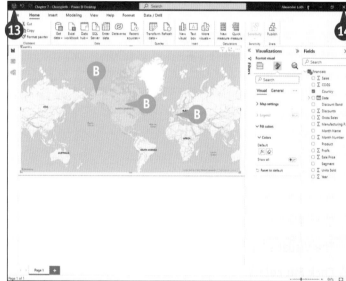

How can I interactively show key figures on the map?
Add the Profit field and the Gross Sales field to the Tooltips section of the chart. To do so, click the visual, and then click **Build visual** (▦) to display the Build Visual tab in the Visualizations pane. In the Fields pane, click the Profit field and drag it to the Tooltips box on the Build Visual tab. Then click the Gross Sales field in the Fields pane and drag it to the Tooltips box too. You can then display the profit and gross sales figures when you position the mouse over one of the countries in the dataset.

Enable Power BI's Preview Features

As well as a wide range of regular features that are enabled by default, Power BI also offers preview features that are still in development and testing. These features are not enabled by default, but you may want to enable some of them for specific use cases.

As of this writing, Power BI offers Azure Maps integration as a preview feature. The following two sections use Azure Maps, so you will need to enable Azure Maps to work through these sections. If Azure Maps integration has been finalized by the time you read this, you can skip this section.

Enable Power BI's Preview Features

Ⓐ If Azure Maps visuals are not enabled, the message "Azure Maps visuals are not enabled for your organization. Contact your tenant admin to fix this." appears.

Note: Despite the message's wording, you may be able to enable Azure Maps without contacting the administrator of the *tenant*, your company or organization's subscription to the Power BI service. Try this section's steps before contacting the administrator.

1 Click **File**.

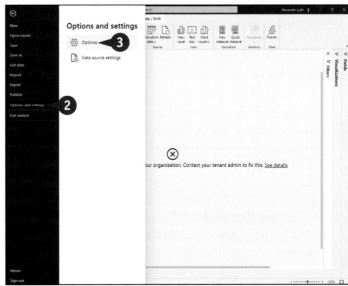

Backstage View opens.

2 Click **Options and settings**.

The Options and Settings pane appears.

3 Click **Options** (⚙️).

The Options dialog box opens.

4 In the Global section of the sidebar, click **Preview features**.

The Preview Features pane appears.

5 Click **Azure map visual** (☐ changes to ☑).

Note: If the Azure Map Visual check box is not available, ask your Power BI administrator to enable the Use Azure Maps Visual setting in the Tenant Settings section of the Power BI Admin Portal.

6 Click **OK**.

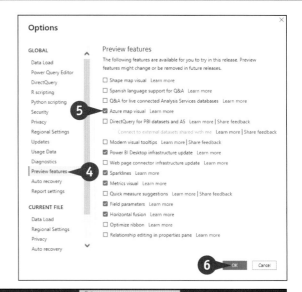

The Feature Requires a Restart dialog box opens.

7 Click **OK**.

The Feature Requires a Restart dialog box closes.

The Options dialog box closes.

8 Click **Close** (☒).

Power BI Desktop closes.

You can now restart Power BI Desktop and start using Azure Maps visuals.

TIP

Which preview features is Power BI offering?
Power BI's preview features include the following as of this writing:

- Azure map visual, Shape map visual, and Scorecard visual
- Sparklines and modern visual tool tips
- Support for field parameters
- DirectQuery for Power BI datasets and Analysis Services

- Power BI Desktop infrastructure update
- Web page connector infrastructure
- Modifying visuals settings for mobile layouts
- Spanish language support for Q&A
- Q&A for live connected Analysis Services databases

Create an Isarithmic Map

You can use isarithmic maps, also called heatmaps, to display a range of quantities. *Isarithmic* maps show data as a third dimension on a map and are therefore well suited for mapping surface elevations or for weather data. You can use an isarithmic map to illustrate sales data.

To create an isarithmic map, you must enable the Azure Maps preview feature; see the previous section, "Enable Power BI's Preview Features," for instructions. The steps in this section are based on the Retail Analysis Sample dataset, which you can download here: docs.microsoft.com/en-us/power-bi/create-reports/sample-retail-analysis#get-the-pbix-file-for-this-sample.

Create an Isarithmic Map

Note: This section uses the Chapter 7 - Isarithmic.pbix database, available at www.wiley.com/go/tyvpowerbi.

1 Open the Chapter 7 - Isarithmic.pbix database in Power BI Desktop.

Note: If the Fields pane and the Visualizations pane are collapsed, expand them.

2 Click **Build visual** (▤).

3 Click **Azure Map** (🔺).

Power BI Desktop adds an Azure Map visual to the canvas.

4 Drag the lower-right handle to expand the visual.

5 Click **Expand** (〉 changes to ✓) to the left of Store.

6 Click **PostalCode** (☐ changes to ✅).

Ⓐ The PostalCode field appears in the Location box.

Ⓑ The PostalCode data appears in the visual.

7 Click **Expand** (〉 changes to ✓) to the left of Sales.

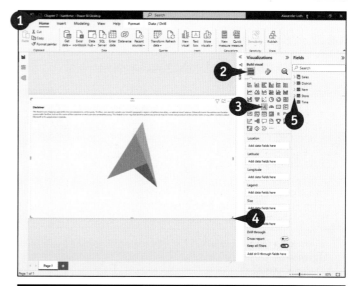

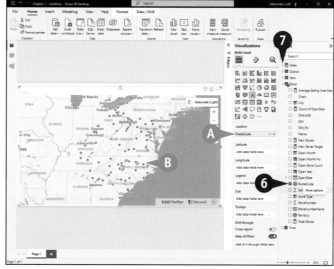

The Sales hierarchy expands.

8 Click **TotalSales** (☐ changes to ✓).

ⓒ The TotalSales field appears in the Size box.

ⓓ Bubbles appear in the visual.

9 Click **Format visual** (🖌).

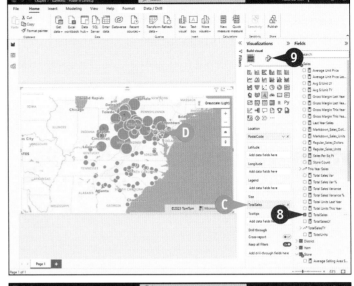

The Format Visual tab appears.

10 Click **Visual**.

The Visual subtab appears.

11 Click the switch (On changes to Off) on the Bubble Layer heading.

Power BI Desktop disables the bubble layer.

12 Click the switch (Off changes to On) on the Heat Map heading.

Power BI Desktop enables the heat map.

13 Click **Heat map**.

The Heat Map section expands.

14 Click **Radius** (◇) and set the radius. This example uses **50 px**.

ⓔ Power BI creates an isarithmic map that shows the countries in the dataset.

15 Click **Save** (💾).

16 Click **Close** (❎).

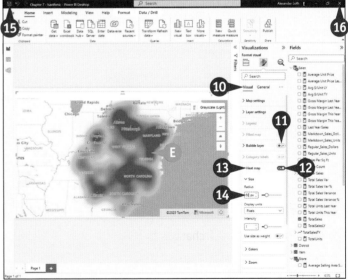

TIP

How can I avoid issues with ambiguous location names in my maps?
Wherever possible, use two or more columns for your location data rather than relying on a single column. For example, you might use a Country column to help distinguish Birmingham, AL, from Birmingham, UK; or you might use a State column to differentiate the many towns named Newport. To apply a second or further column, drag it from the Fields pane to the Location box in the Build Visual pane. Once you have two or more fields in the Location box, you can drag them into the order needed.

Create a Skyscraper Map

Y̶ou can use a skyscraper map, also called a bar chart map or a bar chart on a map, for displaying geodata along values. The *skyscraper* map is a combination of a map with locations and a bar chart. The location can represent a city, a country, or some other geographical entity. As with a bar chart, the height or volume of each bar is proportional to the values it represents.

To create a skyscraper map, you must enable the Azure Maps preview feature; see the earlier section, "Enable Power BI's Preview Features," for instructions. The steps in this section are based on the Retail Analysis Sample dataset, which you can download here: docs.microsoft.com/en-us/power-bi/create-reports/sample-retail-analysis#get-the-pbix-file-for-this-sample.

Create a Skyscraper Map

Note: This section uses the Chapter 7 - Skyscraper.pbix database, available at www.wiley.com/go/tyvpowerbi.

1 Open the Chapter 7 - Skyscraper.pbix database in Power BI Desktop.

Note: If the Fields pane and the Visualizations pane are collapsed, expand them.

2 Click **Build visual** (▦).

3 Click **Azure Map** (◢).

Power BI Desktop adds an Azure Map visual to the canvas.

4 Drag the lower-right handle to expand the visual.

5 Click **Expand** (› changes to ›) to the left of Store.

6 Click **PostalCode** (☐ changes to ☑).

Ⓐ The PostalCode field appears in the Location box.

Ⓑ The PostalCode data appears in the visual.

7 Click **Expand** (› changes to ›) to the left of Sales.

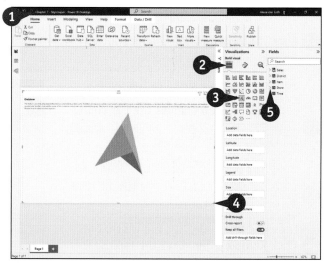

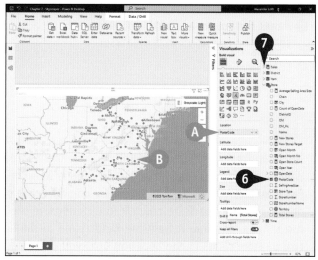

The Sales hierarchy expands.

8 Click **TotalSales** (☐ changes to ✔).

⊙ The TotalSales field appears in the Size box.

⊙ Bubbles appear in the visual.

9 Click **Format visual** (🖌).

The Format Visual tab appears.

10 Click **Visual**.

The Visual subtab appears.

11 Click the switch (On ⬤ changes to ⬤ Off) on the Bubble Layer heading.

Power BI Desktop disables the bubble layer.

12 Click the switch (⬤ Off changes to On ⬤) on the Bar Chart Layer heading.

Power BI Desktop enables the bar chart.

13 Click **Bar chart layer**.

The Bar Chart Layer section expands.

14 Click **Height** (◇) and set the height. This example uses **4 px**.

15 Click **Width** (◇) and set the width. This example uses **3 px**.

⊙ Power BI creates a skyscraper map that shows the countries in the dataset.

16 Click **Save** (💾).

17 Click **Close** (✖).

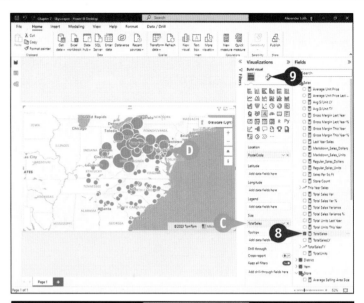

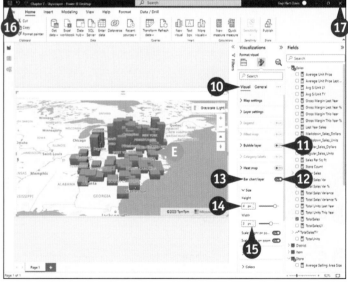

TIP

Can I use latitude and longitude data in Power BI?
Yes, you can use latitude and longitude data in your maps. Power BI retrieves latitude and longitude coordinates based on a set of address values for any country using Bing's unstructured URL template service. If your data source does not contain enough location data, add latitude and longitude columns to the source, and label the columns correctly. You can then drag each field you need from the Fields pane to the Location box in the Build Visual pane. After adding two or more fields to the Location box, drag the fields into the order required.

CHAPTER 8

Using Calculated Columns and DAX

Up to now in this book, you have used Power BI Desktop with data that is fully ready for analysis. But likely you will often use data sources that require further calculation to derive the key figures you need to analyze the data effectively. You can derive these figures by using the DAX language built into Power BI.

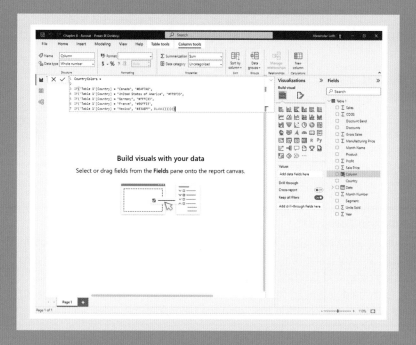

Understanding DAX and Why You Should Use It

To get the most out of your data sources, you will sometimes need to perform calculations on the data they contain. For example, you may need to add all the values in a column to give a single value; or you may need to multiply, say, the number of items sold by their price to give the total sales figure.

Power BI Desktop enables you to perform calculations either by using operators, such as + for addition and * for multiplication, or by using its built-in DAX language. Both approaches work, but using DAX is often the better choice.

What Is DAX?

DAX is the acronym for *Data Analytics Expressions*, a suite of functions and operators used by Microsoft products including Power BI Desktop, PowerPivot, and SQL Server Analysis Services.

Microsoft originally used DAX in Excel before implementing it in Power BI; if you are familiar with Excel's functions and formulas, you will likely see similarities in DAX and find the transition to DAX relatively straightforward, even though DAX is more powerful and complex than Excel.

What Does DAX Enable You to Do?

In Power BI Desktop, DAX enables you to perform calculations by using its functions and operators. By performing calculations, you can derive key values that your data sources do not directly provide. These key values can illuminate different aspects of the data and give you greater insights than the data sources' raw values afford.

DAX enables you to create two types of calculated expressions in Power BI Desktop. The first type is calculated columns. The second type is calculated measures.

What Is a Calculated Column?

A *calculated column* is a column that contains a calculated value. A calculated column uses the data already loaded into your data model as opposed to drawing in data from elsewhere. When you create a calculated column formula, Power BI automatically applies it to the entire table, evaluating the formula separately for each row. Power BI computes a calculated column at the row level within the table that contains the column.

What Is a Calculated Measure?

A *calculated measure* uses an aggregation function to calculate an aggregate value from multiple rows in a table. A calculated measure is a dynamic calculation formula whose results change depending on the context. Power BI evaluates a measure at the cell level rather than at the row level.

How Do You Perform Calculations in DAX?

To perform calculations in DAX, you use formulas and functions. A *formula* is a recipe for a calculation; for example, the easy formula for converting from Celsius to Fahrenheit is to multiply the Celsius value by 9, divide it by 5, and then add 32, which you might write as F = (9C/5) + 32.

You can write formulas in DAX by using the operators, such as + for addition and / for division, explained in the table that follows.

A *function* is a ready-made formula for a standard calculation that is built into DAX. For example, the DB function calculates depreciation using the fixed declining balance method. DB has this syntax:

DB(<cost>, <salvage>, <life>, <period>[, <month>])

Here, DB is the function name, and the parentheses hold its *arguments* — its parameters — separated by commas. An argument in angle brackets, such as <cost> or <salvage>, is required; an argument in square brackets, such as [, <month>], is optional.

Microsoft provides a DAX functions reference at learn.microsoft.com/en-us/dax/dax-function-reference.

Understanding the DAX Operators

To perform operations with DAX, you use the appropriate operator. Table 8-1 explains the four categories of DAX operators: arithmetic operators, comparison operators, logical operators, and the single concatenation operator.

Table 8-1: Operators in DAX

Operator	Meaning	Example	Operator	Meaning	Example
Arithmetic Operators			>=	Greater than or equal to	[TotalUnits] >= 125
+	Addition	7+5	<=	Less than or equal to	[MinUnits] <= 10
–	Subtraction or negative value	7–5 –5	**Concatenation Operator**		
			&	Connects two text strings to produce a single string	[FirstName] & " " & [LastName]
*	Multiplication	2*4			
/	Division	4/2	**Logical Operators**		
^	Exponentiation	2^10	&&	AND condition	([State] = "CA") && ([Orders] > 5)
Comparison Operators			||	OR condition	([State] = "WA") || ([State] = "OR")
=	Equal to	[State] = "AK"			
==	Strict equal to; exact match	[State] == "CA"	IN	OR condition between each row compared to a table	'Customer'[State] IN { "ID", "NV", "AZ" }
<>	Not equal to	[Country] <> "Germany"			
>	Greater than	[TotalUnits] > 125	NOT	NOT returns the logical opposite	NOT('Customer'[State] IN { "CA", "WA", "NV" })
<	Less than	[MinUnits] < 10			

Add All Numbers in a Column

When analyzing your data, you will often need to add all the numbers in a column so that you can use the result in your analysis. Power BI enables you to do this with its SUM function. SUM is so useful that it is the most widely used function in DAX.

In this section, you use the SUM function to create a calculated measure. This is the way you normally use SUM in Power BI: The function is not useful for a calculated column, because it simply returns the same number as the row number.

Add All Numbers in a Column

Note: This section uses the Chapter 8 - Add. pbix database, available at www.wiley.com/ go/tyvpowerbi.

1 In Power BI Desktop, open the file Chapter 8 - Add.pbix.

Note: If the Fields pane and the Visualizations pane are collapsed, expand them.

2 In the Fields pane, right-click the table for which you want to create the calculated measure. This example uses Table 1.

3 In the contextual menu, click **New measure**.

A The formula bar appears, showing the default text MEASURE =.

Note: The default text is selected, so you can type over it without having to delete it.

B The table expands.

C The new measure appears in the table.

4 Type the measure name, **SumOfSales**.

5 Type = to start the DAX formula.

6 Type **SUM(**.

7 In the menu of tables and columns, click **'Table 1' [Sales]**.

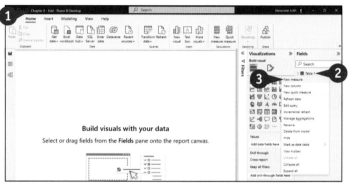

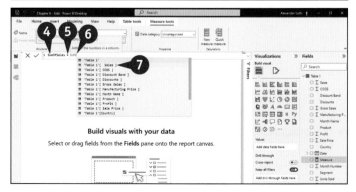

D Power BI Desktop adds the information to the formula.

8 Type **)** to complete the DAX formula.

9 Click **Enter** (✓) or press `Enter`.

E Power BI Desktop creates the SumOfSales measure.

10 Click **Country** (☐ changes to ☑).

Power BI Desktop creates a map visual showing the Country data.

11 Click **SumOfSales** (☐ changes to ☑).

Power BI Desktop adds the SumOfSales data to the map visual.

12 Click **Table** (⊞).

F Power BI Desktop converts the visual to a summarized table using the SumOfSales measure.

13 Click **Save** (💾).

Power BI Desktop saves your changes.

14 Click **Close** (✖).

The file closes.

TIPS

How do I remove a calculated measure or a calculated column?

If the Fields pane is collapsed, click **Expand** (≪ changes to ≫) to expand it. Right-click the calculated measure or calculated column, and then click **Delete from model** on the contextual menu.

Can I change the name of a calculated measure or a calculated column?

Yes. Simply right-click the measure or column in the Fields pane, and then click **Rename** on the contextual menu. Power BI Desktop displays an edit box around the existing name and selects the name. Type the new name and press `Enter` to apply it.

Perform Division

Power BI Desktop enables you to perform mathematical division on your data in two ways. First, you can use the Division operator, the / character. Second, you can use the DIVIDE function in DAX, which is usually the better choice.

Mathematical division requires two numbers: the *numerator*, the number to be divided; and the *denominator*, the number by which to divide it. For example, when you divide 10 by 2, 10 is the numerator and 2 is the denominator. The DIVIDE function can automatically handle divide-by-zero cases or cases where either the numerator or the denominator is blank.

Perform Division

Note: This section uses the Chapter 8 - Division.pbix database, available at www.wiley.com/go/tyvpowerbi.

1 In Power BI Desktop, open the file Chapter 8 - Division.pbix.

Note: If the Fields pane and the Visualizations pane are collapsed, expand them.

2 In the Fields pane, right-click the table for which you want to create the calculated measure. This example uses Table 1.

3 Click **New measure**.

Ⓐ The formula bar appears, showing the default text MEASURE =.

Ⓑ The table expands.

Ⓒ The new measure appears in the table.

4 Type the measure name, **PercentageProfit**.

5 Type = to start the DAX formula.

6 Type **DIVIDE(SUM('Table 1'[Profit]), SUM('Table 1'[Sales]), "0")** to complete the DAX formula.

7 Click **Enter** (✓) or press Enter.

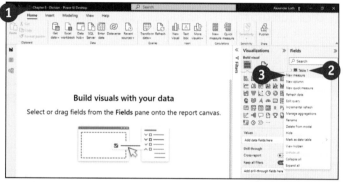

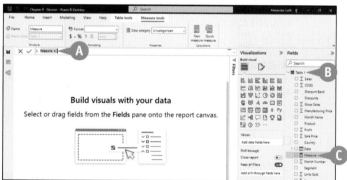

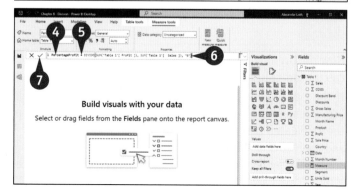

Power BI Desktop enters the formula.

8 Click **Country** (☐ changes to ☑).

Power BI Desktop adds the Country field to a default visual placeholder.

9 Click **PercentageProfit** (☐ changes to ☑).

Power BI Desktop adds the PercentageProfit data to the default visual.

10 Click **Table** (▦).

D Power BI Desktop changes the default visual to a summarized table using the PercentageProfit measure.

E By default, the measure appears in a decimal format.

11 Click **PercentageProfit**.

F The Measure Tools contextual tab appears on the ribbon.

12 Click **Percentage** (%).

G Power BI Desktop displays the data in percentage format.

13 Click **Save** (▣).

Power BI Desktop saves your changes.

14 Click **Close** (✕).

The file closes.

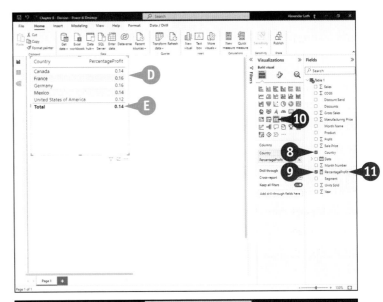

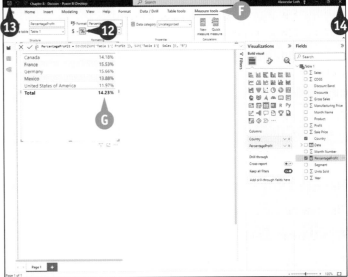

TIP

What is the syntax for the DIVIDE function in DAX?

The DIVIDE function has the following syntax:

name = DIVIDE(<numerator>, <denominator> [, <alternateresult>])

Here, Part is the name you are giving the calculated measure. <numerator> is the value or expression that produces the numerator, and <denominator> is the value or expression that produces the denominator. <alternateresult> is an optional value for the function to return when the denominator is zero or blank.

Check a Condition

When you need to make a decision in Power BI, you can use the IF function. IF evaluates the given expression and determines whether it is true or false; the function returns one value if the expression is true and another value if the expression is false.

You can nest IF functions within each other as needed to create logical loops or conditional columns, measures, or formatting. This flexibility enables you to create a wide range of conditions in your Power BI projects. In this section, you use the IF function to create a calculated column.

Check a Condition

Note: This section uses the Chapter 8 - Condition.pbix database, available at www. wiley.com/go/tyvpowerbi.

① In Power BI Desktop, open the file Chapter 8 - Condition.pbix.

Note: If the Fields pane and the Visualizations pane are collapsed, expand them.

② In the Fields pane, right-click the table for which you want to create the calculated column. This example uses Table 1.

③ Click **New measure**.

Ⓐ The formula bar appears, showing the default text Column =.

Ⓑ The table expands.

Ⓒ The new column appears in the table.

④ Type the column name, **SumOfSalesForCanada**.

⑤ Type = to start the DAX formula.

⑥ Type **IF('Table 1'[Country] = "Canada", 'Table 1'[Sales], 0)** to complete the DAX formula.

⑦ Click **Enter** (✓) or press Enter.

D Power BI creates the SumOfSalesforCanada calculated column.

8 Click **Country** (□ changes to ☑).

E Power BI Desktop creates a map visual showing the Country data.

9 Click **SumOfSalesForCanada** (□ changes to ☑).

Power BI Desktop adds the SumOfSalesForCanada data to the visual.

10 Click **Table** (⊞).

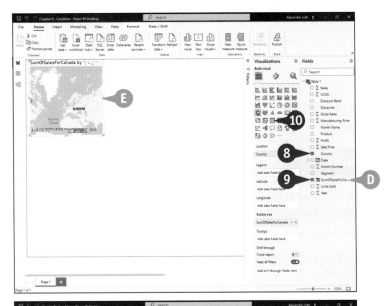

F Power BI Desktop displays a summarized table using the SumOfSalesForCanada calculated column.

Note: For any country other than Canada, the table shows zero sales value because of the formula you created in step **6**.

11 Click **Save** (💾).

Power BI Desktop saves your changes.

12 Click **Close** (✕).

The file closes.

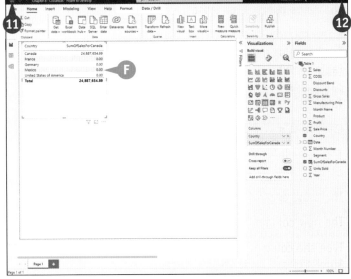

TIP

What is the syntax for the IF function in DAX?

The IF function has the following syntax:

name = IF(<logical_test>, <value_if_true>[, <value_if_false>])

Here, *name* is the name you are giving the calculated column. <logical_test> is the expression you are testing for truth or falsity. <value_if_true> is the value the IF function returns if the expression evaluates to True. <value_if_false> is an optional value for the function to return when the expression evaluates to False.

Count the Number of Cells in a Column

To analyze your data effectively, you may need to count the number of cells in a column that contain values, ignoring any blank cells in the column. To this end, Power BI provides the COUNT function, which makes such counting easy.

Normally, you would use the COUNT function to create a calculated measure rather than a calculated column. This is because, when used in a calculated column, COUNT returns the value 1 if the row's cell contains data and returns the value 0 if the row's cell has no data.

Count the Number of Cells in a Column

Note: This section uses the Chapter 8 - Count. pbix database, available at www.wiley.com/go/tyvpowerbi.

1 In Power BI Desktop, open the file Chapter 8 - Count.pbix.

Note: If the Fields pane and the Visualizations pane are collapsed, expand them.

2 In the Fields pane, right-click the table for which you want to create the calculated measure. This example uses Table 1.

3 Click **New measure**.

Ⓐ The formula bar appears, showing the default text Measure =.

Ⓑ The table expands.

Ⓒ The new measure appears in the table.

4 Type the measure name, **CountOfCellsContainingData**.

5 Type = to start the DAX formula.

6 Type **COUNT('Table 1'[Country])** to complete the DAX formula.

7 Click **Enter** (✓) or press Enter.

D Power BI creates the
CountOfCellsContainingData
calculated measure.

8 Click **Country** (☐ changes to ☑).

E Power BI Desktop creates a map visual
showing the Country data.

9 Click **CountOfCellsContainingData**
(☐ changes to ☑).

Power BI Desktop adds the
CountOfCellsContainingData
data to the visual.

10 Click **Table** (▦).

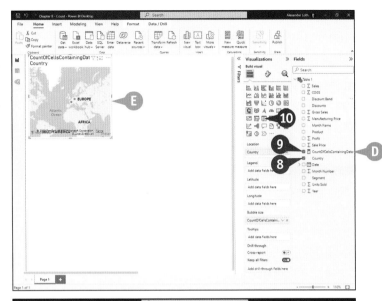

F Power BI Desktop creates a
summarized table using the
CountOfCellsContainingData
calculated measure.

11 Click **Save** (💾).

Power BI Desktop saves your changes.

12 Click **Close** (✖).

The file closes.

TIP

What other counting operations can I perform with DAX?

Apart from the COUNT function, DAX also offers the counting functions COUNTA, COUNTAX, COUNTBLANK, COUNTROWS, and COUNTX. You use COUNTA to count the number of rows in a given column that contain nonblank values. COUNTAX is similar to COUNTA but includes in its count any cells containing expressions that result in empty strings. COUNTBLANK returns the number of blank cells in the specified column, and COUNTROWS returns the number of rows in the specified table. COUNTX returns the number of rows containing nonblank values or expressions that evaluate to nonblank values. For more detail, see Microsoft's DAX functions reference at learn.microsoft.com/en-us/dax/dax-function-reference.

Return the Average of All Numbers in a Column

Power BI Desktop's AVERAGE function returns the average of all numeric values in one or more columns. AVERAGE adds each numeric value, including zeros, and then divides the result by the number of values.

You can use AVERAGE to create either a calculated column or a calculated measure. For a calculated column, you can specify two or more columns; in this case, AVERAGE adds the values and divides them by the number of values and the number of columns. For a calculated measure, AVERAGE adds each numeric value matching your criteria and then divides the result by the number of values.

Return the Average of All Numbers in a Column

Note: This section uses the Chapter 8 - Average.pbix database, available at www.wiley.com/go/tyvpowerbi.

1 In Power BI Desktop, open the file Chapter 8 - Average.pbix.

Note: If the Fields pane and the Visualizations pane are collapsed, expand them.

2 In the Fields pane, right-click the table for which you want to create the calculated measure. This example uses Table 1.

The contextual menu opens.

3 Click **New measure**.

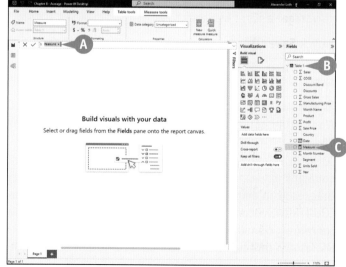

A The formula bar appears, showing the default text Measure =.

Note: The default text is selected, so you can type over it without having to delete it.

B The table expands.

C The new measure appears in the table.

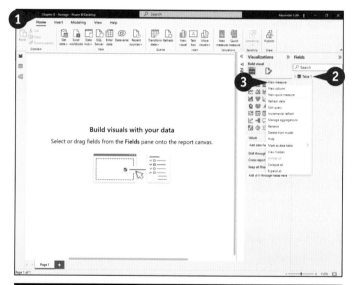

④ Type the measure name, **AverageManCost**; *Man* is short for *Manufacturing*.

⑤ Type = to start the DAX formula.

⑥ Type **AVERAGE(**.

⑦ Click **'Table 1' [Manufacturing Price]**.

Power BI Desktop adds that information to the formula.

⑧ Type **)** to complete the DAX formula (not shown).

⑨ Click **Enter** (✓) or press Enter.

Ⓓ Power BI creates the AverageManCost calculated measure.

⑩ Click **Country** (☐ changes to ✓).

Power BI Desktop creates a map visual showing the Country data.

⑪ Click **AverageManCost** (☐ changes to ✓).

Power BI Desktop adds the AverageManCost data to the visual.

⑫ Click **Table** (▦).

Ⓔ Power BI Desktop creates a table that shows a summarized table using the AverageManCost measure.

⑬ Click **Save** (▣).

⑭ Click **Close** (✕).

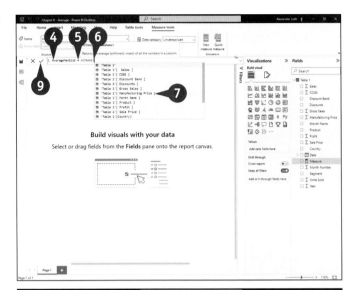

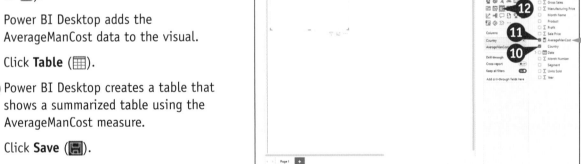

How does the AVERAGE function handle text values?

If any cells in the column or columns you specify for the AVERAGE function to use for a calculated column or calculated measure contain text values rather than numeric values, AVERAGE performs no aggregation and returns blanks.

If a column you want to average may include cells containing text values, use the AVERAGEA function instead of the AVERAGE function. AVERAGEA treats both text values and empty text values as zero, treats values that evaluate to False as zero, and treats values that evaluate to True as 1.

Join Two Text Strings into One Text String

When you need to join two or more text strings into a single string, you can use the CONCATENATE function in DAX. For example, when working with customer data, you might need to join the first name and the last name to make a single name, or you might need to assemble a full mailing address from fields such as Street, City, State, and ZIP.

The CONCATENATE function limits you to joining two items at a time, but you can use multiple instances of the function to join more items.

Join Two Text Strings into One Text String

Note: This section uses the Chapter 8 - Concatenate.pbix database, available at www.wiley.com/go/tyvpowerbi.

1 In Power BI Desktop, open the file Chapter 8 - Concatenate.pbix.

Note: If the Fields pane and the Visualizations pane are collapsed, expand them.

2 In the Fields pane, right-click the table for which you want to create the calculated column. This example uses Table 1.

The contextual menu opens.

3 Click **New column**.

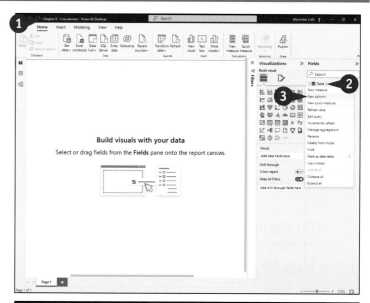

Ⓐ The formula bar appears, showing the default text Column =.

Note: The default text is selected, so you can type over it without having to delete it.

Ⓑ The table expands.

Ⓒ The new column appears in the table.

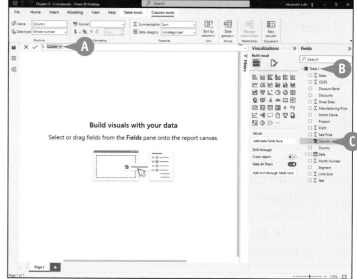

4 Type the column name,
Country_DiscountBand.

5 Type **=** to start the DAX formula.

6 Type **CONCATENATE('Table 1'**
[Country],'Table 1'[Discount
Band]) to complete the DAX
formula.

7 Click **Enter** (✓) or press `Enter`.

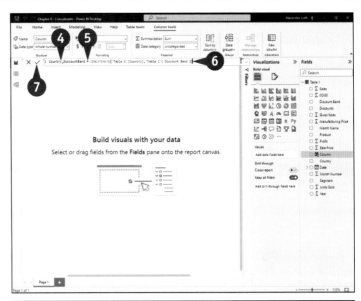

D Power BI creates the Country_
DiscountBand calculated column.

8 Click **Country** (☐ changes to ☑).

Power BI Desktop creates a map
visual showing the Country data.

9 Click **Discount Band** (☐ changes
to ☑).

10 Click **Country_DiscountBand**
(☐ changes to ☑).

11 Click **Table** (▦).

E Power BI Desktop creates a
summarized table using the
Country_DiscountBand
calculated column.

12 Click **Save** (▣).

13 Click **Close** (✕).

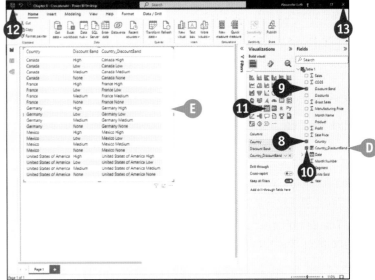

TIP

How do I concatenate more than two items using the CONCATENATE function?
The syntax for the CONCATENATE function is simply CONCATENATE(<text1>, <text2>), meaning that you can
concatenate only two text strings at a time. But you can nest the CONCATENATE function to concatenate
further strings. The following example concatenates the Country column in Table 1 with the result of
concatenating the Product column in Table 1 with the word Analysis and a leading space.

Cat3 = CONCATENATE('Table 1'[Country], CONCATENATE('Table 1'[Product], " Analysis"))

Apply Conditional Formatting in Tables

Power BI Desktop offers conditional formatting for tables, enabling you to define formatting to apply automatically to a table when the conditions in a measure are met. For example, you might want to apply standout formatting to highlight positive results in a table of sales. You can choose from a wide range of formatting, including the font face, the font size, and the font color.

Apply Conditional Formatting in Tables

Note: This section uses the Chapter 8 - Format.pbix database, available at www.wiley.com/go/tyvpowerbi.

① In Power BI Desktop, open the file Chapter 8 - Format.pbix.

Note: If the Fields pane and the Visualizations pane are collapsed, expand them.

② In the Fields pane, right-click the table for which you want to create the calculated column. This example uses Table 1.

The contextual menu opens.

③ Click **New column**.

Ⓐ The formula bar appears, showing the default text Column =.

Ⓑ The table expands.

Ⓒ The new column appears in the table.

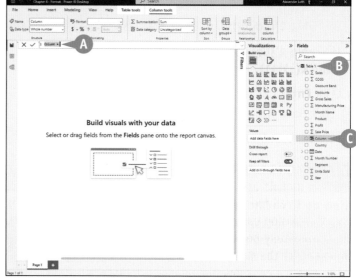

④ Type the column name, **CountryColors**.

⑤ Type = to start the DAX formula.

⑥ Press `Shift`+`Enter` twice to create two new lines.

Note: You must press `Shift`+`Enter` to create a new line. Pressing `Enter` gives the command for entering the formula.

Ⓓ Power BI Desktop numbers each line for your reference.

⑦ Type **IF('** to start creating the DAX formula.

⑧ Click the **'Table 1' [Country]** item.

⑨ Type **= "Canada", "#DAF7A6",** to complete this line of the formula.

⑩ Press `Shift`+`Enter` to create a new line (not shown).

⑪ Enter the remainder of the DAX formula on multiple lines, pressing `Shift`+`Enter` to create each new line:

IF('Table 1'[Country] = "United States of America", "#FF9F33",

IF('Table 1'[Country] = "Germany", "#FFFC33",

IF('Table 1'[Country] = "France", "#99FF33",

IF('Table 1'[Country] = "Mexico", "#33A8FF", BLANK()))))))

⑫ Click **Enter** (✓) or press `Enter`.

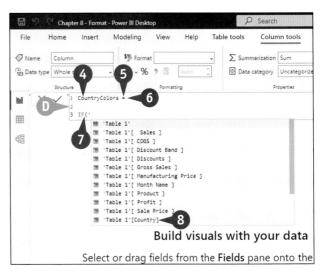

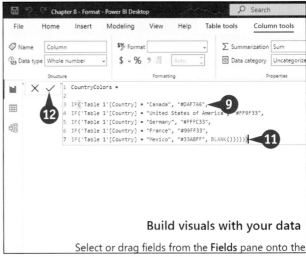

TIP

Why does this section's DAX formula end with six closing parentheses?
The DAX formula uses four nested IF statements, each with its opening parenthesis immediately after the IF keyword; all four of the corresponding closing parentheses appear at the end of the statement, together with the closing parenthesis of the first, and non-nested, IF statement. That makes five closing parentheses; but immediately before these is the closing parenthesis of the BLANK() function, which provides the third argument for the most deeply nested IF function. As you enter each closing parenthesis, Power BI Desktop highlights the corresponding opening parenthesis, helping you see which function you are closing.

continued ▶

Apply Conditional Formatting in Tables (continued)

To apply conditional formatting, you create a condition using an IF function. In this section, you use a complex IF statement, including four nested IF clauses, to test the value of the Country column in a table, assigning a hexadecimal color code depending on the country that appears in the row.

See the section "Check a Condition," earlier in this chapter, for more information about the IF function.

Apply Conditional Formatting in Tables (continued)

Ⓐ Power BI Desktop creates the CountryColors calculated column.

⑬ Click **Country** (☐ changes to ☑).

Ⓑ Power BI Desktop creates a visual using the Country data.

⑭ Click **CountryColors** (☐ changes to ☑).

Power BI Desktop adds the CountryColors data to the visual.

⑮ Click **Table** (▦).

Ⓒ Power BI Desktop creates a summarized table using the CountryColors measure.

⑯ Click **Format Visual** (🖌).

The Format Visual tab appears.

⑰ Click **Visual**.

The Visual subtab appears.

⑱ Click **Cell elements**.

The Cell Elements section expands.

⑲ Click the **Background color** switch (◉Off changes to On◉).

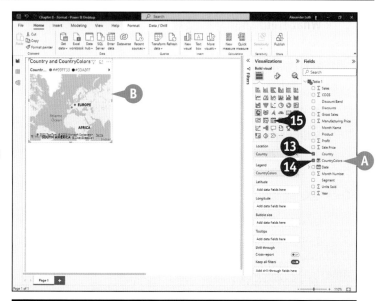

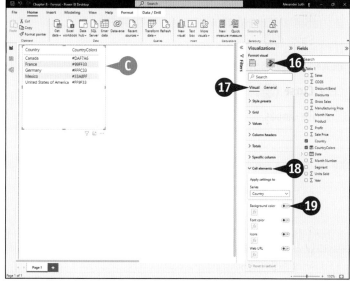

The Background Color – Background Color dialog box opens.

20 Click **Format style** (∨), and then click the style. This example uses **Field value**.

21 Click **Apply to** (∨), and then click Values Only, Values and Totals, or Totals Only. This example uses **Values only**.

22 Click **What field should we base this on?** (∨).

The drop-down menu opens.

23 Click the field to use. This example uses the **CountryColors** calculated column.

24 Click **Summarization** (∨), and then click First or Last, as needed. This example uses **First**.

25 Click **OK**.

The Background Color – Background Color dialog box closes.

D Power BI Desktop changes the background color of each cell in the Country column to the colors you assigned those countries.

26 Click **Save** (▯).

Power BI Desktop saves your changes.

27 Click **Close** (✕).

The file closes.

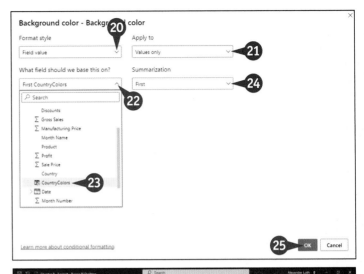

TIP

What does the error "Argument '3' in IF function is required" mean?
This error indicates that you have omitted the IF function's third argument, the <ResultIfFalse> argument. For lines 3, 4, 5, and 6, this argument is the IF function on the next line. For line 7, this argument is the **BLANK()** function at the very end of the DAX statement. To resolve this error, edit the statement and enter the missing argument.

CHAPTER 9

Using Analytics and Machine Learning

Power BI enables you to perform statistical analysis with just a few clicks, simplifying tasks such as identifying outliers and finding groups of similar data through clustering. Power BI also offers the AutoML feature for building machine-learning models with binary prediction, general classification, and regression.

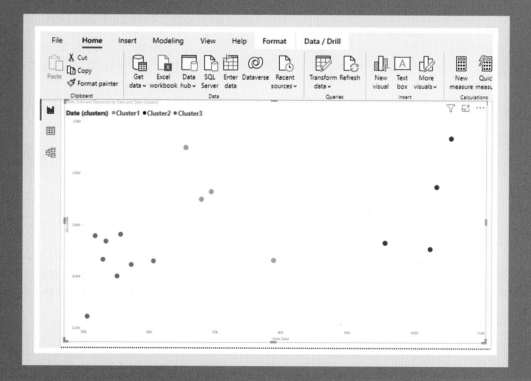

Identify Outliers

When analyzing your data, you will likely sometimes want to identify outliers. *Outliers* are data points that deviate from the norm. If enough outliers are present, they can skew the expected results of data analytics, so it is important to be aware of what outliers your data contains.

Identifying outliers in tables of data tends to be difficult, because they do not jump out at you. But using visuals — such as scatter charts, bar charts, or line charts — makes outliers far easier to spot. In this section, you use a scatter chart to identify outliers.

Identify Outliers

Note: This section uses the Chapter 9 - Outliers. pbix database, available at www.wiley.com/go/ tyvpowerbi.

1 Open the Chapter 9 - Outliers.pbix database file.

Note: If the Fields pane and the Visualizations pane are collapsed, expand them.

2 Click **Build Visual** (▦).

The Build Visual tab appears.

3 Click **Scatter chart** (⋰).

Ⓐ Power BI adds a Scatter Chart visual to the canvas.

4 Click **Expand** (⟩ changes to ⌄) to the left of TransactionTable.

The TransactionTable table expands, showing its fields.

5 Click **COGS** (☐ changes to ☑).

Ⓑ The COGS field appears in the X Axis box.

Ⓒ The COGS data appears in the Scatter Chart visual.

6 Click **Profit** (☐ changes to ☑).

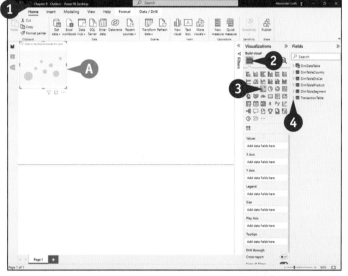

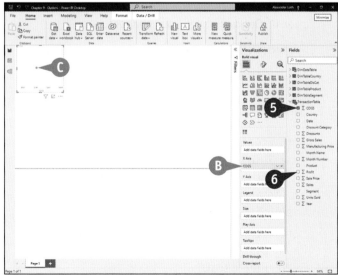

D The Profit field appears in the Y Axis box.

7 Click **Date** (☐ changes to ☑).

E The Date field appears in the Values box.

F Plotted circles appear in the Scatter Chart visual.

8 Drag the lower-right handle to resize the visual.

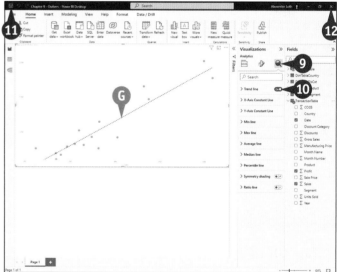

9 Click **Analytics** (🔍).

The Analytics tab appears.

10 On the Trend Line heading, click the switch (●Off changes to On●).

G A dotted trend line appears.

The position of the circles enables you to see deviation from the median clearly.

11 Click **Save** (💾).

Power BI Desktop saves your changes.

12 Click **Close** (✖).

The file closes.

TIP

How can I control what data points Power BI Desktop shows?

In Power BI Desktop, you can specify which data points to exclude. To exclude a single data point, right-click it in the visual, and then click **Exclude** on the contextual menu. To exclude multiple data points, click the first data point you want to exclude, and then Shift+click each other victim. Next, right-click anywhere in the selection, and then click **Exclude** on the contextual menu.

The contextual menu also contains the Include command. Select all the data points you want to include before right-clicking the selection and clicking **Include**, because this command removes all other data points from the visual.

Find Groups of Similar Data by Clustering

ata clusters are groups of data that are closely related or share similar properties. The easiest way of identifying a data cluster is to use a scatter chart. A scatter chart clusters closely related data, making them easy to spot visually.

If your dataset contains no predetermined categories, clustering can be a great tool for establishing what the system performance and data relations are. This information will help system designers and data analysts in optimizing and enhancing system performance and analytics.

Find Groups of Similar Data by Clustering

Note: This section uses the Chapter 9 - Clustering.pbix database, available at www.wiley.com/go/tyvpowerbi.

1 Open the Chapter 9 - Clustering.pbix database file.

Note: If the Fields pane and the Visualizations pane are collapsed, expand them.

2 Click **Build Visual** (▦).

3 Click **Scatter chart** (⸬).

A Power BI adds a Scatter Chart visual.

4 Click **Expand** (> changes to ∨) to the left of TransactionTable.

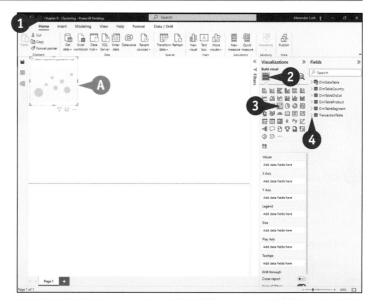

The TransactionTable table expands.

5 Click **Units Sold** (☐ changes to ☑).

B The Units Sold field appears in the X Axis box.

6 Click **Discounts** (☐ changes to ☑).

C The Discounts field appears in the Y Axis box.

7 Click **Date** (☐ changes to ☑).

D The Date field appears in the Values box.

8 Drag the lower-right handle to resize the visual.

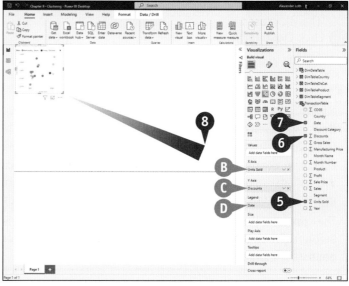

9 Click **More options** (⋯).

The More Options menu opens.

10 Click **Automatically find clusters** (⚬⩊).

The Clusters dialog box opens.

11 Optionally, change the default name for the cluster field.

12 Optionally, change the default description.

13 Optionally, type the number of clusters in the Number of Clusters box. The default setting is Auto. This example uses **Auto**.

14 Click **OK**.

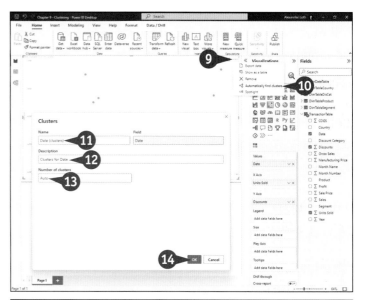

The Clusters dialog box closes.

E Power BI Desktop applies color coding to the data points to show the clustering.

F The legend explains the color coding for the clusters.

15 Click **Save** (🖫).

Power BI Desktop saves your changes.

16 Click **Close** (✕).

The file closes.

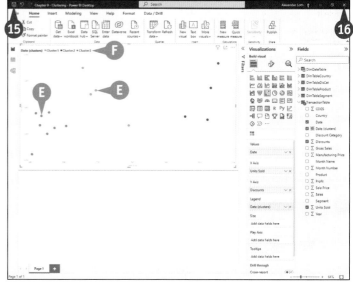

TIP

How do I change the cluster colors to make the clusters easier to see?

Click the scatter chart visual to select it, click **Format Visual** (📊) to display the Format Visual tab, and then click **Visual** to display the Visual subtab. Click **Markers** to expand the marker section. In the Color box, click **Cluster1** (⌄), and then click the color you want. Repeat the previous move for each of the other clusters.

For greater differentiation, give each series a different shape. In the Apply Settings To box, click **Series** (⌄), and then click the series, such as **Cluster1**. In the Shape box, click **Type** (⌄), and then click the shape, such as ▲ or ■.

Create a Dataflow

When data volumes are growing, you may find that keeping the data organized and updated becomes a challenge. The data should be well-formed, actionable, and ready for analytics that can populate visuals reports and dashboards. Power BI enables you to create a dataflow that takes you from raw data to implementable insights in a few clicks.

To create a dataflow, you must first create a Premium workspace. For this, you require a Premium Per User Power BI license.

Create a Dataflow

1. In a web browser, go to powerbi.microsoft.com/en-us (not shown).

2. Click **Sign in**, and then follow through the sign-in process (not shown).

   Once you are signed in, your home page appears.

3. Click **Workspaces** (🗐).

   The Workspaces pane opens.

4. Click **New workspace** (🔡).

   The Workspaces pane closes.

   The Create a Workspace pane opens.

5. In the Workspace Name box, type the name to give the workspace. This example uses **PracticalDemo**.

6. Optionally, type a description of the workplace to help yourself and others identify it.

7. Click **Advanced**.

   The Advanced section of the Create a Workspace pane expands.

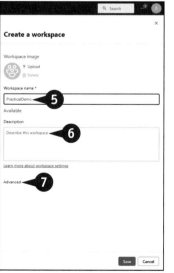

8. In the License Mode area, click **Premium per user** (○ changes to ◉).

9. Click **Save**.

The Create a Workspace pane closes.

Power BI creates the new workspace and displays it.

10 Click **New** (∨).

The New menu opens.

11 Click **Dataflow** (◌°).

The Want to Build a Datamart (Preview) Instead? dialog box opens, prompting you to create a self-service datamart rather than a dataflow.

12 Click **No, create a dataflow**.

The Want to Build a Datamart (Preview) Instead? dialog box closes.

The Start Creating Your Dataflow page appears.

13 Click **Add new tables**.

continued ▶

TIP

What are the benefits of creating a dataflow?

By creating a dataflow, you generate reusable transformations that you can share among different datasets and reports. To get the most benefit from a dataflow, you will normally want to focus on creating a data transformation pipeline that transforms raw data into usable data.

Creating a dataflow enables you to provide your colleagues with a single, standard source of data rather than allowing them to data-shop by connecting to disparate underlying systems. This "single source of truth" can help your company or organization evaluate data following approved principles and deliver consistent results.

Create a Dataflow (continued)

Power BI enables you to use a wide variety of data sources in your dataflows — everything from an Excel workbook or a CSV file to a full-on database in SQL Server or Oracle format. In this example, you use an Excel workbook as the data source.

If your data source is a data table, as in this example, the data is clean, so you can load it immediately. If you load another data source, you may need to clean and shape it in Power Query before loading it into Power BI.

Create a Dataflow (continued)

The Choose Data Source page appears.

⑭ Click **Excel workbook** (▦).

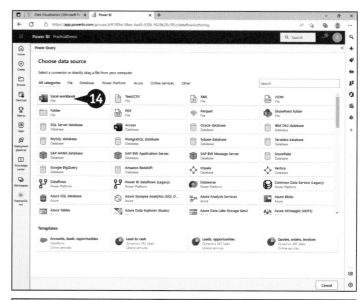

The Connect to Data Source page appears.

⑮ In the Connection Settings area, click **Upload file** (◯ changes to ◉).

⑯ Click **Browse**.

The Open dialog box appears.

⑰ Navigate to the folder that contains the file.

⑱ Click the file.

⑲ Click **Open**.

The Open dialog box closes, and the file name appears in the Connection Settings area.

⑳ Click **Next**.

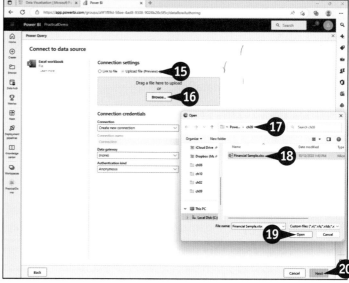

The Choose Data page appears.

21 In the left pane, click the item you want to load (☐ changes to ✓). This example uses **Table1**.

Ⓐ The data appears in the main pane.

22 Click **Transform data**.

The data appears on the Power Query page.

Note: You can now clean and shape the data if necessary. See Chapter 3 for coverage of some of the techniques you can use.

23 Click **Save & close**.

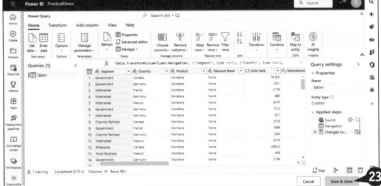

The Save Your Dataflow dialog box opens.

24 Type the name for the dataflow.

25 Optionally, type a description.

26 Click **Save**.

The Save Your Dataflow dialog box closes.

Power BI saves the dataflow.

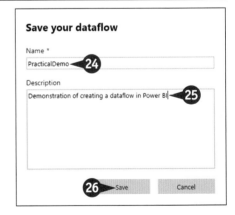

Save your dataflow

Name *

PracticalDemo

Description

Demonstration of creating a dataflow in Power BI

TIP

How can a dataflow protect my data sources?

By creating dataflows that produce consistent data from your approved sources, you can establish an impenetrable barrier between your company or organization's analysts and the data sources actually providing the data. No matter what horrors the analysts inflict on the transformed data delivered by the dataflow, your data sources maintain their integrity. Another benefit of this approach is that you reduce load on the systems providing the data by preventing the analysts from accessing them constantly.

Apply Binary Prediction with AutoML

Power BI includes AutoML, a tool that allows nonexperts to develop machine learning models. AutoML, short for Automated Machine Learning, enables you to tackle thorny problems using machine learning and artificial intelligence without programming. AutoML's no-code interface allows any Power BI user to quickly build, train, and employ machine-learning models. All you need is a Power BI Premium account.

As of this writing, AutoML enables you to perform binary prediction, general classification, and regression. In this section, you perform binary prediction, but the steps for general classification and regression are similar. See the tips for explanations of these three types of analysis.

Apply Binary Prediction with AutoML

① In a web browser, go to powerbi.microsoft.com/en-us.

② Click **Sign in**, and then follow the sign-in procedure.

Your home page appears.

③ Click **Workspaces** (🖳).

The Workspaces page appears.

④ Click the workspace you created in the previous section, "Create a Dataflow."

The workspace's page appears.

5 Click the dataflow you built in the previous section, "Create a Dataflow."

The dataflow's page appears.

6 Click **Machine learning models**.

The Machine Learning Models tab appears, showing the main steps for creating a machine learning model.

7 Click **Get started**.

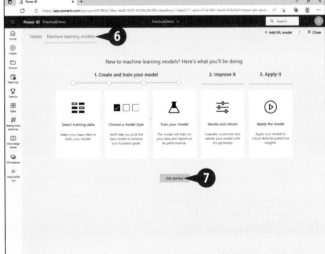

TIP

What are binary prediction and general classification?

Binary prediction is an AutoML classification algorithm that predicts whether an outcome will be achieved. Power BI trains the model's algorithm by providing it with previously achieved results — the more influencing parameters can be provided, the better. The model will then analyze the current set of parameters, predict the results, and share the accuracy percentage of the prediction.

General classification is a classification algorithm for distinguishing between three or more outcomes. When you have only two outcomes, use binary prediction; when you have more than two, use general classification.

continued ▶

Power BI's AutoML feature enables you to create and train a machine learning model using a straightforward web-based interface. You first select the base data to use for training your machine-learning model. Second, you choose what model type to use; as of this writing, the three choices are binary prediction, general classification, or regression, but Microsoft plans to introduce other model types, such as time-series forecasting. Third, you set your model to train on the data provided.

Apply Binary Classification with AutoML (continued)

The What Do You Want to Predict? page appears.

8 Click **Table** (∨), and then click the table, **Table1** in this example.

9 Click **Outcome** (∨), and then click the column you want to predict, **Discount Band** in this example.

10 Click **Next**.

The Choose a Model page appears, with a suggested model.

11 If the model is suitable, click it. If not, click **Select a different model**, click a different model on the resulting page, and click **Next**. Power BI then displays the Choose a Model page again, this time with the model you selected. This example uses **Binary Prediction**.

12 Click **Choose a target outcome** (∨), and then click the target outcome. This example uses **Medium** — the Medium level for the Discount Band field.

13 Change the default label in the Match Label box.

14 Change the default label in the Mismatch Label box.

15 Click **Next**.

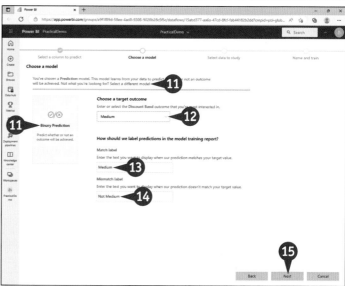

The Select Data to Study page appears.

16 Select (☑) each column you want the model to study.

Ⓐ You can click **Clear** to deselect the check boxes that Power BI has selected.

17 Click **Next**.

The Name and Train Your Model page appears.

18 Type a name for your model. This example uses **BinaryPredictionModel**.

19 Optionally, type a description.

20 Drag the Training Time slider to set the length of time for which to train the model.

Note: Increase the training time if your dataset is large, complex, or both. Longer training times will usually deliver more accurate predictions.

21 Click **Save and train**.

Power BI saves your changes and starts training the machine-learning model.

The workspace page appears again, and you can work on other tasks while the model trains.

What is AutoML regression?

Regression is the study of the relationships between all the values in a dataflow. This allows the machine learning model to predict sales in the near term and the long term, assess inventory levels, understand supply and demand, and review and understand how different variables impact these factors.

Regression is generally used to forecast numerical key performance indicators (KPIs). You provide the machine learning model with data on past performance; the model creates a forecasting algorithm that allows it to predict future performance for a specific time frame. The further away the time frame from the current date, the less accurate the predictions become.

CHAPTER 10

Creating Interactive Reports

Power BI Desktop enables you to create interactive reports that provide a detailed examination of a company's or organization's performance. Power BI reports typically consist of multiple pages that contain visuals and data as well as analysis of the past results and implications for the future.

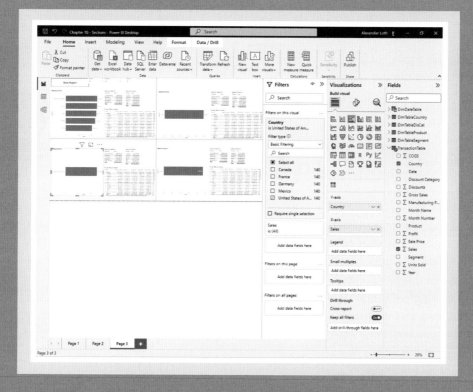

Planning to Create a Report

Power BI Desktop enables you to create detailed reports that you can share online with your colleagues. Before you start creating a report, you should understand the essentials of what reports are in Power BI and what tools you have at your disposal. You should establish your goals in creating the report so that you can assess the types of information the report will need for maximum effectiveness. You should decide whether to create a static report or a dynamic, interactive report. You should also grasp some straightforward design principles, test your report, and keep it updated.

Understanding What Power BI Reports Are

A *report* is a document that presents information derived from a single dataset in easy-to-understand format, using visuals — such as charts, key performance indicators, and maps — to present information graphically. The purpose of a report is typically to present findings in a forum where participants can discuss them logically and derive conclusions and recommendations.

Power BI Desktop gives you a great deal of flexibility in creating reports. A report can contain anything from a single page up to many pages. In a multipage report, you can navigate from page to page by clicking the tabs at the bottom of the pages, but you can also provide enhanced navigation by adding page navigator controls and bookmarks.

Establish the Audience and Goals of Your Report

Before you start putting your report together, make sure you have a clear understanding of the audience and the goals of the report. This clarity will help ensure you design the report to be relevant and useful for the audience and target the report's goals accurately.

Use a Clean Design and a Unified Color Scheme

To make your report easy to read, keep the design clean and simple. Avoid using too many fonts or other visual elements, as doing so will tend to make the report harder to read and interpret.

To help the report present a cogent appearance, use a unified color scheme rather than using different color palettes on different pages. For example, if you use the orange-blue diverging color palette to show profits and losses, continue to work with this throughout your report. Your choice of color palettes may be constrained by corporate or organizational guidelines.

Keep Data Relevant and Use the Right Level of Detail

Chances are that your dataset contains far more detail than will fit in the report. This means you need to choose the right level of detail to include in the report. Avoid including too much data, because it can make the report overwhelming and prevent readers from seeing the forest for the trees. At the other extreme, include enough data to make the report informative.

When selecting data to include, make sure it is relevant to the report's audience and goals. Including irrelevant data risks making the report cluttered and confusing.

Pick Suitable Visuals for the Report

To convey information visually and vividly, most reports include visuals, such as charts and graphs. A report can contain anything from a single visual to multiple pages full of visuals.

For maximum impact, you will need to select visuals that present your data most clearly and effectively. This will depend on the dataset and data you are using for your report.

Make a Report Interactive

A report can be either static (unchanging) or interactive (changing in response to the user's actions). In most cases, making a report interactive is the better choice, because the user can explore the report's data in greater detail and gain a better understanding of it.

You can add interactivity to a report by adding slicers or by adding drill-through. A *slicer* is a control that enables the user to refine the data presented on a report page — for example, by displaying only one sales territory instead of all the sales territories. *Drill-through* enables the reader to move down through a hierarchy of data — such as years, quarters, and months in a three-level date hierarchy — to see finer detail.

Test and Update Your Report

After creating a report, test it with users to ensure that it is effective and easy to use. Solicit user feedback to identify any functional or conceptual problems with the report, and make changes accordingly.

Even when the report is working satisfactorily, do not rest on your laurels, but keep the report up to date so that it can deliver the most value to your company or organization. Update the data to keep the report current and accurate, and consider using real-time data to make the report more dynamic and interactive.

Start a Report and Add a Title

You can start a report in Power BI Desktop in two ways. First, you can create a new file and connect the appropriate data source to it, as explained in Chapter 2. Second, you can open an existing file with the data source connected, as you do in this section.

After starting the report, you can add a title to it to explain what the report covers and what its purpose is. For the title, you can use either a text box control or a Blank button control. Either works fine, but a Blank button gives you much greater flexibility.

Start a Report and Add a Title

Note: This section uses the Chapter 10 - Start Report.pbix database, available at www.wiley. com/go/tyvpowerbi.

1 Open the Chapter 10 - Start Report.pbix database file.

Note: If the Fields pane and the Visualizations pane are collapsed, expand them.

2 Click **Insert**.

3 In the Elements group, click **Buttons**.

The Buttons gallery opens.

4 Click **Blank** (☐).

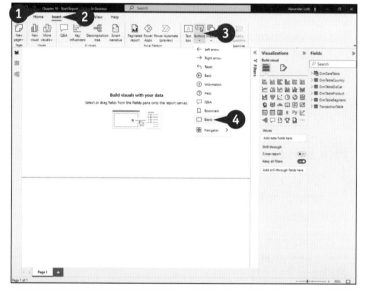

Ⓐ Power BI Desktop inserts a blank button.

Ⓑ The Format pane replaces the Visualizations pane.

5 Move the pointer over the lower-right corner of the blank button so that it becomes a diagonal double-headed arrow (↘), and then drag the corner down and to the right.

The button expands.

6 Click **Button**.

7 Click **Style** to expand the Style section.

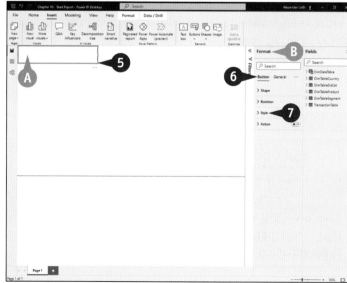

8 Click the Text heading switch (⬤Off changes to On⬤).

9 Click **Text**.

10 Click **Text**, and type **Sales Report**.

11 Click **Font** (∨), and then click the font.

12 Click **Font size** (◌), and then specify the font size.

13 Click **Font color** (∨), and then click the text color.

14 Click a horizontal alignment: **Left** (☰); **Center** (☰), as shown here; or **Right** (☰).

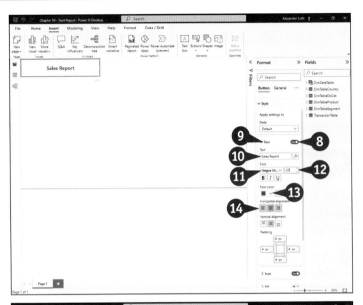

15 Click a vertical alignment: **Top** (☰); **Middle** (☰), as shown here; or **Bottom** (☰).

16 Click a padding option (◌), **Top**, **Right**, **Bottom**, or **Left**, and adjust the padding distance.

Note: *Padding* is the minimum distance between the text and the edge of the button.

Ⓒ The button takes on the formatting.

17 Click **Save** (🖫).

18 Click **Close** (✖).

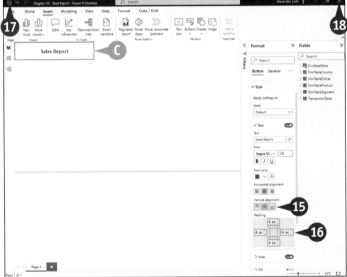

Add Visuals to a Report

Your next step in creating the report is to add visuals. A typical report will benefit from using two distinct types of visuals. The first type is visuals used for summarization, such as bar charts, pie charts, or line charts. The second type is visuals that elaborate on this first type of visual.

The specific visuals you create will depend on the type of report you are creating. Choose a type of graph or chart that clearly communicates the data, and use labels and other visual elements to make the data easy to understand and assimilate.

Add Visuals to a Report

Note: This section uses the Chapter 10 - Report Visuals.pbix database, available at www.wiley.com/go/tyvpowerbi.

1 Open the Chapter 10 - Report Visuals.pbix database file.

Note: If the Fields pane and the Visualizations pane are collapsed, expand them.

2 Click **Build Visual** (▦).

3 Click **Clustered bar chart** (📊).

A A clustered bar chart visual appears on the canvas below the title button.

4 Click **Expand** (⟩ changes to ⌄) to the left of TransactionTable.

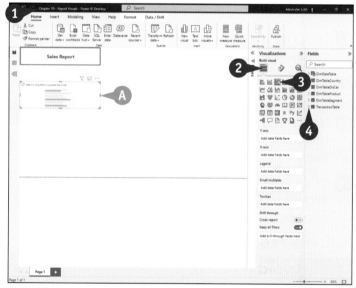

5 Click **Country** (☐ changes to ✅).

B The Country field appears in the Y-axis box.

6 Click **Sales** (☐ changes to ✅).

C The Sales field appears in the X-axis box.

D The Sales data and Country data appear in the visual.

7 Click the canvas to deselect the visual.

8 Click **Table** (▦).

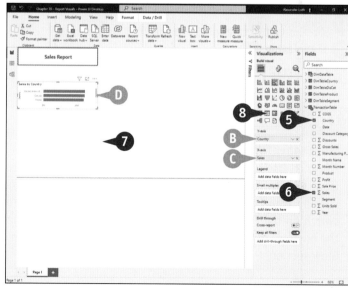

E A table visual appears.

9 Click **Segment** (☐ changes to ✅).

F The Segment field appears in the Columns box.

G The Segment data appears in the first column of the table.

10 Click **Sales** (☐ changes to ✅).

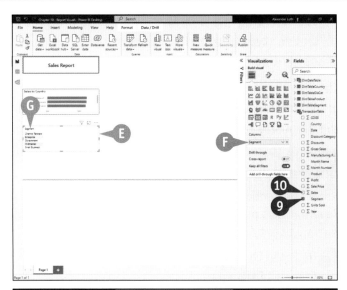

H The Sales field appears below the Segment field in the Columns box.

I The Sales data appears in the second column of the table.

11 Click the canvas to deselect the visual.

12 Click **Table** (▦).

J A second table visual appears.

13 Click **Product** (☐ changes to ✅).

K The Product field appears in the Columns box.

L The Product data appears in the first column of the table.

14 Click **Sales** (☐ changes to ✅).

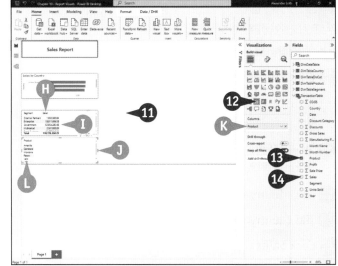

TIP

How many visuals should I include on a report page?

For most pages, it is best to restrict yourself to two to four visuals so as not to clutter the page and make it confusing. Experiment with different types of visuals, and use those that most clearly convey the message you want the page to deliver to the reader. Remember that you can create multiple pages, each containing an easy-to-read number of visuals, to tell a story or to let your audience explore the data in successive steps.

continued ▶

Add Visuals to a Report (continued)

After creating the first four visuals, you drag the visuals to where you want them on the canvas, resize them to suit their contents, and format them for readability and impact. This section provides example stops for placing, sizing, and formatting the visuals, but you may prefer a different layout, a different look, or both. Either way, use the skills you have learned in the earlier chapters of this book.

Finally, you add a matrix visual to the report. This matrix will allow the reader to drill down to any segment to analyze the data and draw inferences from it.

Add Visuals to a Report (continued)

Ⓐ The Sales field appears below the Segment field in the Columns box.

Ⓑ The Sales data appears in the second column of the table.

15 Drag the Product table to the upper-right quadrant of the canvas, and then resize the table to fit its contents.

16 Drag the Segment table up and to the right, positioning it to the left of the Product table, and then resize the table to fit its contents.

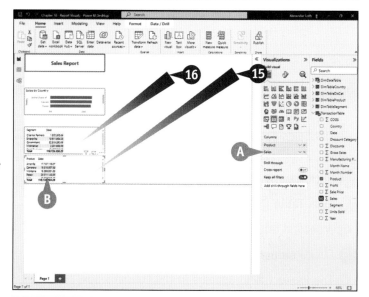

17 With the Segment table still selected, click **Format Visual** (🖌).

18 Click **General**.

19 Set the switch on the Title heading to On (On⬤).

20 Click **Title** to expand the Title section.

21 Click **Text**, and type the title text. This example uses **Sales by Segment**.

22 Format the title as needed.

23 Click the Product table, and then repeat steps **19** to **22** to apply a title. This example uses **Sales by Product**.

24 Click outside the table to deselect it.

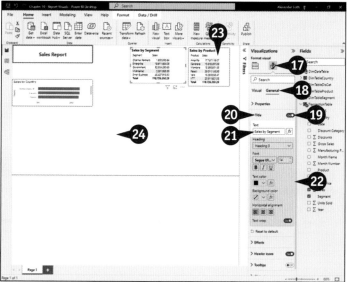

25 Click **Matrix Visual** (▦).

26 Click **Country** (☐ changes to ☑).

27 Click **Segment** (☐ changes to ☑).

C The Country field and Segment field appear in the Rows box.

28 Click **Product** (☐ changes to ☑).

D The Product field appears in the Columns box.

29 Click **Sales** (☐ changes to ☑).

E The Sales field appears in the Values box.

F The data appears in the matrix visual.

30 Drag the matrix to below the two Sales tables, and then resize it to display most of its contents with some of the Country rows expanded.

31 With the matrix visual still selected, repeat steps **19** to **22** to apply a title. This example uses **Product Matrix (Sales)**.

32 Reposition, resize, and format the clustered bar chart. See the tip.

33 Click **Save** (💾).

34 Click **Close** (✖).

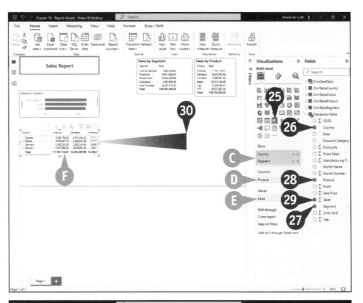

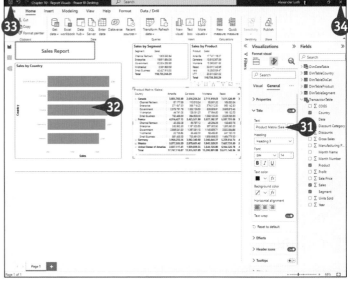

How should I format the clustered bar chart?
You can format the clustered bar chart however you prefer. The example shows font formatting applied to the Y-axis title, the X-axis title, and the title of the visual to make the subject matter and axes clearly visible; data labels added to the bars for reference; and the visual resized to occupy the available space.

How do I hide the borders around the visuals?
Click the visual you want to affect, click **Format Visual** (🖌) to display the Format Visual tab, and then click **General** to display the General subtab. Click **Effects** to expand the Effects section, and then click the switch on the Visual Border heading (On changes to Off).

Add Slicers to a Report

A slicer is a control that enables the user to refine the data presented on a report page. For example, the sample report contains visuals tied to the Country field. If you add a slicer for the Country field, the user's selecting a country in the slicer makes the other visuals display only that country's data. You can add multiple slicers to a page.

Power BI Desktop enables you to display a slicer in three ways: as a drop-down list, as in this section; as a vertical list of check boxes; or as a row of buttons.

Add a Slicer to a Report

Note: This section uses the Chapter 10 - Slicers.pbix database, available at www.wiley.com/go/tyvpowerbi.

1 Open the Chapter 10 - Slicers.pbix database file.

Note: If the Visualizations pane and Fields pane are collapsed, expand them.

2 Click **Expand** (⟩ changes to ⌄) to the left of TransactionTable to expand the listing.

3 Click **Build Visual** (▦).

4 Click **Slicer** (▧).

Ⓐ A slicer appears on the canvas.

5 Click **Country** (☐ changes to ☑).

Ⓑ The Country field appears in the Field box.

Ⓒ The Country data appears in the slicer.

6 Drag the slicer to above the Sales by Segment table.

7 Click **Format Visual** (🖌).

8 Click **Visual**.

9 Click **Slicer settings**.

10 Click **Style** (⌄), and then click **Dropdown**.

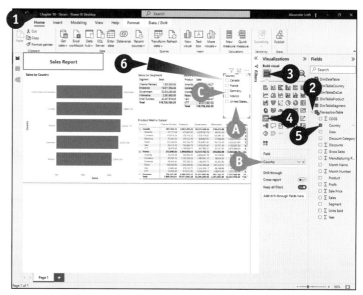

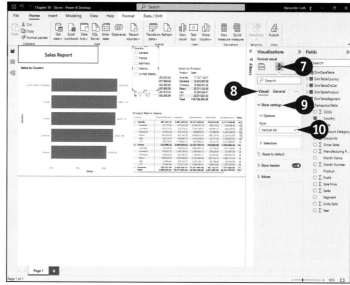

The slicer changes to a drop-down list.

11 Resize the slicer to suit the heading and drop-down list.

12 Click **More options** (⋯).

The More Options menu opens.

13 Click **Search** (🔍).

The slicer takes on search capabilities.

14 Click a blank area of the canvas.

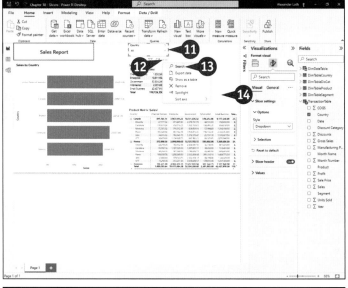

15 Repeat steps **4** to **13** to create a second search-capable slicer in drop-down format. Assign the Segment field to this slicer, and position the slicer to the right of the Country slicer.

16 Repeat steps **4** to **13** again to create a third search-capable slicer in drop-down format. Assign the Product field to this slicer, and position the slicer to the right of the Segment slicer.

17 Click **Save** (💾).

Power BI Desktop saves your changes.

18 Click **Close** (❌).

The file closes.

TIP

Why should I add slicers to a report page?

Adding slicers can help readers of your report more easily find the data they need. The reader can select a value in a slicer to filter all the visuals and slicers on that value. Alternatively, the reader can select a value on a visual to filter all the visuals on that value without affecting the slicers.

Turning on search capabilities for a slicer enables the reader to type in the search box to display matching items. "Typing down" like this is a fast and convenient way of navigating longer lists, but it may not be needed for shorter lists.

Control Which Visuals and Slicers Interact

By default, every visual on a page interacts with every other visual, and every slicer on a page interacts with every other slicer and every visual on the page. However, Power BI Desktop enables you to configure a slicer to control which visuals and which other slicers it affects. Similarly, you can configure a visual to control which other visuals it affects. Using these customization features, you can create comparative visuals and add sections within a report.

Control Which Visuals and Sliders Interact

Note: This section uses the Chapter 10 - Interact.pbix database, available at www.wiley.com/go/tyvpowerbi.

1 Open the Chapter 10 - Interact.pbix database file.

2 Click the Country slicer.

Note: Click the Country label to select the slicer without opening the drop-down list.

3 Click **Format.**

4 Click **Edit interactions.**

Power BI Desktop enables Editing mode for interactions.

Note: Editing mode remains on until you turn it off by clicking **Edit interactions** on the Format tab of the ribbon again.

Ⓐ The controls for editing interactions appear.

Note: The Country slicer is still selected at this point, so the changes you make affect this slicer's interaction with the other slicers and visuals.

5 For the Sales by Segment visual, click **None** (⊘ changes to ⦸).

Ⓑ When the None icon becomes active (⬤),
the Filter icon becomes inactive
(⬛ changes to ⬜).

Note: To enable filtering again, click **Filter**
(⬜ changes to ⬛). The None icon becomes
inactive (⬤ changes to ◯).

❻ For the Sales by Product visual, click **None**
(◯ changes to ⬤).

Note: At this point, you can click another
slicer and configure interactions for it.

❼ Click **Edit Interactions**.

Power BI Desktop disables Editing mode
for interactions.

The controls for editing interactions
disappear.

❽ Click **Save** (💾).

Power BI Desktop saves your changes.

❾ Click **Close** (✖).

The file closes.

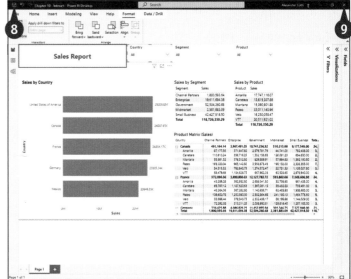

TIP

How can I guide users through a report?

If your visuals are linked via report actions, move the visual that serves as a window into the data to the top left, and move visuals that are not meant to be filtered to the bottom right. That will implicitly provide a path for your audience along which you expect them to explore the report: from top left to bottom right. For instance, you could go from a high-level overview of different product categories to a more detailed visual showing the evolution over time of categories that are clicked. Use explanatory text fields and numbers to guide the user through the report. For example, you might start with "Step 1: Select a category."

Enable and Control Drill-Through Actions

Slicers are a powerful way of adding interactivity to your reports, but you can also add interactivity by enabling drill-through actions. A *drill-through action* enables the user to navigate easily from a field in a visual on one page to a different page whose visuals are automatically filtered by that field. In this section, you add a drill-through action to the Country column of the Sales by Country visual.

To implement a drill-through action, you add a landing page to the report. The *landing page* is the page the user reaches when they drill through from the source page.

Enable and Control Drill-Through Actions

Note: This section uses the Chapter 10 - Drill-Through.pbix database, available at www.wiley.com/go/tyvpowerbi.

1 Open the Chapter 10 - Drill-Through.pbix database file.

Note: If the Fields pane and the Visualizations pane are collapsed, expand them.

2 Click **New page** (➕).

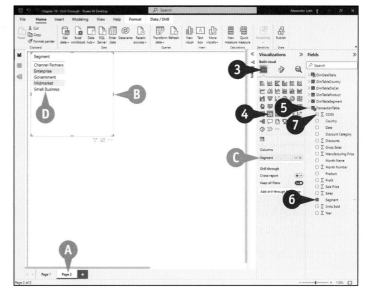

A A new page appears.

3 Click **Build Visual** (▦).

4 Click **Table** (▦).

B Power BI adds a table visual to the canvas.

5 Click **Expand** (❯ changes to ❯) to the left of TransactionTable to expand the TransactionTable listing.

6 Click **Segment** (☐ changes to ☑).

C The Segment field appears in the Columns box.

D The Segment data appears as the first column in the table.

7 Click **COGS** (☐ changes to ☑).

E The COGS field appears below the Segment field.

F The COGS data appears as the second column in the table.

8 Click **Manufacturing Price** (☐ changes to ☑).

9 Click **Gross Sales** (☐ changes to ☑).

10 Click **Sales** (☐ changes to ☑).

11 Click **Discounts** (☐ changes to ☑).

G The Manufacturing Price field, Gross Sales field, Sales field, and Discounts field appear in the table.

12 Drag the lower-right corner to resize the table visual so that you can see all its columns.

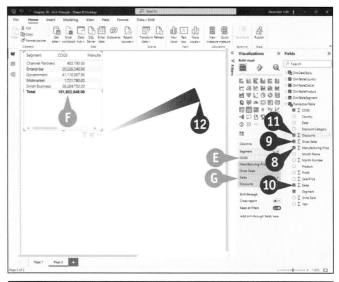

H The columns appear in the order in which you added the fields.

Note: You can rearrange the table columns by dragging the fields in the Columns box up and down.

13 Click the canvas to deselect the visual.

14 Click **Table** (▦).

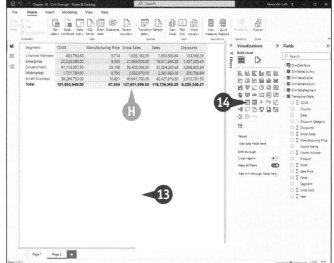

TIP

Can I drill through from one report to another?

Yes. Power BI includes a feature called *cross-report drill-through* that enables you to connect multiple reports that have related content. Each report must be in the same Power BI app or in the same Power BI service workspace, such as the workspace belonging to your company or organization, and the tables and fields on which you want to drill through must have identical names in each report's data model. You then set up the drill-through by right-clicking a data point in a visual in the source report, clicking or highlighting **Drill through** on the contextual menu, and then clicking the drill-through target in the destination report on the continuation menu.

continued ▶

After creating the two table visuals and populating them with fields from the TransactionTable table, you specify the Country field as the key drill-through field for the new page. Specifying the key drill-through field designates the new page as the drill-through landing page and causes Power BI Desktop to add a Back button that you can click to return to the page whence you came.

Enable and Control Drill-Through Actions (continued)

Ⓐ Power BI adds a second table visual to the canvas.

⑮ Click **Product** (☐ changes to ☑).

⑯ Click **COGS** (☐ changes to ☑).

⑰ Click **Manufacturing Price** (☐ changes to ☑).

⑱ Click **Gross Sales** (☐ changes to ☑).

⑲ Click **Sales** (☐ changes to ☑).

⑳ Click **Discounts** (☐ changes to ☑).

Ⓑ The Product, COGS, Manufacturing Price, Gross Sales, Sales, and Discounts fields appear in the Columns box in that order.

㉑ Click a blank space on the canvas.

The second table visual becomes deselected.

㉒ Drag the Country column to the Add Drill-Through Fields Here box on the Build Visual tab of the Visualizations pane.

㉓ Click **Page 1**.

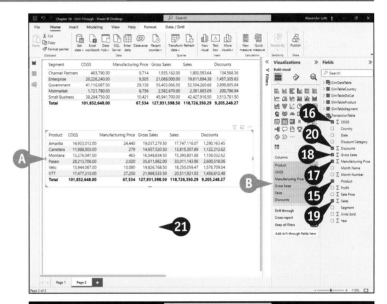

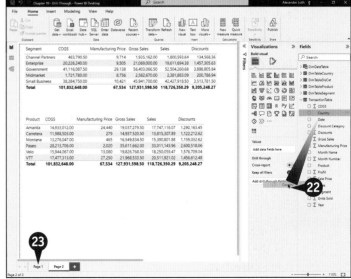

Page 1 appears.

24 Right-click **France** in the Sales by Country visual.

The contextual menu appears.

25 Click or highlight **Drill through**.

The continuation menu opens.

26 Click **Page 2**.

Note: In this example, Page 2 is the only item on the Drill Through continuation menu. Typically, a report would have multiple drill-through pages.

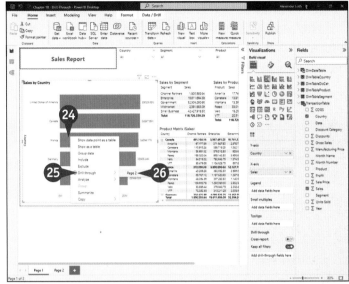

Page 2 appears.

Ⓒ The visuals show data for France, because that is the country from which you clicked through to Page 2.

27 Click **Back** (⊜).

Power BI Desktop again displays Page 1, the page from which you drilled through to Page 2.

28 Click **Save** (💾).

Power BI Desktop saves your changes.

29 Click **Close** (✖).

The file closes.

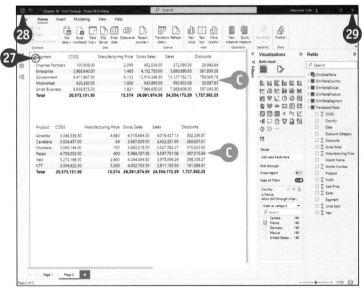

TIP

What settings must I choose to enable cross-report drill-through?

In Power BI Desktop, click **File** to open Backstage view, click **Options and settings**, and then click **Options** (⚙) to open the Options dialog box. In the sidebar on the left, click **Report settings** in the Current File section, go to the Cross-Report Drillthrough section, and click **Allow visuals in this report to use drillthrough targets from other reports** (☐ changes to ☑). Click **OK** to close the Options dialog box. Then, on the Build Visual tab of the Visualizations pane for the report, click the **Cross-report** switch (●Off changes to On●) in the Drill Through section.

Split a Page into Sections

When you need to make a direct comparison between different categories in a report, you can split a page into sections. To help the reader compare the categories visually, you would normally make each section the same size and use the same visuals in each section. You can separate the sections by using different colors, by adding horizontal or vertical lines, or both.

Here, you add a new page to the report and set its dimensions to 2560 pixels wide by 1440 pixels high, big enough to provide space for four sections. Each section will show one country's performance.

Split a Page into Sections

Note: This section uses the Chapter 10 - Sections.pbix database, available at www. wiley.com/go/tyvpowerbi.

1. Open the Chapter 10 - Sections.pbix database file.

Note: If the Fields pane and the Visualizations pane are collapsed, expand them.

2. If Page 1 is not already displayed, click **Page 1** to display it.

3. Press Ctrl + A to select all the visuals on the page (not shown).

4. Click **Home** to display the Home tab.

5. Click **Copy** to copy the visuals to the Clipboard.

6. Click **New page** (➕).

Ⓐ A new page appears and becomes the active page.

7. Click **Format Page** (◳).

8. Click **Canvas settings** to expand the Canvas Settings section.

9. Click **Type** (⌄), and then click **Custom**.

10. Click **Height**, and specify **1440**.

11. Click **Width**, and specify **2560**.

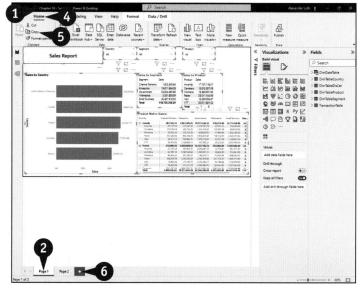

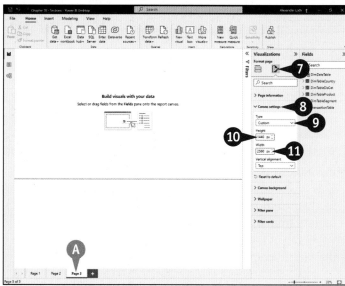

12 Click **Insert**.

The Insert tab of the ribbon appears.

13 Click **Shapes**.

The Shapes gallery opens.

14 Click **Line** (╲).

A horizontal line appears on the page.

15 Drag the line to halfway down the page.

B A midline guide appears when the line is halfway down.

16 Extend the line all the way across the page.

17 Repeat steps **12** to **14** to insert another line.

18 Click **Shape**.

The Shape tab of the Format pane appears.

19 Click **Rotation**.

The Rotation section expands.

20 Click **Shape** (◯), and specify **90°**.

C The line becomes vertical.

Note: When turned 90 degrees, the line should be in the middle of the canvas by default. If not, drag it to the middle.

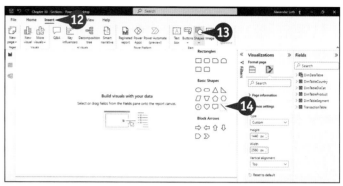

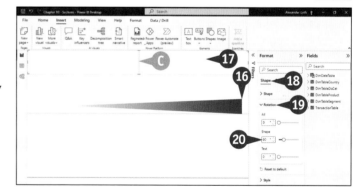

TIP

How can I encourage the reader to make the comparison between different sections?
First, design the layout of the page to make the comparison clear. This typically means allocating a similar amount of space to each category in the comparison; using a visual means, such as lines or color shading, to distinguish the categories; and using the same visuals in each. Second, keep the design as clean and uncluttered as possible to reduce distractions. Third, use text labels to provide unambiguous instructions — for example, telling the reader what to look at. Fourth, use shapes where appropriate for emphasis or direction.

continued ▶

After adding the new page to the report, you add a centered horizontal line and a centered vertical line to divide the page into four equally sized sections. You populate the upper-left section by pasting all the controls from Page 1 of the report. You then populate the other three sections by copying most of these controls and pasting them three times. After that, you adjust the filtering in the sections to make each show data for a different country.

Split a Page into Sections (continued)

21 Extend the line all the way to the bottom of the page, so that the canvas contains four equally sized rectangular sections.

22 Click **Home**.

23 Click **Paste**.

A Power BI Desktop pastes the visuals into the upper-left section.

Note: If the Sync Visuals dialog box opens, click **Don't Sync**.

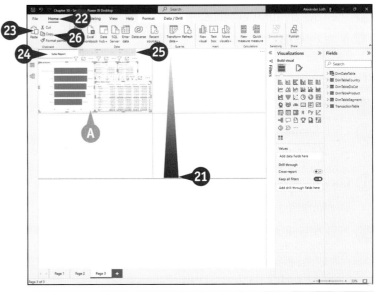

24 With the visuals still selected from you pasting them, press Ctrl+click the Sales Report title to deselect it.

25 Press Ctrl+click the label at the top of each of the three slicers to deselect them.

26 With the remaining visuals still selected, click **Copy**.

Power BI Desktop copies the visuals to the Clipboard.

27 Click **Paste**.

The pasted visuals appear on top of the existing visuals. They remain selected.

28 Press → and ↓ to move the pasted visuals to another section.

29 Repeat steps **27** and **28** to populate the two remaining sections.

30 Click **Expand** (≪).

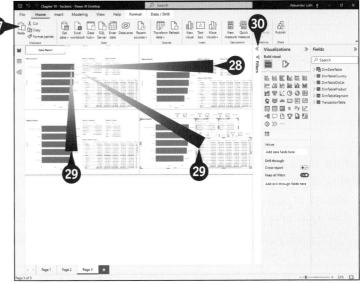

31 In the upper-right section, click the Sales by Country clustered bar chart.

The chart becomes selected.

32 Drag **Country** from the Fields pane to the Filters on This Visual box.

33 Click **Country** in the Filters on This Visual box.

The Country filter expands.

34 Click **Canada** (☐ changes to ☑).

35 Click each other visual in the upper-right section in turn, and then repeat steps **32** to **34** to make each visual show data for Canada.

36 Repeat steps **31** to **35**, but this time work in the lower-left section and set the country to a different country, such as Germany.

37 Repeat steps **31** to **35** a second time, but this time work in the lower-right section and set the country to a third country, such as United States of America.

38 Click **Save** (🖫).

39 Click **Close** (✖).

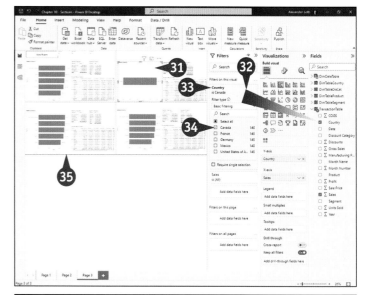

TIP

How can I make my report's filters and legends easy to understand?

Here are two suggestions. First, make sure all filters and legends are necessary. Once you have created your first draft of the report, see if there are any filters or legends that you can remove without affecting functionality or comprehensibility. Second, arrange the filters and legends logically and consistently. Group filters and legends that relate to the same content so that their affiliation is clear. Move them near to the visuals in question or format them with the same background to make the link obvious.

Add Bookmarks and Navigation to a Report

To enable the reader to navigate the pages and contents of a report easily, you can add bookmarks and a page navigator control. Bookmarks are especially useful, because they let you create different states of the report between which the reader can easily switch. For example, you can use a bookmark to save the settings you have made to a page's filters, slicers, and visuals. You can then click a button to return the page to the saved state stored in that bookmark.

Add Bookmarks to a Report

Note: This section uses the Chapter 10 - Bookmarks.pbix database, available at www.wiley.com/go/tyvpowerbi.

Add Bookmarks to a Report

1. Open the Chapter 10 - Bookmarks.pbix database file.

Note: If the Fields pane and the Visualizations pane are expanded, collapse them.

2. Click **View**.

The View tab of the ribbon appears.

3. Click **Bookmarks**.

Ⓐ The Bookmarks pane opens between the Filters pane and the Visualizations pane.

4. Click **Add** (☐).

Power BI Desktop creates a bookmark and assigns the default name Bookmark 1.

5. Double-click **Bookmark 1**.

6. Type **Default** and press Enter.

7. Repeat steps **4** to **6** to create a bookmark named **Change View**.

8. Right-click the Change View bookmark.

9. Click **Selected Visuals**.

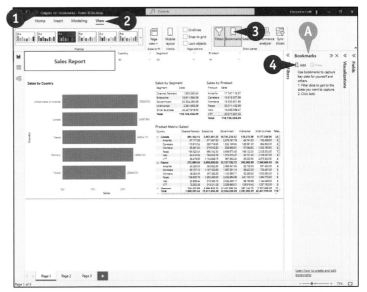

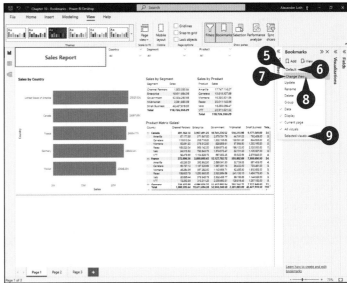

10 Click **Selection**.

B The Selection pane opens between the Filters pane and the Bookmarks pane.

11 Click **Hide Visual** (👁 changes to 👁‍🗨) next to Sales by Country, next to Sales by Segment, next to Sales by Product, and next to Product Matrix (Sales).

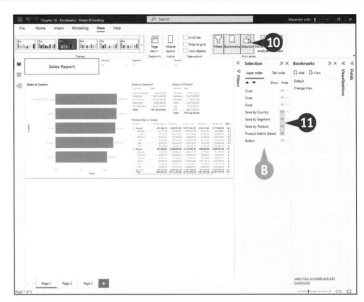

C Power BI Desktop hides those four visuals.

12 In the Selection pane, click **Sales by Country**.

The Sales by Country button becomes selected.

13 **Shift**+click **Product Matrix (Sales)**.

The buttons for the four visuals become selected.

14 Right-click the **Change View** bookmark.

The contextual menu opens.

15 Click **Update**.

Power BI Desktop updates the Change View bookmark to include the four visuals being hidden.

16 Click the **Default** bookmark.

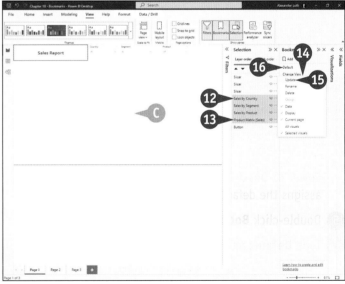

TIP

What is the best way to organize many bookmarks?

Try using the bookmark navigator control that Power BI Desktop provides. Click **Insert** to display the Insert tab of the ribbon, click **Buttons** in the Elements group to open the Buttons gallery, click or highlight **Navigator** to open the Navigator gallery, and then click **Bookmark navigator**. Power BI Desktop inserts a bookmark navigator control, which shows a named button for each bookmark. You can position and resize the bookmark navigator control as needed, and you can format it by working on the Visual tab of the Format pane.

continued ▶

Power BI Desktop enables you to add a page navigator control that lets the user navigate easily between the pages in a multipage report. Any time you create a report that has more than a handful of pages, you should evaluate whether adding a page navigator control would benefit the reader. If so, you can add the control quickly and easily.

Power BI Desktop links the page navigator control dynamically to all the pages in the report. As a result, when you change the name of a page, the page's button in the page navigator control automatically changes as well.

Add Bookmarks and Navigation to a Report (continued)

A Power BI Desktop displays the page's default state.

17 Click **Collapse** (») to collapse the Selection pane.

18 Click **Collapse** (») to collapse the Bookmarks pane.

19 Click **Expand** («) to expand the Visualizations pane.

20 Click **Insert**.

21 Click **Buttons**.

22 Click **Bookmark** (⌑).

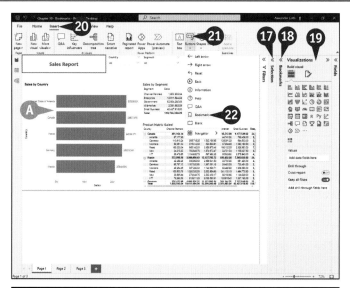

A bookmark button appears.

23 Reposition and resize the bookmark button.

24 Click **Button**.

25 Click **Action** to expand the Action section.

26 Click **Bookmark** (⌄), and then click **Default**.

27 Repeat steps **20** to **26** to create a second bookmark, this time clicking **Change View** in the Bookmark drop-down list.

You can now test your bookmarks by clicking the first bookmark to switch to the default view and then clicking the second bookmark to switch to the alternate view.

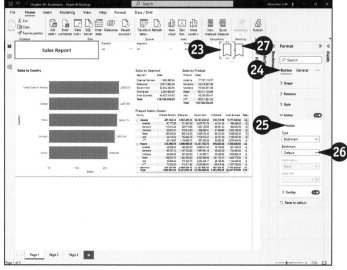

Add Page Navigation to a Report

Note: Continue to use the Chapter 10 - Bookmarks.pbix file for this subsection.

① Click **Insert**.

The Insert tab of the ribbon appears.

② Click **Buttons**.

The Buttons gallery opens.

③ Click **Navigator** (⊞).

The Navigator gallery opens.

④ Click **Page navigator**.

Ⓑ Power BI Desktop inserts a page navigator control. This control consists of a button for each page.

Note: The highlighted button in the page navigator control indicates the active page.

⑤ Drag the page navigator control to where you want it.

Note: You can also resize the page navigator control if you want.

You can now test the page navigator control by clicking the button for the page you want to display.

⑥ Click **Save** (💾).

⑦ Click **Close** (❌).

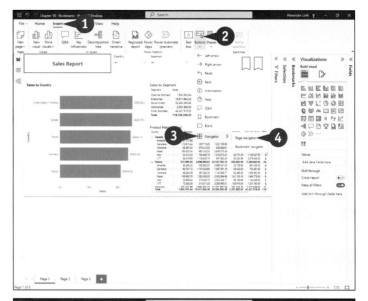

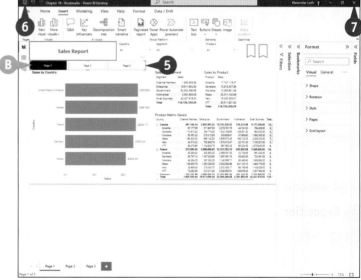

How do I create a vertical page navigator control?

Start by inserting the page navigator control following the steps in the main text. With the control selected, click **Visual** in the Format pane to display the Visual tab. Click **Grid layout** to expand the Grid Layout section, click **Orientation** (⌄), and then click **Vertical**. Power BI Desktop arranges the page buttons in a vertical stack.

The Orientation drop-down list also offers the Grid option, which arranges the page numbers in a grid. After selecting Grid, you can click **Columns** (◇) and adjust the number of columns.

CHAPTER 11

Publishing Reports and Dashboards

In this chapter, you learn how to share your Power BI analysis and reports with your colleagues by using the Power BI service. You set up workspaces, implement row-level security, and create and share dashboards. You also schedule data refreshes for datasets you have published, and even publish reports to the web so that anybody can access them.

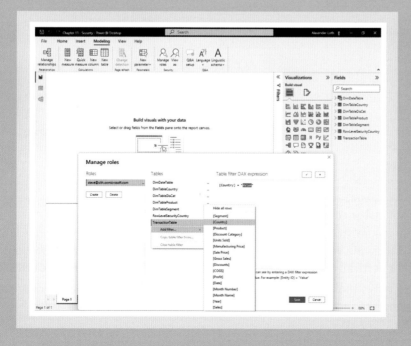

Set Up a Workspace

In Power BI, a *workspace* is a container for dashboards, reports, workbooks, datasets, and dataflows. Workspaces enable you to make content available to the people who need to work with it.

Each Power BI user has a personal workspace, called My Workspace, that only that user can access and that contains the content that the user has created. To collaborate with members of your organization, you can create four other types of workspaces: Pro workspaces, Premium per-user workspaces, Premium per-capacity workspaces, and Embedded workspaces. Premium workspaces require a Power BI Premium subscription.

Set Up a Workspace

1. In a web browser, go to powerbi.microsoft.com/en-us.

   The Data Visualization: Microsoft Power BI web page appears.

2. Click **Sign in**, and then follow the steps of the sign-in procedure using your credentials for Power BI.

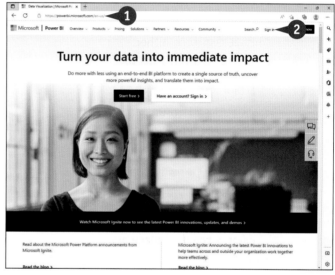

Once you have signed in, your Power BI Home page appears.

3. Click **Workspaces** (🗔).

   The Workspaces pane opens.

4. Click **New Workspace** (⊞).

224

The Create a Workspace pane appears.

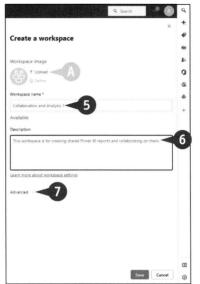

Ⓐ You can click **Upload** (⤒) to upload an image file for the workspace. For example, you might upload a corporate logo.

⑤ Click in the **Workspace name** box, and type the workspace name.

⑥ Click in the **Description** box, and type a description.

⑦ Click **Advanced** (⌄).

⑧ In the Contact List area, either leave **Workspace admins** selected (⦿) or click **Specific users and groups** (◯ changes to ⦿); then click **Enter users and groups** and enter the users and groups.

⑨ In the License Mode area, click **Premium per user** (◯ changes to ⦿).

⑩ Click **Save**.

Power BI creates the workspace and displays its home page.

Ⓑ You can click **Add content** to start adding content to the workspace.

When I publish a Power BI report on a workspace, how does it receive updates?

When you publish a dataset in Power BI, you publish not only the report but also the entire data model and any transformations you have created. However, when that dataset is updated depends on the type of data source to which you have connected it. If you have connected it to an online data source or a SQL Server data source, the dataset can receive real-time updates. By contrast, if you are using a local data gateway, you can enable scheduled updates. For more information about connecting Power BI to your data, see Chapter 2.

Ask Questions About the Data

ower BI's Q&A feature enables the user to ask questions about the data using natural language. Q&A also creates a visual demonstration of the question asked. Q&A enables the user to explore the data in their own words.

Q&A, which is available on both Power BI Desktop and Power BI Services, is interactive and fun. Often, asking one question can reveal other information about the dataset that prompts further exploration by asking other questions. The user can dig into the results or can pin them as a visual on the page.

Ask Questions About the Data

Note: This section uses the Chapter 11 - Ask Questions.pbix database, available at www.wiley.com/go/tyvpowerbi.

1 Open the Chapter 11 - Ask Questions. pbix database file.

Note: If the Fields pane and the Visualizations pane are collapsed, expand them.

2 Click **Build Visual** (▦).

The Build Visual tab appears.

3 Click **Q&A** (▭).

A A Q&A visual appears on the canvas.

4 Drag a handle to resize the Q&A visual.

B You can click a button to run one of the suggested queries.

5 Click **Ask a question about your data**.

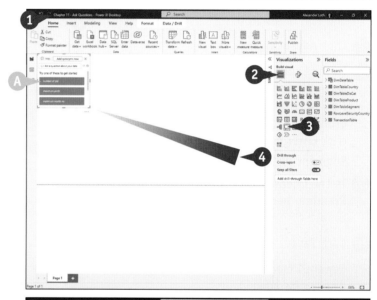

6 Type your question. This example uses **Sum of Sales by Country**.

C Power BI Desktop displays suggestions related to what you typed. You can click a suggestion to display the related visual.

D Power BI Desktop displays a suggested visual. This example shows the sum of sales ranked by country.

7 Select the text you typed, and then type **Sum of Sales by Country by Segment matrix** over it.

E The visual appears.

8 Click **Save** (🖫).

Power BI Desktop saves your changes.

9 Click **Close** (✕).

The file closes.

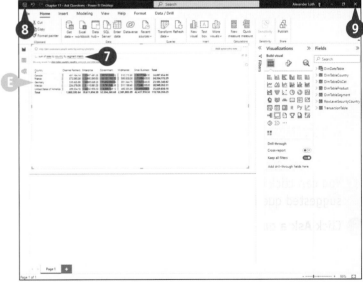

What other way can I add a Q&A visual?
Double-click blank space on the canvas to add a Q&A visual quickly.

How do I use the Adding Synonyms feature?
Click **Add Synonyms Now** in the Help Q&A Understand People Better by Adding Synonyms box to display the Field Synonyms tab of the Q&A Setup screen. In the Include in Q&A section, set the switch for each field you want to include to On (⚪) and the switch for each field you want to exclude to Off (⚪). For each field you include, click **Expand** (⌄) to the left of the field's name and use the controls in that section to add synonyms for the field name, as needed.

Publish a Report to the Power BI Service

Once you have created a Power BI report, you will likely want to share it with your colleagues so that they can benefit from your efforts. To make the report available, you do not directly share the file itself; instead, you publish it to the Power BI service.

Publishing the report makes it available to its readers in a form that lets them access only the extracted transformed and loaded dataset, not the whole of the source file. They will not be able to change any of your calculations, but they can create their own reports from your report.

Publish a Report to the Power BI Service

Note: This section uses the Chapter 11 - Publish.pbix database, available at www.wiley.com/go/tyvpowerbi.

1 Open the Chapter 11 - Publish.pbix database file.

2 Verify that you are signed in to your Power BI account.

A Your username appears if you are signed in.

If the Sign In button appears, click **Sign In** and follow the prompts to sign in to your account.

Note: Depending on your account type, you may need to authenticate yourself via Microsoft Authenticator or another means of authentication.

3 Click **Save** ().

Power BI Desktop saves any unsaved changes.

4 Click **Home**.

5 Click **Publish**.

The Publish to Power BI dialog box opens.

B You can click **Search** (Q) to search for a workspace that matches the text you type.

6 Click the appropriate workspace.

7 Click **Select**.

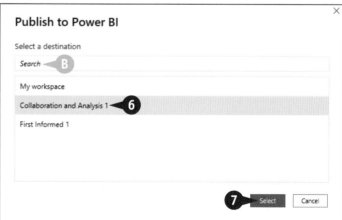

The Publish to Power BI dialog box closes.

The Publishing to Power BI dialog box opens, displaying a progress readout as Power BI publishes the report.

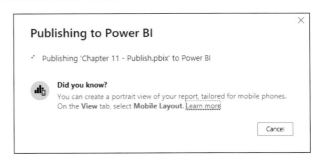

When Power BI has published the report, the Publishing to Power BI dialog box displays a Success! message.

Ⓒ You can click **Open** to open the report in a browser window to check the report's contents.

Ⓓ You can click **Get Quick Insights** to display Power BI's list of Quick Insights from the report, again in a browser window.

⑧ Click **Got It**.

The Publishing to Power BI dialog box closes.

⑨ Click **Close** (☒).

The file closes.

Why should I not share my Power BI report directly with my colleagues?
If you share a report by making the PBIX database file available to your colleagues, each of them receives direct access to the source file and all the transformations you have performed on the data set. This gives your colleagues free rein to make changes to the file, which is not what you normally want when sharing a report. Instead, you would typically share the report by publishing it to the Power BI service. Doing this enables your colleagues to use your report but not to change it wholesale.

Set Up Row-Level Security

hen you share a report with members of a workspace, those members by default have access to all the data the report contains. Often, this is what you want, but in other cases, you may want to restrict what data some users can see. Power BI enables you to implement such restrictions by using row-level security, which creates customized views for different users.

To set up row-level security on a table, you need the users' IDs and a key column that defines the restrictions that will be applied. This section's example implements row-level security using email IDs filtered on the Country column.

Set Up Row-Level Security

Note: This section uses the Chapter 11 - Security.pbix database, available at www.wiley.com/go/tyvpowerbi.

1 Open the Chapter 11 - Security.pbix database file.

2 Click **Modeling**.

3 Click **Manage roles**.

The Manage Roles dialog box opens.

4 Click **Create**.

A new role, provisionally entitled New Role, appears under the Roles heading.

5 Type the email address for the new role.

6 In the Tables column, right-click **TransactionTable**.

7 Click or highlight **Add filter**.

The continuation menu opens, showing a list of the table's rows.

8 Click **[Country]**.

Ⓐ A placeholder expression, [Country] = "Value", appears in the Table Filter DAX Expression box.

9 Double-click **Value** to select it, and then type **Canada** over the selection, creating the filter expression **[Country] = "Canada"**.

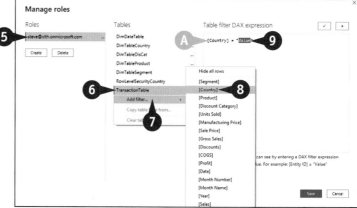

10 Repeat steps **4** to **9**, this time adding another email address and specifying **[Country] = "France"**.

11 Repeat steps **4** to **9** once more, this time adding another email address and specifying **[Country] = "Germany"**.

12 Repeat steps **4** to **9** once more, this time adding another email address and specifying **[Country] = "Mexico"**.

13 Repeat steps **4** to **9** once more, this time adding another email address and specifying **[Country] = "United States of America"**.

14 Click **Save**.

Power BI Desktop applies the row-level changes you made.

15 Click **Save** (🖫).

16 Click **Home**.

17 Click **Publish**.

The Publish to Power BI dialog box opens.

18 Click the destination.

19 Click **Select**.

The Publishing to Power BI dialog box replaces the Publish to Power BI dialog box.

20 Click **Got it**.

21 Click **Close** (✖).

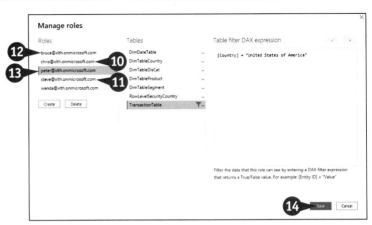

TIPS

How can I test what another user would see on the report?
Click **Modeling** to display the Modeling tab of the ribbon, go to the Security group, and click **View as** to open the View as Roles dialog box. Click the role you want to view (☐ changes to ☑), and then click **OK**.

How do I remove a role I have created?
Click **Modeling** to display the Modeling tab, go to the Security group, and click **Manage roles** to open the Manage Roles dialog box. In the Roles list, click the role to delete, and then click **Delete**. In the Delete Role dialog box, click **Yes, delete**. Click **Save** to apply your changes and close the Manage Roles dialog box.

Add Tiles to a Dashboard

Much like the dashboard in a motor vehicle, a *dashboard* in Power BI is a single page that uses visuals to present a quick overview of a dataset. Power BI enables you to create a dashboard quickly by adding *tiles*, snapshots of data that you pin to the dashboard. In this section, you use Power BI's Auto-Create Report feature, which assembles a dashboard for you automatically.

To share a dashboard you create, you must have a Power BI Pro user license or a Premium Per User license.

Add Tiles to a Dashboard

1. In a web browser, go to powerbi.microsoft. com/en-us.

   The Data Visualization: Microsoft Power BI web page appears.

2. Click **Sign in**, and then follow through the steps of the sign-in procedure using your credentials for Power BI.

   Once you have signed in, your Power BI Home page appears.

3. Click **Workspaces** (▦).

   The Workspaces pane opens.

4. Click the workspace to which you published the report in the section "Publish a Report to the Power BI Service," earlier in this chapter.

The workspace appears in a new tab.

5 Move the pointer over the row for the dataset you created.

Extra controls appear in the row.

6 Click **More Options** (···).

The More Options menu opens.

7 Click **Auto-create report**.

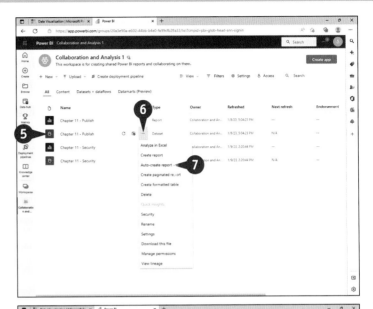

Power BI creates a complete report with tiles based on the data you have uploaded.

8 Click **Save** (🖫).

The Save Your Report dialog box opens.

9 Click **Enter a name for your report**, and type a name, such as **AutoGeneratedReport**.

10 Click **Select a destination workspace** (⌄), and select the workspace in which to save the report.

11 Click **Save**.

You can now edit the report as needed. For example, you can add further tiles to the report manually.

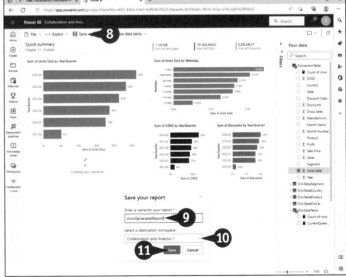

TIP

How do I edit the report I have created?

Click **Edit** (✐) on the toolbar at the top of the workspace window, and then click **Continue** in the Switch to Edit Mode dialog box that opens. The Your Data pane on the right of the web interface disappears, replaced by the Visualizations pane and the Fields pane. You can use these panes in much the same way as in Power BI Desktop — for example, you can use the controls on the Build Visual tab of the Visualizations pane to create new visuals. Similarly, you can click **New page** (➕) to create a new page in the report.

Share a Dashboard

After creating a dashboard or a report, you can share it with your colleagues by using the Power BI service to send each colleague a link to it. You can either share the dashboard or report freely, allowing your colleagues to share it further with other people as they see fit and to use the dataset's content to build reports of their own, or restrict either sharing or report-building.

To share a dashboard you create, you must have a Power BI Pro user license or a Premium Per User license.

Share a Dashboard

Note: This section assumes that you have completed the previous section, "Add Tiles to a Dashboard," and created a dashboard named AutoGeneratedReport.

1 In a web browser, go to powerbi. microsoft.com/en-us.

The Data Visualization: Microsoft Power BI web page appears.

2 Click **Sign in**, and then follow the steps of the sign-in procedure using your credentials for Power BI.

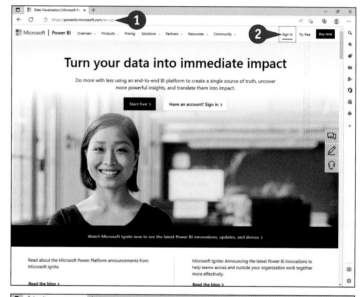

Once you have signed in, your Power BI Home page appears.

3 Click **Workspaces** (▥).

The Workspaces pane opens.

4 Click the workspace to which you published the report in the section "Publish a Report to the Power BI Service," earlier in this chapter.

The workspace appears in a new tab.

5 Move the pointer over the row for the report you created — in this example, the AutoGeneratedReport report.

Extra controls appear in the row.

6 Click **Share** (⤷).

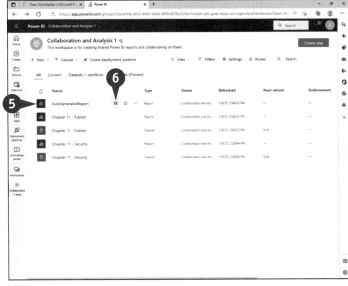

The Send Link dialog box opens.

7 Click **Enter a name or email address**.

8 Type the name or email address of each recipient in turn, clicking to accept the names or addresses after Power BI verifies them.

9 Optionally, click **Add a message**, and type a message to the recipients.

10 Click **Send**.

Power BI sends the link to the recipients and displays a message saying it has done so.

11 Click **Close** (✕).

The Send Link dialog box closes.

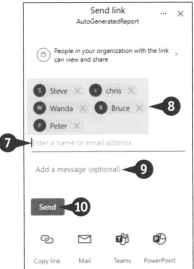

TIP

How can I restrict the users with whom I share a link?

Click **Share** (⤷) to open the Send Link dialog box, and then click **People in your organization with the link can view and share** to display further controls in the dialog box. In the Settings section, select **Allow recipients to share this report** (☑) if you want recipients to be able to share the report with others; if not, clear the check box (☐). Similarly, select (☑) or clear (☐) the **Allow recipients to build content with the data associated with this report** box to control whether recipients can use the report's data to build content. Click **Apply**. Enter the recipients, optionally add a message, and then click **Send.**

Schedule Data Refreshes

To keep your Power BI reports and dashboards up to date, you will need to refresh the data they contain. Power BI Services enable you to refresh a dataset's data either manually or automatically via the Schedule Refresh function.

Automatic updates save time and effort, so they are the better choice in most cases. To schedule automatic refreshes, you must use valid credentials for the data source from which you will refresh the data. If you published the data source, as in this section's example, your credentials should be valid.

Schedule Data Refreshes

Note: This section requires you to have completed the earlier section, "Publish a Report to the Power BI Service." In this section, you schedule data refreshes for the dataset for the report you published.

① In a web browser, go to powerbi.microsoft.com/en-us.

The Data Visualization: Microsoft Power BI web page appears.

② Click **Sign in**, and then follow the steps of the sign-in procedure using your credentials for Power BI.

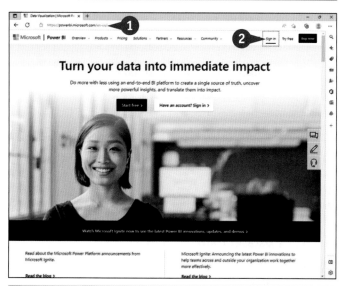

Once you have signed in, your Power BI Home page appears.

③ Click **Workspaces** (▦).

The Workspaces pane opens.

④ Click the workspace to which you published the report in the section "Publish a Report to the Power BI Service," earlier in this chapter.

The workspace appears.

5 Move the pointer over the row for the dataset you published for the Chapter 11 - Publish report.

Extra controls appear in the row.

6 Click **Schedule refresh** (🕓).

The Settings screen for the dataset appears.

7 Click **Scheduled refresh**.

The Scheduled Refresh section expands.

8 Set the **Keep your data up to date** switch to On (⬤▬).

9 Click **Refresh frequency** (⌄) and click **Daily** or **Weekly**.

10 Click **Time zone** (⌄) and click the time zone.

11 Click **Add another time**, and use the resulting controls to set the refresh time.

12 Select **Dataset owner** (☑) to receive notifications of refresh failures.

13 Click **Apply**.

Power BI schedules data refreshes for the dataset.

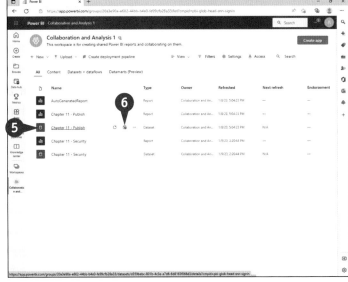

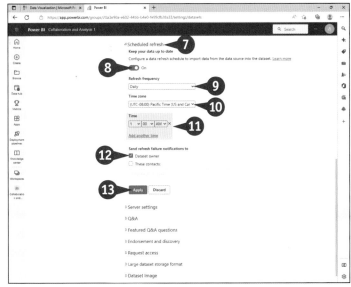

TIP

Why are the Scheduled Refresh options grayed out?

Most likely, no gateway connection is configured for the dataset. On the Settings screen for the dataset, click **Gateway connection** to expand the Gateway Connection and see if a gateway is listed with Running status. If not, ask your Power BI administrator to configure a gateway connection for you. If you have no Power BI administrator, you can download Microsoft's On-Premises Data Gateway from go.microsoft.com/ fwlink/?LinkId=820925&clcid=0x409, run the installer, click **On-premises data gateway (personal mode)**, and follow through the resulting screens. After installing the gateway, run it, and then visit the Settings screen for the dataset again.

Publish a Report to the Web

As well as sharing a report with your colleagues in a workspace, Power BI enables you to publish a report to the web so that anybody who has internet access can read it. To let others know about a publicly shared report, you can email a link to the report on the Power BI service or paste HTML code into a page on your website to enable access to the report from there.

To share a report on the web, you need a Power BI Premium subscription. You should also have the right to distribute the material contained in the report.

Publish a Report to the Web

1 In a web browser, go to powerbi. microsoft.com/en-us (not shown).

The Data Visualization: Microsoft Power BI web page appears.

2 Click **Sign in**, and then follow the steps of the sign-in procedure using your credentials for Power BI (not shown).

Once you have signed in, your Power BI Home page appears.

3 Click **Workspaces** (▣).

4 Click the workspace to which you published the report in the section "Publish a Report to the Power BI Service," earlier in this chapter.

The workspace opens.

5 Click the report you want to publish (not shown).

The report opens.

6 Click **File** (∨).

7 Click or highlight **Embed report**.

The Embed Report continuation menu opens.

8 Click **Publish to web (public)**.

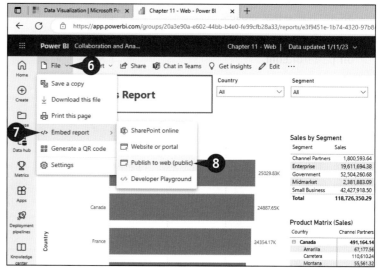

The first stage Embed in a Public Website dialog box opens.

9 Click **Create embed code**.

The second stage of the Embed in a Public Website dialog box replaces the first stage.

10 Click **Publish**.

The Embed in a Public Website dialog box closes.

The Success! Your Report Is Ready to Share dialog box opens.

A You can click **Copy** to copy the link to share via email.

B You can click **Copy** to copy the HTML for pasting into a web page.

C You can click **Size** (∨) and select the size to use.

D You can click **Upload** (⬆) to upload a placeholder image for the report.

E You can click **Default Page** (∨) and select the default page to display.

11 Click **Close**.

The Success! Your Report Is Ready to Share dialog box closes.

Your report is now publicly available on powerbi.com.

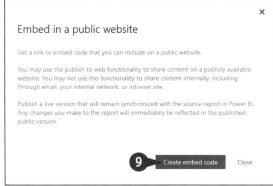

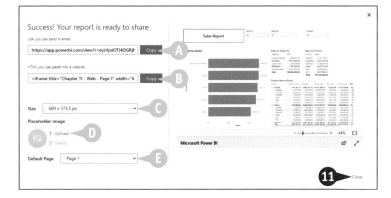

TIP

Why does the Publish to Web (Public) command not appear on the Embed Report continuation menu?
Most likely, the report contains one or more items that Power BI cannot currently publish to the web. As of this writing, Power BI cannot publish reports using row-level security, reports shared with you by others, reports from a workspace in which you do not have Edit privileges, reports containing report-level DAX measures, reports containing Q&A visuals, and reports containing Python visuals or R-language visuals. Go to learn.microsoft.com/en-us/power-bi/collaborate-share/service-publish-to-web and see the Considerations and Limitations section for the latest list of restrictions.

Index